Advance Praise for
Dying and Living in the Arms of Love...

What does it demand of us to hold the self endlessly with love? What must we die to? In *Dying and Living in the Arms of Love*, we are invited to be witness to one woman's search to find those answers and, without bargaining or compromise, to do it with endless compassion for herself and the world.

Receiving a heart-calling to travel the holy path around one of the world's most sacred mountains, Tracey Alysson takes us on this thirty-four mile path not by walking but by doing endless prostrations. Travelling a path filled with rocks and boulders, a path often underwater or covered with ice and snow at higher elevations, requires more than physical stamina. Here we are brought to the essence of a spiritual journey as she and we learn that the physical body alone cannot accomplish this task; yet, the physical demands strip away all illusions and all defenses to lay bare the emotional, psychic, and spiritual bones of her being. It is a heart-rending and heart-felt pilgrimage.

In reading her journal of the path around Mt. Kailash and her introspections following in the *Epilogue* and *Lessons and Changes*, I begin to grasp what it truly means to live and die in the arms of love – naked love – devoid of all the delusions we wrap ourselves in everyday. Regardless of one's spiritual intentions or path, this story offers the reader a mirror for the hard work of learning to receive oneself in love so that we may hold others, all the planet, in love. It is necessary work for this time on the planet. After all, "All there is is love...and the love is endless."

Barbara Meyers, MSW, author of *Common Ground, Uncommon Gifts: Growing Peace and Harmony Through Stories, Reflections, and Practices in the Natural World*

Dying and Living in the Arms of Love is at once extraordinary and humble. Battling rain, exhaustion, and her own mind, Tracey Alysson intently makes her way along Mt. Kailash toward the ferocious heart of infinity. This book invites you into the preparation, her inner and outer experiences, and the joyful triumph of her surrender to the mountain. Like Tracey, the writing is honest, unyielding, graceful, and human. I was delighted to find myself experiencing the pain, the enormity, and the beautiful rhythm of her journey.

Jeremy Parise, singer/songwriter of CD
The Year I Clung to Fantasy

We all live in just the one moment we draw a breath. This book is about the experience of one woman's journey through those moments, being present and experiencing each of them fully. This is not an adventure story about a three-day trek around Mt. Kailash with a few prostrations at key points or an expectation of spiritual reward. This is the journal of a pilgrimage and completion of khora, the act of devotion, in the traditional and most devout manner, prostrating and praying, moving only the length of your body at each prostration around the 34 mile trail that surrounds the home of the Buddha or if you prefer the Throne of Shiva. The purely physical demands would deter all but the most adventurous of us. It is more importantly and significantly an insight into the nature of someone who has, for reasons they may not fully understand, been called by some unknown force to complete an act of pure devotion with no expectation of what the process will reveal or if indeed it can be completed at all. I had concerns about Tracey going to Tibet, to an arduous and potentially dangerous journey into a remote and inhospitable part of the world, occupied and controlled by military forces foreign to its culture, religion, and inhabitants. I cannot think of her without being transported to an image of her in that remote place and wonder how she came to be there.

David Galluccio, Owner, *Raven Computers*

Dying & Living
in The Arms of Love

One Woman's Journey
around Mount Kailash

Tracey Alysson, Ph.D.

Parts of this manuscript were previously published in the journal of the Theosophical Society in America.

To order additional copies of this book, contact:
Xlibris Corporation
1-888-795-4274
www.Xlibris.com
Orders@Xlibris.com
107399

This book is dedicated to

My friend and teacher, Marcus Daniels

My classmates:
Patrick, Dorothy, Jeremy,
Sherri, Beth, German, Dea, Kevin, Kellie, John, Anna, and Silvia,
and all those who have shared this work with me

My sister, Marian Zalis DeBardeleben

My crew, Dorjee La, Jigme La, Rikjin La, and Nima La,
who tended to the needs of both my body and my soul

Mt. Kailash, for all time

All Beings

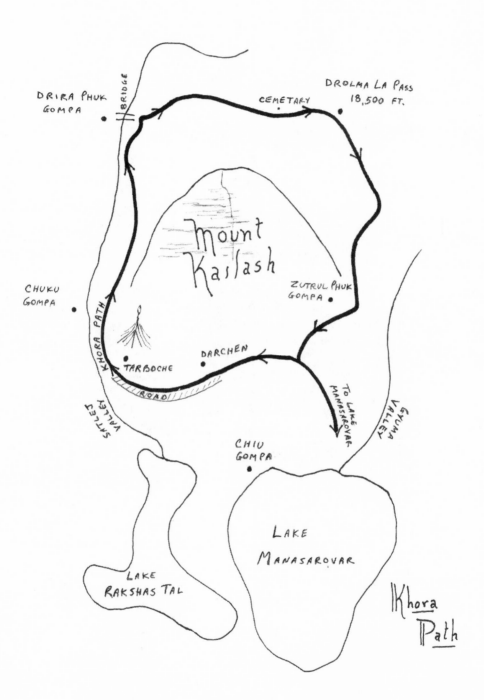

DRIRA PHUK
GOMPA

BRIDGE

CEMETARY

DROLMA LA PASS
18,500 FT.

Mount Kailash

CHUKU
GOMPA

ZUTRUL PHUK
GOMPA

KHORA PATH

DARCHEN

TARBOCHE

ROAD

SATLEJ VALLEY

TO LAKE MANASAROVAR

GYUMA VALLEY

CHIU
GOMPA

LAKE
MANASAROVAR

LAKE
RAKSHAS TAL

Khora
Path

The center of the spiritual universe already exists in your human heart. Meet your mirror.
~ Marcus Daniels

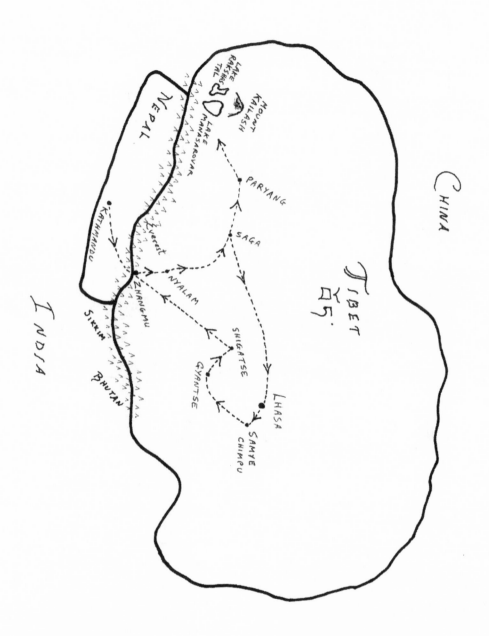

Table of Contents

Foreword
Marcus Daniels

The Buddha said, "Life is suffering." One can experience suffering as an act of kindness, which is an act of service and evolution. One can also experience suffering as an agenda, a mission, as a victim, or even a death march. The first is held in love, the second is held in tension.

Going on pilgrimage is an act of suffering. On pilgrimage one gets to have an experience of feeling one's naked heart in its relationship to one's authentic love. One is not lonely, but one is alone, sometimes raging in spiritual vitality to attempt to uncover the sublime blessing which lies suppressed in one's tissues. As this occurs, the blessing can no longer be held or hidden in the separations of trance, nervous system, or history.

To be spiritually vital one has to first experience one's relationship to fear. As fear is loved or accepted, one is now available to feel the rage of vitality, the arising of Wisdom Hatred. This brings one through fear to anger in order to empower the moment and eventually allow the experience of being blessed. *In my nakedness, I love this much hate, I hate this much love.* The authentic blessing is now available to self-arise.

Going to Mount Kailash is a pilgrimage. It is an exquisite act of suffering: thirty-four miles around the base of the Mountain, 15,000 feet of elevation at its lowest, 18,500 feet at its highest at Drolma La Pass. One takes step after step into the moment, the only safety being the mala one wears, the mantra one recites, and one's heart self-arising one's blessing. As one shares their blessing with the Mountain, one receives the Mountain's blessings in return. As one loses one's identity love itself will self-arise, free from image and the constraints of the mind. It is the individual's experience itself, not the mind, which determines how long one allows this union to last.

It is said that the first Westerner to walk around Kailash was the explorer Sven Hedin in the first decade of the twentieth century. Tracey Alysson's act of suffering for evolution and her service to humanity was not a walk around Kailash as most do in two to three days. It was an act of surrender which entailed twenty-eight days, five to nine hours a day of full body prostrations: two giant steps, stillness, saying prayers, then falling face down, body touching the ground feeling the earth and exchanging blessings. Wearing a leather apron and special gloves so the rocks on the ground would not cut and bruise her clothes and body, in raw cold and snow, she endured day after day with no days off until the circumambulation was complete.

Prostrations in general are meant to cut the human ego and arrogance, to remove obstacles on the spiritual path. Prostrations at high elevations set a new bar. In all the research I have done, I have never come across a Western woman who did full body prostrations around Kailash. A Kailash area lama's family with whom I am friends also has no recall of a Western woman doing full prostrations. That she might be the first is of no concern to Tracey. She got a vision to go, met her vision head on, finished the circuit around Kailash, dedicated her pilgrimage blessings for humanity and all beings, and went home where she soon re-started her psychotherapy practice. As is usual for her, she did not tell more than a few souls.

I consider her journey equal to a mythic epic, an inspiration for all to embrace. For those on a spiritual quest and non-believers alike, please enjoy this sharing from a very remarkable woman.

Preface

As I was completing the Korah, I knew in my own mind that I wanted to write a book about it. My friends, Marcus and Patrick, had both separately encouraged me to keep a journal as I went around the Mountain. I was puzzled – it was only my personal pilgrimage, what would there be to write about? Who would be interested? I had no concept of what I was undertaking. But I took journals anyway, and I wrote, and I am so grateful for their foresight in urging me to do this. As I completed Korah, I wondered how my guides and those Tibetans and others who had supported me around the Mountain would feel as I wrote not only about me but about them. Would Tibet feel offended that this Westerner, this foreigner, had dared to undertake a most sacred ritual? I did not want to offend this country and culture that is of towering spiritual magnificence. Yet a Rinpoche in Nepal said to me, "You are going to write a book, aren't you?" One guide said, "You must write about this, history must have this for others to know about." My teacher urged me to do magazine articles, interviews, a book, saying this is a monumental achievement which I should share to inspire others to follow their authentic hearts. None of these people knew each other. These were all separate conversations in different times. I took them to mean that it would not be offensive for me to write of this journey, to let Mt. Kailash stand visibly in me.

It took me a number of months to realize that I was afraid to write this book. I would begin, and get distracted. I would make plans to begin again, but somehow my pace was as a glacier moving across a landscape. Then I realized that I was as afraid to write this book as I had been to go to Mt. Kailash. However, it was clear to me that the opportunity to go to Tibet, to go to Mt. Kailash, and the enormous gift of completing the Korah with prostrations had to be shared. It never belonged to me. It is not an individual achievement. Thus, while I have spent my life living deeply inside myself and seeking quietness and invisibility, it is necessary that I share this experience.

What follows are notes from my personal evolution. I am neither Buddhist nor non-Buddhist, Christian nor non-Christian, Sufi nor non-Sufi, Muslim nor non-Muslim. I am Tracey, with a Soul in a Personality and a Body, with a spiritual evolution and a psychological evolution as my body moves through time. My teacher Marcus Daniels is the only teacher I have found in a lifetime of searching who holds and helps my body, mind, and soul. My classes with him have changed my life on all levels, and my gratitude is unrepayable. Before I met Marcus, my sole concern was spiritual. As a psychologist I studied and worked with what is called mind or personality, and later as a bodyworker, I struggled to understand how the body lives and speaks. But my search has always been one of faith, of soul. My journals reflect this language. What I am really attempting to do is to find a way to live, to live as a human, to live this life on this planet.

I was raised Roman Catholic, and loved the high ritual of that tradition, the purity of Jesus in the entirety of his commitment to who he was. When I came across Tibetan Buddhist Practices, they spoke to me in new ways, opening not only soul space but clarifying so much that psychology strives to address. Marcus' teachings, too, draw from Tibetan Buddhist wisdom. Much of what follows from my journals has much Buddhist language about it. I must emphasize that I am not writing from scholarship, and that undoubtedly the way I use many of the words and concepts is imperfect. I do not speak from mastery. I speak from moments where I have been touched by an experience of a concept which I have put into my own words. I apologize for errors in understanding, and I mean no offense to those who are purists in the tradition.

I will also refer to personages from the Buddhist tradition that have touched and taught me. Guru Rinpoche, also known as Padmasambhava, is the master who brought Buddhism to Tibet in the eighth century. Yeshe Tsogyal was his main consort, and remained to teach in Tibet for many years after Guru Rinpoche walked through to the other side. Certain prayer rituals or practices are mentioned. These practices have held me, comforted me, and taught me. They and the deities and saints they address have walked with me in my lostness and my faith.

Just as I did not know how to do my journey, I do not know how to write about it either. I kept journals while in Tibet, as well as before and after, in my simple, direct voice. Since this is not a story but an experience, I have turned to my journals for my words. Thank you for walking with me through this experience. May the multitude of blessings that have graced me grace you.

Tracey Alysson
West Chesterfield, New Hampshire
2012

Acknowledgements

My gratitude forever is to my friend and teacher, Marcus Daniels. Marcus has held space for me with a generosity and depth that is unrepayable. He held both reality and possibility as I approached my pilgrimage to Kailash, and helped me prepare in innumerable ways.

My classmates in our work with Marcus have been a home to me, a family that has gathered and held both whole and broken pieces of me as I have continued my journey. They have helped me stay on the path, taking myself less seriously and more kindly. As is clear in the pages of this book, my classmates were a lifeline as I dared to journey to Kailash.

My friend David Galluccio regularly saves me as my computer does incomprehensible things. But more than that, he is one of the most intelligent and profound friends in my life. David urged me to get this book published, and when I asked him one day why he felt so passionately about this, he answered simply, "So many people talk and talk about things. You didn't talk about it, you just did it. This needs to be shared." I was struck by David's perception. He is right. I did not stay home and theorize.

Cathy, Bob, and April Martel, Emily Franzen-Langa, and Sandy Chase and Maryann Gallagher took my precious golden retriever Connor into their homes as I journeyed to Tibet. Connor was my closest family and a treasure to my heart. Loving him was loving me, and I am forever grateful for their generous hearts. My wonderful neighbors, Sheena and Joe Derosias, and their daughters Lilly and Lucy, cared for Jesse and Liam, my sweet cats, and watched over my home while I journeyed. In particular, I was touched by Lilly's keen interest in my travels, of how people lived in other parts of this world, and I was glad to share gifts and learnings from my travels with her.

My dear friend, Ed Hutchins, made my leather apron to protect my body as I prostrated around Mt. Kailash. My sister, Marian Zalis

DeBardeleben, kindly made sure my pre-paid bills got mailed on time. While this sounds perhaps mundane, our journey as sisters has been very difficult. My willingness to ask for her help, and her offer before I asked, was a testament to the love that has always been deeper than any of our struggles. My friend and financial advisor Torrey Greene realized I had not anticipated my quarterly health insurance bill and paid it for me, surely a step above and beyond.

Many friends took time to read and comment on the manuscript: Maryann Gallagher, Sandy Chase, Barbara Meyers, David Galluccio, Marian Zalis DeBardeleben, Jeremy Parise, Emily Franzen-Langa, Dorothy Pietracatella, Snow Frye, David Palmer, Edwin Hill, and Elaine Schierioth. Their experience and feedback on this endeavor was an act of generosity that was a most helpful reality check. Catherine Conrey, without being asked, performed the magic of putting the manuscript in PDF. On very short notice, and as an act of complete kindness and generosity, Dianna Noyes worked electronic magic to make the maps readable.

At the eleventh hour, Ruth H. G. Cohen made space at a tremendously busy time in her life to read this manuscript through the eye of a professional editor. Her feedback significantly improved this book. Both her experienced eye and her willing heart have blessed me and this work, and I am grateful to her.

I have to thank Prof. Dan Toomey of Landmark College in Putney, Vermont. Dan teaches a course on Pilgrimage, and invited me to speak to his students. Although I had already written the book, this helped me tremendously to begin to speak aloud about my experiences and to begin to learn how to speak of them. His welcoming and feedback as I have spoken to his students over the past few years has been a great gift to me. Karen Kallie (www.livingenergyworks.com), a friend and colleague, invited me to share my experiences at Kailash with a gathering of her friends, again another opportunity encouraging me to learn how to share the many blessings I received at Kailash.

I have to specially thank my friend and colleague Barbara Meyers for so many ways in which she cares for and supports me. In particular, Barbara had the prescience to insist on picking me up at Logan International Airport when I arrived home. How could I have thought I could ever have stepped off a plane, returning from Mt. Kailash, and safely driven myself home from Boston to New Hampshire! What was I thinking! I remember seeing Barbara at the airport and allowing her to shepherd my disoriented self to her car while experiences and feelings poured non-stop out of me. As always, she held a loving, perceptive, and generous space for me, getting me safely home before heading off to her busy work day.

Finally, my gratitude to Rangrig Rinpoche and Michael Sangpo in Nepal, for their counsel and blessings, and for the generous time they spent with me prior to and following my Khora.

The Invitation

In July, August, and September of 2006, I made a journey that I knew would change my life. When I agreed to go to Tibet and do prostrations around Mount Kailash, there were some things that I did not know. I did not know that this journey would change every piece of my life, shattering the old and leaving me naked, lost, and grateful as the realization dawned that I could not return to my old life. While I knew that the journey around Kailash would change me, I did not consciously understand that the change does not stop. Once this kind of door is opened, it is an invitation that evolves, walking slowly in front of me, inviting me to keep coming forward.

I came to be invited to do Korah with prostrations in July 2005. Two of my dearest friends, David and Ed, invited me to join them in a week's vacation at their time-share condo in North Carolina. I said yes immediately! There is so much busyness in my life. A week with my friends, a week away in a beautiful State, a week to do my Tibetan practices, to read novels, rest, be in the love of our friendship: the answer was yes.

It was the first morning I awoke there, in a bedroom with my own bath, a little enclave of peace and beauty and rest. I got up, and did some practice. I was not inspired, or particularly adept or "in." I was just doing my practice, grateful for no time limit on how long I could pray, free from schedule. I was just learning prostrations, and had managed twenty-one that morning. In Buddhist thought, there are spiritual beings, dakinis, which are self-manifesting beings of love. Buddhist thought tells us there are five classes of dakinis, one of which guards Kailash. The dakinis are feminine, while dakas are masculine. As I was doing practice, three dakinis arrived and told me that it was time for me to return to Tibet, sometime in the next two years. They told me to do prostrations around Mt. Kailash when I was there. When I say dakinis arrived, I do not mean

I saw them. I am not gifted that way. But I felt them, and I received their transmission.

Days later, I was chatting with my friend and teacher, Marcus Daniels, who has traveled to Tibet and Mt. Kailash. I told him with happiness that I was going to Tibet, and he was excited for me. I told him I was going to do prostrations around Mt. Kailash, and he said, "You don't want to do that." I thought, *Oh, that must be a silly idea, impossible idea, ridiculous.* I was quiet. We talked about other things.

In October, I was visiting Marcus in New Jersey where he lived at that time, prior to a training I was there for. While we were just hanging out, I told him I wanted to do prostrations around Mt. Kailash. He said I didn't want to do that. I paused. A bit later, I said I was going to do prostrations around Mt. Kailash. He asked why I wanted to do that. In a quiet, clear voice from the center of my being, I told him it was because I wanted to. He stood up, and with love and enthusiasm, asked me if I knew how to do a walking prostration. I said I did not, did he? He showed me. Later that evening, he asked his dear wife to bring a videotape of his journey in Tibet, a book on Guru Rinpoche, and a stone he had brought back from Mt. Kailash to my room.

Between my initial conversation with Marcus in North Carolina, and my taking ownership of my own decision resulting in the conversation in New Jersey, there had been a journey. While I knew I would go to Tibet, I waffled on the commitment to do prostrations around Mt. Kailash. My self esteem, my sense of worthiness, was insufficient: Who was I to undertake such an act? Who was I to think I could prostrate in such a holy land, at such a holy site? Then one day in October 2005, I was struggling in the preparation of a workshop I was to teach. It was bringing out all my horror and fear of speaking in public, of being seen, every nightmare of school and exams and articulation that had ever visited me. In the midst of the agony of trying to organize thoughts that insisted on remaining nonverbal impressions, I finally burst out to myself, "What, after all, do I want or expect! I ask for spiritual guidance, I ask for the next steps in my life. Dakinis show up and answer me. They tell me the next step, *if I want it.* What do I do? I respond like a tourist: I'll go to Tibet, but I am deftly avoiding comment on whether I shall go to Mt. Kailash and circumambulate on my belly." Clearly, I am interested, but I put my poor self esteem before the invitation. I hesitate. So what do I expect in my life? I ask for guidance, I refuse it, and then I struggle in the agony of my not-good-enoughness.

Clearly confronted with my foot-dragging, I made a decision. Sitting in my office at home, I gave my word that I would do prostrations around

Mt. Kailash. My heart quieted. I was terrified, but I was clear. My word was given. It began a teaching I had never experienced, of what it meant to give my word and keep it, keep it in the tiniest moments and the biggest. It took away, or rather, I gave up wiggle room. Wiggle room was always there, but now I saw it in the context of having given my word to divinity. How could I be wishy-washy with divinity, with the divine in me and outside of me? It was unthinkable. My journey had begun.

The Destination

Lama Anagarika Govinda, the eminent Buddhist teacher and practitioner, wrote of his pilgrimage to Tibet and to Kailash in *The Way of the White Clouds*. He speaks with a simple lucidity of some of the metaphysical truths that live in our physical reality.

> There are mountains which are just mountains and there are mountains with personality....Personality consists in the power to influence others, and this power is due to consistency, harmony, and one-pointedness of character.... If these qualities are present in a mountain we recognise it as a vessel of cosmic power, and we call it a sacred mountain....The power of such a mountain is so great and yet so subtle that, without compulsion, people are drawn to it from near and far, as if by the force of some invisible magnet; and they will undergo untold hardships and privations in their inexplicable urge to approach and to worship the centre of this sacred power. Nobody has conferred the title of sacredness on such a mountain, and yet everybody recognizes it; nobody has to defend its claim, because nobody doubts it; nobody has to organise its worship, because people are overwhelmed by the mere presence of such a mountain and cannot express their feelings other than by worship. (Govinda, 1966, p. 197)

Mt. Kailash is one of three sacred mountains in Tibet. It stands at the center of a rich tapestry of geography, history, and mythology. Out of respect for the sacredness of this mountain, it has never been climbed. Kailash lies in the wilderness of Western Tibet. John Snelling, who has written a classic text on Kailash, sets the scene:

> The landscape of the corner of the great plateau of Tibet
> in which Kailas is situated is one of desolate beauty. In the
> high altitudes prevailing there – 13,000 feet and more –
> virtually no trees grow and little vegetation clothes the
> rugged terrain. Due to the transparency of the rarefied air,
> however, colours reach the eye with unfiltered intensity:
> rich reds, browns, yellows, purples – and in fine weather
> both sky and mirroring water are a deep, noble blue.
> Climate, on the other hand, is unpredictable, at times
> violent, and always prone to extremes of heat and cold....
> Not surprisingly, therefore, this has always been a scantily
> populated area. (Snelling, p. 22)

From this landscape of truly "desolate beauty" rises Kailash, 22,027 feet in altitude. To Tibetans, Kailash is known as Kang Rinpoche (Jewel of Snow). With its white and black markings, the geometry of Kailash stands out as a symmetrical cone graced by a cap of perpetual snow. Brian Beresford, in Gyurme Dorje's *Tibet,* notes that Kailash makes the Himalayas "seem ordinary." Geologically, Kailash arose fifty million years ago, "up through the depths of the great ocean, the Tethys Sea....The Great Himalayas on the other hand are one of the newest ranges on the planet, arbitrarily wrenched out of the Asian landmass as it met the tectonic plate of the Indian subcontinent...some 20 million years ago." (Gyurme Dorje, p. 360)

Materially, four major rivers arise within some sixty miles of Kailash. Govinda comments that "Kailas forms the spire of the 'Roof of the World', as the Tibetan plateau is called, and radiating from it, like the spokes from the hub of a wheel, a number of mighty rivers take their course towards the east, the west, the north-west, and the south....All these rivers have their source in the Kailas-Manasarovar region, which forms the highest tier of the Tibetan plateau." (Govinda, 1966, p. 199)

The Brahmaputra flows east, transversing Tibet to the Himalayas and India. The Indus flows north, flowing through Tibet, India, Ladakh, Baltistan, and Pakistan. The Karnali flows south, leading to the Ganges. The Satlej flows west. Snelling points out that "Meru (Kailash) is the source of all the life-giving waters of the world." (Snelling, p. 49) Beresford speaks of the far-reaching effects of these generous waters:

> Grudgingly through the valleys and folds of the land it
> then manifests into four, the great rivers of the world
> flowing in the four cardinal directions: the sacred rivers

which are the courses of civilizations and knowledge: north the Indus, spawning the earliest, the Indus Valley civilization; east, the Brahmaputra feeding the mystics of Tibet before cutting through the eastern Himalayas and cascading down into Bengal and the source of the great philosophy and knowledge of ancient India; south via the Karnali into the Ganges, India's life-blood and the well-spring of its spiritual inspiration and ongoing timeless presence; and west, along the Sutlej, little known but in fact the link with the mystics of the Indian Himalayas and the sustainer of the richness of life in the northwest of India. (Gyurme Dorje, p. 360)

Spiritually, Mt. Kailash is home to four major religions. The Bon religion or the Bonpos are the original shamanistic religion of Tibet, and their founder Shenrab is said to have descended to earth on Mt. Kailash. Kailash is sacred to the Buddhists, Jains, and Hindus as well. It was here that the Bonpo master Naro Bonchung battled Milarepa, Tibet's greatest saint. Milarepa's transcendence in that battle established Buddhism as the dominant religion in the country. For the Buddhists, Mt. Kailash is the home of Demchog who dwells atop the mountain with his consort Dorje Phamo. For the Hindus, it is Shiva who dwells here with his consort Parvati. My guides told me that when Indian pilgrims die from the cold and exertion atop Drolma La Pass, the highest point on the circuit around Mt. Kailash, they die in great happiness because they are close to Shiva.

Govinda points out that geographically Kailash "forms the hub of the two most important ancient civilizations of the world, whose traditions remained intact for thousands of years: India and China. To Hindus and Buddhists alike Kailas is the centre of the universe....not only the physical but the metaphysical centre of the world...." (Govinda, 1966, p. 198) Hindu, Buddhist, and Jain cosmologies all speak of a cosmic mountain which is the *axis mundi*, the center of all that is, both physically and metaphysically. This cosmic mountain is known as Mount Meru (also Sumeru or Sineru).

The geography of this region seamlessly reflects the spiritual totality that calls pilgrims to Kailash. Beneath Mt. Kailash sit two lakes, Lake Manasarovar, the Lake of Wisdom, and Rakshas Tal, the Lake of Power.

...at the southern foot of Kailas there are two sacred lakes, Manasarovar and Rakastal, of which the former is shaped

like the sun and represents the forces of light, while the
other is curved like the crescent moon and represents
the hidden forces of the night, which – as long as they
are not recognized in their true nature and directed
into their proper channels – appear as the demonic
powers of darkness. These ideas are also expressed in
the names of the two lakes. 'Manas' (Skt.) means mind or
consciousness: the seat of the forces of cognition, of light,
and finally of enlightenment. 'Rakas' or, more correctly,
'Rakshas', means demon, so that Rakastal means 'Lake of
the Demons'. (Govinda, 1966, p. 200)

The belief that Kailash is Mt. Meru reaches back across ancient
civilizations. Snelling notes that Swami Pranavananda circumambulated
Kailash and cites references he found at Drira Phuk and Gyantra Gompas
(monasteries). These sources provide the names used by Tibetans for the
four great rivers:

> In the West: the *Langchen Khambab* or Elephant-mouthed
>   river – the Sutlej
> In the North: the *Singhi Khambab* or Lion-mouthed river
>   – the Indus
> In the East: the *Tamchok Khambab* or Horse-mouthed river
>   – the Brahmaputra
> In the South: the *Mapcha Khambab* or Peacock-mouthed
>   river – the Karnali
> These names are almost identical with the old Puranic
> names for the four waters that flowed from Mount Meru.
> (Snelling, p. 56)

Snelling notes that the old Puranic names are "the Sita, supposed
to flow from an elephant's head; the Alakanada, supposed to flow from
a cow's head; the Chaksu, from a horse's head; and, finally the Bhadra,
from a lion's head." (Snelling, p. 49) The similarity of these names across
Tibetan and Hindu cultures suggests that the belief that these four rivers
of Mt. Meru emanate from Mt. Kailash, that is, Mt. Meru, is ancient.

Again and again, this sacred mountain is experienced as a temple.
Snelling quotes T. Burckhardt's *Sacred Art in East and West* regarding the
far-reaching significance of the *axis mundi:*

The axis of the world corresponds to the transcendent

reality of *Purusha,* the Essence that passes through all planes of existence, linking their respective centres with unconditioned Being, situated symbolically at the highest point of the axis, clear of the pyramid of existence, the likeness of which is the temple with its many storeys. (Snelling, p. 56)

Snelling himself comments:

The sacred Mount Kailas stands out of this elemental landscape, a compelling and uncannily symmetrical peak. Sheer walls of horizontally stratified conglomerate rock form a monumental plinth thousands of feet high that is finally capped by a cone of pure ice. Such is the regularity of the mountain that it looks as though it might have been carved by human – or more accurately, *superhuman* – hands: those of the gods in fact. Kailas has been frequently compared to a great temple, a cathedral, or a *stupa* – one of those characteristically Buddhist monuments known in Tibet as *chortens.* The analogy almost invariably has religious connotations, for in some mysterious ways Kailas seems to have the power to touch the spiritual heart of man; in the past this has been as true for hard-headed explorers as it has been for the more impressionable pilgrims. (Snelling, p. 22)

In Govinda's memoire, he states:

And, indeed, to the devotee it is a celestial temple, the throne of the gods, the seat and centre of cosmic powers, the axis or hub which connects the earth with the universe, the super-antenna for the influx and outflow of the spiritual energies of our planet....What the pilgrim sees with his naked eyes is only the sub-structure and emanation of something much more grand and far-reaching. To the Tibetan the mountain is inhabited and surrounded by thousands of meditating Buddhas and Bodhisattvas, radiating peace and bliss, and sowing the seeds of light into the hearts of those who want to liberate themselves from the darkness of greed, hatred, and ignorance. (Govinda, 1966, p. 215)

It is with interest that I have read these records of pilgrims' experiences of Mt. Kailash upon my return from my pilgrimage to that holy mountain. The path I follow with my teacher is that of bringing spirit into density, of slowly bringing the divine through my humanness. My path is not to rise above the dark aspects of my being but to encompass within love every part of my being. The union of dark and light is the quest of the mystic. It is my quest as I struggle to bring together the lightness of my soul with the dead, dragging weight not only of my body but of my personality, my psyche. From the moment I gave my word to go to Kailash and do prostrations around the mountain, I felt a commitment that seized all of me in its grip, body, mind, and soul. I felt no bravado and no confidence. I felt fear but it was unimportant. Without knowing any of this history or geography, still my heart knew that this temple is approached only in the context of surrender, of being devoured by the divinity that suffuses this sacred place. I expected to break apart psychologically, and I had no idea if my body could prostrate thirty-four miles through mountainous terrain in high altitudes and cold weather. Govinda speaks of all this:

> Nobody can approach the Throne of the Gods, or penetrate the *Mandala* of Shiva or Demchog, or whatever name he likes to give to the mystery of ultimate reality, without risking his life – and perhaps even the sanity of his mind. He who performs the Parikrama, the ritual circumambulation of the holy mountain, with a perfectly devoted and concentrated mind goes through a full cycle of life and death. (Govinda, 1966, p. 214)

When I went to Tibet, I wanted to go with the eyes of my soul and my human heart. I wanted Kailash and Tibet to teach me, rather than bringing the expectations of my intellect from other journeyers' perceptions. Reading these sources now, I remember walking back from a day of prostrations, looking at the mountainous foothills of Kailash rising up – always up - around me, struck by the vividness of the colors in the barren rock walls. Purples, reds, greens reflected back at me. The colors did not diminish as the angle of the sun shifted with the passing of the day. Reading Snelling's comment that the rarified air allows the natural colors of the mountains to shine through recalled that experience to me. Now, the voice of science whispers that the perception of my heart was true: the colors shone deeper and brighter, truer. But for me, there, I was at the center of the universe. I was at the only place that existed. Living in that profound endless moment, why would I think of science, or rarified air or light refracted through thicker air? There was only the experience, not to be analyzed or proved, but to be savored.

Govinda spoke of the accessibility yet overwhelming infinity of Mt. Kailash. I heard in his words what I had experienced:

> The mountain is so near that it seems to the pilgrim as if he could just walk over and touch it – and at the same time it is intangible in its ethereal beauty, as if it were beyond the realm of matter, a celestial temple with a dome of crystal or diamond. (Govinda, 1966, p. 215.)

Circumambulating Kailash is called Korah or parikrama. Many pilgrims from Tibet and many countries in the world come each year to walk Korah around Mt. Kailash. This circuit is thirty-four miles in length. Its highest point is Drolma La Pass, at an altitude of 18,500 feet. As with nearly this entire journey, I had never heard of Drolma La, and even once I was in Tibet and at Kailash, it took me a long time to connect those words, her Tibetan name, with Tara. Drolma La is the home of Tara, the enormously compassionate and powerful female Buddha of Tibet. It is said that in one incarnation, she was told that if she re-incarnated as a man, she would attain Buddahood quickly. She declined, saying there were many male Buddhas, and that she would persist to bring enlightenment through her female body. Although I did not know why, each time I thought of Drolma La, I would break down into tears. What was it that called me about Drolma La? I still do not know. I just prayed that if I was too weak or not meant to complete the Korah with prostrations that I would at least be allowed to reach Drolma La Pass.

Circumambulating Kailash is a cycle of death and life. It does destroy your mind and change your body. It does take away the illusion of knowledge and mastery, the blessing of Shiva/Demchog. As Govinda states, the fear of death loses its power because one learns "through the mercy of Tara, the Saviouress, [that] mercy is stronger than Karma." (Govinda, 1966, p. 217) Elsewhere, Govinda expresses the effect of the encounter with Kailash:

> There is no more need even for any 'armour', because he is the dragon and the knight, the slayer and the slain, the demon and the God....there is only one prayer in his mind: 'May I never forget it! May I ever be able to keep this realization alive within me!' (Govinda, 1966, p. 208)

Most pilgrims walk Korah around Mt. Kailash. A very small number circumambulate Kailash through prostrations. Tibetans call this by various names, including Korah with prostrations, Korah with puja, and Korah with prayer. I was told that it takes Tibetans seventeen days to prostrate around Kailash. My travel agent allocated twenty-five days for my effort. In August 2006, I completed my Khora with prostrations in twenty-eight days.

Prostrations are done while saying a mantra (a prayer) on the descent to the ground, and again on the re-ascent to standing. To begin a prostration, I join my hands above my head, in the transpersonal space above my head, begin the mantra, bring my hands down pausing at my forehead (Body), throat (Speech), and heart (Mind), and then kneel down, reach out with my hands in front of me and lower my body flat down onto the earth. I stretch my arms out in front of me. Then I pull my arms back, lift my upper body back to my knees, and stand up, with my hands above my head, coming down to my forehead, throat, and heart as I say the mantra. I used mantras in the Tibetan language, and occasionally used one in an English translation. For a walking prostration, one does the above, and then takes steps to where one's fingertips reached when lying flat on the ground. After stepping to that place, the next prostration begins.

When I felt called to go to Tibet and do prostrations around Mt. Kailash, I had never heard of Korah and did not know that doing prostrations around Kailash is a sacred ritual of the Tibetans. My friend Patrick had said to me one day, "Hey, Trace, I hear you're going to do Korah." My response had been, "What's Korah?" Korah is what I had committed to do, from the deepest level of my heart without knowing that it was called Korah. I only knew I was called to do it. A number of people told me that I was the first Westerner to do Korah with prostrations. One of my Nepalese travel agents told me that some Japanese have done this, and Tibetans have done this, but that he was unaware of any Westerner who had done this. One of my Tibetan guides told me that very few Tibetans do this, although one of his friends had just completed Korah with prostrations through heavy snow conditions. I met perhaps eight or ten Tibetans prostrating as I went around Kailash. Most moved much more quickly than I, and I do not know how many completed the circuit. I do know that Mt. Kailash is a small region in the wilderness, so news is of great interest in this isolated place, and travels quickly around the mountain. I received feedback at various times that some people expected me to be walking the end of Korah, not prostrating. I guess few expected me to be able to do the rigorous thirty-four mile journey.

I am not surprised! Nothing could have prepared me for any aspect of this journey, including the unbelievably rough terrain of the mountain. I was constantly prostrating on rocks, from small jagged stones to sizable boulders, unless I was going through shallow streams, or along the edges of rivers, rock-filled deltas, areas where runoff from the mountains had washed out the path and left a thick layer of stones cast about everywhere, or fields of foot-high mounds or hillocks formed as the waters ran through flat areas on their way down from the hills towards the river. I prostrated up and down hillsides and mountainsides on trails no wider than my body, and on some trails that canted at a thirty-degree angle just above an embankment dropping down into white water. I prostrated on the skinny Korah trail snaking around the edges of ravines. I prostrated up and through the streets Darchen, the one town at the base of Mt. Kailash, and through a construction site there. There were one or two stretches of flattened, road-like area on the thirty-four mile path, but all terrain of the Korah was simply what it was, loved for what it asked of and gave to me.

Buddhist thought recognizes manifestations of wisdom referred to as Body, Speech, and Mind. Of the three sacred mountains, Kailash holds the wisdom of Body, while Lapchi holds the wisdom of Speech, and Tsari holds the wisdom of Mind. (Tsewang Lama, p. 116) Govinda articulates the subtle mystery of Body, Speech, and Mind.

> To the enlightened man...whose consciousness embraces the universe, to him the universe becomes his 'body', while his physical body becomes a manifestation of the Universal Mind, his inner vision an expression of the highest reality, and his speech an expression of eternal truth and mantric power....The Mystery of the Body is here not that of materiality, of physical embodiment, but the mystery of the boundlessness, the all embracing wholeness, of the 'universal body'. The Mystery of Speech is more than that of mere words or concepts, it is the principle of all mental representation and communication...in which highest knowledge is represented and imparted. It is the mystery of creative sound, of mantric speech, of sacred vision, from which flows the *Dharma*-revelation of a saint, an Enlightened One, a Buddha. The Mystery of the Mind... is more than what can be conceived and grasped by way of thoughts and ideas: it is the principle of spiritualization, the realization of the spirit in the realm of matter, of the

infinite in the finite, of the universal in the individual; it
is the transformation of the mortal body into the precious
vessel...." (Govinda, 1969, p. 225-226)

How perfect that it was Kailash that called me, Kailash that holds
the wisdom of Body. Through the Khora or parikrama, the ritual
circumambulation around Mt. Kailash, it felt like the ego or the
separateness of my individual body was broken down and broken open.
Although I had not read Govinda's elegant exposition of the meaning
of Body, Speech, and Mind, his description of the mystery of Body is in
fact what happened to me at Kailash. The concerns of my ego, my self,
my physical body gave way to the universality, the infinity that radiates
from every atom of Kailash. The linearity of my intellect dissolved in its
irrelevance to the door in which I stood at that great mountain. Linear
thinking, explanation, control in any form collapsed into the heart of this
mountain which melted the very thought of reductionistic explanations,
of limitation. All time and space is held here. It is indeed the center,
the heart of existence. When I chose to go to Kailash, I knew I would
be stepping into the Void, the great generative emptiness that is the
nothingness that holds everything. I knew it would devour me, dissolve
and purify me, in its profound act of loving me. Govinda articulates the
destruction of illusion that allows re-birth in the pilgrim of Kailash:

> The interrelationship of these forces – solar and lunar
> energy, conscious and subconscious forces, the principles
> of light and darkness, male and female energies, action
> and contemplation, emptiness and form – is the great
> discovery of Tantric philosophy. He who realizes its
> truth is fit to worship the awe-inspiring Master of Kailas,
> whether he sees him in the form of Shiva, the destroyer
> of this world of illusion, or in the form of Demchog, who
> like Shiva tears asunder the elephant-hide of ignorance....
> (Govinda, pp. 202-203)

Kailash is a liminal space, a living doorway, linking the finite and
the infinite, the mundane and the sublime. More than anything else I
have ever done, this journey of prostrating around this sacred mountain
brought my life into a dance with infinity. Divinity, the sacred, the
infinite, was no longer a place I went to pray and rest. Divinity had come
into the fibers of every moment of my life. It was now here. It was now
everywhere.

The Preparation

My Human Heart

How does one prepare for a journey that is beyond the edges of one's understanding? Again and again, it was only settling into my heart that guided me. Obviously, my intellect, my head, did not understand or it would have guided me. But I have traveled little, I know little of Buddhism, and I am not an athlete, so my store of historical experience was not to be a bulwark on which I relied as I attempted prostrations around Mt. Kailash! In preparing this account of my journey, I read through my journals from the year before I left for Mt. Kailash. In August 2005, I wrote of a mantra or saying that came into my awareness: *My human heart is big enough to hold me.* I realized in that moment that I was beginning to trust my heart again, instead of my intellect first. There is still a battle. I want to know first, I want to understand before I take a step. Yet there it was: My heart is big enough...to hold me. I have safety, whenever I want to rely on it. Trust was beginning to re-awaken, an event that is both pretty amazing and tenderly vulnerable. What will I do if I don't think first all the time? What will I do if I live before I think?

In the way that I have been working with my teacher and with my own path in this life, I have been striving to go deeper than my intellect. Even though I work as a psychologist, it has always been clear to me that it is not the personality that is important. Personality is just a packaging, it is not the contents. And often, because there is so much spin in our public presentation, the information on the package is erroneous. My personality is a crystallization of my life history, the events that I have experienced as I was born and grew up, in a family, in this society, as an individual. My personality is a dynamic but repetitive structure, a cage, really. It is a package or enclosure that I created as I came into this life, trying to figure out how to be, and mostly how to survive. I created concepts with

15

my intellect to organize an understanding of my experiences. I created sensory perceptions to organize my physical experience.

I also created emotions, which are different from feelings. Feelings are core felt responses: grief, fear, anger, pain, joy. Emotions are situational variants, superficial distortions of pure feeling, attached to some event. When I returned from Tibet, I spent one evening organizing gifts I had brought back for my precious friends in class. Sitting in my living room, pouring water from Lake Manasarovar into small bottles for my friends, sorting out packets of incense, organizing small medals I had brought back to commemorate my Khora with prostrations: I could not stop a wrenching wailing and crying. I was so lonely for Tibet! I could not bear to not be there! Then I remembered my teacher's teachings, that there is historical reaction and there is true feeling. So I paused to sort out what was historical and what was true feeling. Everything just *stopped*, immediately. I realized I had been wailing in history, as it were, wailing from the memory of losses throughout my life that I was still resisting and coveting. Then, the true grief arose, and I felt consumed with it. I felt like I was in the center of a white hot furnace that completely surrounded me. I knew I would not die from this feeling. Death would have been easy. Instead, I would live with my heart so open to the beauty of Tibet that my heart was saturated, drowned, and uplifted in an ocean of the feeling of grief.

It seems to me, too, that personality does a poor job with the notion of choice. I have found little true open-heartedness in my personality. When I choose from the level of personality, I generally have numerous strings attached, consciously or unconsciously, but there nonetheless. I will choose something with an expectation of how it will play out, of what will come back to me. When I have true open-heartedness, I choose with a willingness that encompasses a number of things. I choose with a knowledge that I do not know what the outcome will be, and that I will stand by my choice regardless. I choose with a willingness to take responsibility for the outcome of that choice, pleasant or unpleasant, to stay in that moment, that experience, rather than holding onto it to try to get it to continue, or pushing it aside to try to deny or delete it. Such open-hearted choice does not control the moment. It stays with each moment until the next moment arises, whether the moment is a second or a year in length.

Some place much deeper than my personality has always been my focus as I have lived through the years of my life. I now call that place my human heart. For many years, I lived in my spiritual or energetic heart, my beautiful light body where I could live separately from my human body and my human history. I could not straighten out the mess of my human life deeply enough to make sense of it, so I lived in meditative states, trance states, bliss states. Wonderful states! When I began to study with Marcus, I learned for the first time a way to begin to integrate my body, mind, and soul, all the levels of me, into my act of living this life. It is not at all that everyone should or needs to do this. But it is essential for me to live in my human form as completely as in my spiritual form. Thinking, which psychology does very well, is not integration. Meditation, which spirit does very well, is not integration. It is only in feeling my dense, human body, and receiving the gift of spirit, knowledge, and feeling in my human body as well as in my soul and mind that I feel I am honoring the human path of my life. When the realization that my human heart was big enough to hold me arose, it was a wonderful moment. It was a re-opening of trust that my human heart is a safe and encompassing place for me to live. I made a note in my journal which reflected this step towards living from my heart instead of warring against or succumbing to my personality:

> A kindness to my personality. Like a member of the family that I am always having to apologize for, understanding that "she is just that way," reactive, brittle, greedy, totally self-interested, fearful for her survival, attacking, and very paranoid: that's my personality. Non-resilient. Slowly, I am being kind with her instead of trying to get rid of her, realizing that the defects of my personality reflect the strategies that it took for me to survive, not random and gratuitous, but specifically designed. Being kind with her, but not letting her drive the car. A first moment of compassion for my personality. Because my heart holds me, I can have compassion for my personality.

My self-hate would continue to arise at times, and slowly there was compassion for it instead of resistance to it. I slowly realized it was not something I needed to withstand or suppress, but something I needed to receive with kindness and love. Hate was ravaging me. My ravaging me in the hate was surely not a remedy. It was surely not an act of kindness. Loving me is not an action. It is a state, a state of being; a state of just receiving what is there instead of doing something with it. My personality will not do this because it will die. My personality has a self-interest in maintaining its point of view, in justifying the way it is. My personality is not interested in the present moment. It is only scanning to find where the past is happening again. I often feel at loose ends, rather unemployed, when I leave the past behind and meet the present moment without expectations, as new and fresh and unknown. Only my love will do this. As my heart opens, there is more love supporting me than I have trusted, and I am trusting more.

St. Francis has a famous prayer that begins, *Lord, Make me an instrument of your peace. Where there is hatred, let me sow love; where there is injury, pardon; where there is doubt, faith; where there is despair, hope; where there is darkness, light; where there is sorrow, joy....* I had left my family for fourteen years. I prayed that prayer every day for two years before I had the strength to re-contact my father to begin to mend my relationship with him. Several years after re-connecting and healing this piece of family history, I visited Easter Island. The Franciscans had sent missionaries there. During a week on Easter Island that changed my life, I was sitting in one of the Churches there, just looking at the iconography. There was a statue of St. Francis in his friar's robe, but with the head of the Birdman, the main deity of the local religion of Easter Island. Sitting before this statue, Francis gave me the understanding that his prayer is a prayer for me. It is not a prayer for peace between others, but for peace within me. It was peace with me that I needed to find before I could approach my father. As I work with my human heart, not just my spiritual heart, feeling and receiving love through my humanness, I realize that it is my own hatred that is transformed into love, my own darkness that is transformed into light, my own despair that is transformed into hope. And from there, I step out onto this planet, into this life, not for others, but as who I am.

Shortly after I received the call to go to Tibet, I was reading Milarepa's biography. Milarepa is Tibet's greatest saint. At the beginning, a student asked him about his evil deeds, and there is a whole chapter where he explains what he did. What touched me so deeply was the dispassionate way Milarepa spoke. He did not apologize, express regret, suffer, or rationalize. He just said what he did. There was a resonant quality of emptiness in his words. I felt the hope in my heart that someday I might love from such emptiness. In my journal in August 2005 I wrote:

> I am broken, and I will always be broken. And I am Tracey
> and I am a blessing. I will always have my history and maybe
> it will always hurt. I will not always be attached to it.

Preparations

Not being a very physically oriented person, I thought it might make sense if I put some time into developing more physical strength and endurance. So one evening, in the hustle and bustle of my usual schedule, I stopped by the local department store to check out exercise machines. I had it in my head that a recumbent bicycle was the thing I needed, but the single overburdened salesman made me wait so long that I finally began passing the time by trying out everything in the store. The minute I stood on the ellipsis machine, I knew it was going to work what my body needed working. The recumbent bikes paled by comparison. I explored machines from a variety of brands, picked the one that suited me best, and purchased it. I had to return later to pick it up from the warehouse, and the stockboy muscled it into the back of my suv. It was in a box, and I incorrectly assumed it was mostly assembled. I muscled the box into my living room, and tore it open, which was a job in itself. I found containers of bolts, screws, and wrenches, directions, and a packet of axle grease. I was overwhelmed, and decided to go to sleep rather than having a meltdown in the face of this task. Thankfully, I am pretty good with mechanical things, but the soup-to-nuts presentation was a bit much for that night. Eventually, I returned to the task, assembling the arms of the machine and the base. Then I tackled the electrical part, and finally put the whole thing together, applying axle grease at the spots where the rather indistinct diagram indicated. It wasn't perfect, but it worked. I remember my first effort on the ellipsis: I stood on the huge foot pedals and pumped...for one minute, according to the timer. I was exhausted! I remember later attempting again, and in a day, I had doubled my time to two minutes, after which I was utterly spent! But I must say I was so proud of myself for doing two minutes. I persisted, and over time, I began to do half an hour, and eventually an hour. A friend of mine asked how I was doing, and I mentioned I was doing half an hour. She enthusiastically told me that that was what the Hollywood stars do with their trainers. It seemed too easy to me, but I was happy to think that maybe I was working at a level that was a respectable benchmark for getting in shape.

There is a beauty in doing prostrations, and for me, there was an essential need to do them once I had experienced them. If I do not integrate my body into what I am doing, it is not as complete an experience. I can meditate, and feel nourished. But if my mediation is doing T'ai Chi, I am more completely nourished since I am also moving. I found learning to do prostrations a great gift. I began to practice doing them in my room during my morning prayers. Later, I went out onto my big, beautiful deck, and found that eighteen circuits around the deck required one hundred eight prostrations, which is one mala of prostrations. A mala is the Eastern prayer beads, like the Christian rosary, and contains one hundred eight beads.

I gradually increased the number of prostrations I would attempt. When I first was able to do a whole mala, I thought it a great accomplishment. Then I began doing more than one mala at a session. In my journal for June 2006, I noted that I had an unexpectedly free weekend, and decided to do ten malas of prostrations. I did, and then slept for ten hours! I wrote

> Going to Mt. Kailash is like the difference between dying when you don't know you are going to die, and going knowing I am going to die step by step every step of the way. I did ten malas of prostrations yesterday. I was so exhausted, I was surprised how exhausted. I am encouraging myself to do ten malas today. It will take most of my day. Trying to get myself to find socks and add my new boots instead of prostrating barefoot, I finally had a small meltdown, and now continue forward, finding my socks, moving into a day of preparation through my body and my heart for Kailash, Blessed Kailash, Blessing of Kailash.

> I won't understand this until it is over.

> Today I feel that I cannot do this by momentum. It is the dead weight of choice, in the dead weight of joy. From nowhere else can I attempt this. All there is to do this from is Love.

I managed to do the ten malas for a second day in a row. In my simple way, I was trying to build endurance. I felt it was one thing to do ten malas and rest for a day or a week, but it was another to do ten day after day. Following this I wrote:

> It is the commitment to prepare as best I can, more than the effort itself that is preparing me. I just don't know what will happen at Kailash, and I don't really think I have any control over it either, nor do I need control. This experience is so large I have no concept of why I am going or what needs to happen or what will meet me there. But today, doing another ten malas, at times I felt so sick, at times I felt like I would just shake apart. I wondered how I would manage to keep going when I am in Tibet, in a strange

land with less air and out in the open and not knowing the language, and not being very strong physically. My knees hurt; I'm still searching for the right knee protectors. But I did wear my hiking shoes for the first time, and I was able to manage the prostrations with that addition. Afterwards, I can't really do anything. It's been about eight hours since I finished, and in the last hour or two, I have been able to think and do things a bit, but very little, and very soon I am going to sleep. When I do that many prostrations, it's really all I can do for the day, pretty much. I am surprised it reaches so deeply into me. I don't think it is all the physical demands, although my whole body has been used by the time I'm done. I am very slowly learning to listen better to my body/heart and less to my anxiety/control issues. I worry if I stop to rest, I will not have time to go around Kailash. I know finishing is not the point, but I have not quite let go of that one yet. I am continually realizing just how immense this is for me. It is not bigger than what I signed up for; it's just bigger than anything my intellect can grasp. It is so far beyond me. No matter what happens at Kailash, I have already been shown how infinitesimally small I am in the expanse of what is possible. A very tiny little sparkly diamond chip. How come I cannot yet hold this awareness every day? Why do I get lost in routine and lose awareness? It is coming. It is coming.

It's all just so much, and it's only the beginning. I don't know what I'm going to, and I don't know what I'm coming back to. Really, how blessed is that, even though it's a little big. Only after the prostrations today did I start having meltdowns, and I don't even know what they're about. It just feels better when I am not so controlled, when I do not suppress the tears. There's so much to let go of, and it is not happening on the level of my conscious mind.

A dear friend Ed is a leather worker. I asked him to make me an apron for my prostrations. I had read that the Tibetans wear a leather apron to protect their bodies from the constant contact with the ground. He not only made me the most wonderful apron. He gave me the very fine quality leather, and did not charge me for his labor, not even for the adjustment on the straps which I needed in the midst of his busy schedule. For the last week and a half of prostrations around Mt. Kailash, I stopped wearing my knee protectors, as they seemed to be creating pain in one knee rather than protection. I felt the cushioning of that thick high quality leather apron then.

Now, that apron is an amazing creation. It belongs in a museum. As I prostrated around Mt. Kailash, many people who were walking the Khora would stop me. Almost all immediately were interested in the leather. They would touch it, check the thickness of it, turn it over, examine the apron, and ask me questions about it. A young man who seemed quite the wheeler-dealer conveyed to me in Tibetan that when I had finished Khora with prostrations, he wanted to buy the apron from me. I refused. He thought I did not understand him due to the language barrier, but I understood him perfectly, and refused as many times as he asked, which was very many.

When I was learning prostrations, I would add more and more of what would be with me at Kailash. I prostrated one day in the rain, on my deck, with my coat, leggings, and skirt on. I felt strongly that I wanted to wear a skirt over my hiking pants or leggings as a sign of respect to the culture. I added socks and hiking boots, which was quite different and much heavier than prostrating barefoot. It is all about weight. Marcus had told me I would not want to be carrying a backpack because of the weight. I had thought, *What's the big deal about a small daypack?* Well, let me tell you what the big deal is: *Any* weight is more weight. Carrying the weight of my body was sufficient challenge. There was no gratuitous weight, no weight that was just an add-on. Every single ounce mattered. I recall when I first added the apron while doing prostrations at home. The leather apron weighs four pounds. The day I added the apron, I did five malas with it on, on a hot day. The five malas took me two hours and twenty minutes, a bit longer than prostrating without the apron. But just that additional four pounds wiped me out. I am very sensitive to any pressure on my body, and the additional four pounds of weight hanging on my body affected me deeply. I just sat for the rest of the day, literally too tired to organize my thoughts, much less move around or do things physically. The following day, I did five malas again with the apron, and recovered more quickly physically. I was developing resilience as I entered this space. While this is true, more than resilience is arising within me. After the second day of prostrations with the apron, my journal entry notes: *Longing to do prostrations tomorrow.* The nature of this endeavor, this calling to come home to Kailash, is filling not only my intention but my body. I am hungry to dance more prostrations.

There was a colossal crisis in my preparations for Tibet. In February 2006, we had a major snowstorm. About two feet of snow fell in New Jersey where I was for a training. I went out in the morning to help shovel out the drive and walkways where I was staying. I had just picked up a shovel, not even taken one shovelful, and I felt something shift in my back. I knew I could not lift anything. I could perhaps push snow, a bit, but really I knew I could not do any physical labor. I had herniated a disc thirteen years ago for which I had surgery. I have had no problems since, and I have not abused or overused my body. But I recognized the feeling. I was frightened and overwhelmed by this sudden onset of a back that was not going to let me move, walk, or certainly do prostrations.

I got home to New Hampshire, struggling with the impact of my back going out. I sent this e-mail to Marcus in February 2006:

> ...Whatever is going on with my back, it is just shoving around a lot. I keep crying and crying, I don't even know why. When I find the poor-me part, I can choose deeper, something other than victim, but frankly I just don't know what's going on. I feel like Tibet is being taken away from me, and there are a million thoughts about that. I know it doesn't matter. If I can commit to Tibet, I can commit to this moment, even though I keep losing that. It's harder to see how I lie and cheat in this moment than in my preparations for Tibet. I know I often turn being in my moment, vulnerability, whatever, into rising above it, being in spite of it, being to push past it – rather than being, raging, to receive the love of this very moment. So I'm just letting all this come to me, because when I "do" something, like try to rage instead of letting the rage find me, I am controlling and manipulating and insisting it is my way.
>
> I hurt. It's not terrible, but my back is not really getting better. It's not getting worse, I don't think, and I'm grateful for that. I have an appointment with my orthopedic surgeon on Friday morning, and the anti-inflammatories he put me on are helping. Currently, I can't get up from my futon, so I've moved into the guest room. I miss my room, but I really like the bed. It's showing me that it's time to come up from the floor. I'm going to order a beautiful bed for myself, probably custom made, this weekend. I'm starting to do some practice again. I had stopped everything. I have just been so devastated I haven't known how to exist – I mean, my intellect is saying

"What is my problem?", but I am just shattered on some
level, that Tibet may be taken away, and I'm letting that
devastation find it's way. There is so much self-hate that
is coming again, and I am kinder with me as it arises. I
did one prostration last night, but I am not letting myself
push that 'til I talk to my doc. I am so sad.

I had also called Marcus after sending the e-mail that evening. I was
doing my best to put on a brave front and be accepting, but I needed
to just withdraw into sleep, to get away from the physical pain and the
overwhelming misery of feeling like Tibet would be taken away from
me since I could not really move. I left a message on Marcus' answering
machine, and mentioned I was just going to go to sleep. I did, and an hour
or two later, my phone rang. In the bleariness of interrupted, miserable
sleep, I answered, half awake, and heard a voice that I can only describe
as a bell. Marcus was there. I don't think he even said hello. I remember
his pure, clear voice saying with such simplicity and kindness, "Don't you
understand that the obstacles are coming now so that they don't come
in Tibet? Where is your empowerment?" Really, once he said this, it was
like one of those duh-moments, so obvious once someone says it. Where,
indeed, was my empowerment? Where was my faith?

I never did fully wake up during that phone call. He asked me how I
was, and I realized in that moment that in the pain of this injury, I had
literally gone crazy for the past four days. The place in my body, and its
effect of taking away my ability to move, to escape, to control my pelvis,
had triggered a flashback from my abuse history, and I had just gone
crazy. I had broken up my mind and gone far away to avoid the terror.
That was the moment I suddenly understood what Marcus had taught
so often, and what I had intellectually long understood: if a traumatic
memory comes, do not go to or away from it. Just stay in your human
heart and let it come to you. Do not leave your heart; there is nothing to
do but stay in your heart. I got it. It would not have lessened the terror of
this memory, but I would not again have shattered my mind in a fruitless
attempt to avoid what is. I would simply have stayed and received that
experience, not as a trauma, but as an experience.

I remember, too, in that conversation that Marcus asked me if I was
doing any prostrations. I told him that I had been unable to do any,
but on that day, I had done one. I remember telling him that that one
prostration had been done with so much consciousness and love that it
was like I had done a thousand. I will never forget that learning. It is never
the amount. It is how present I am, how open in love.

Backs take time. Later in February, I noted in my journal:

> I relapsed with my back Saturday, I think, or Sunday. I
> woke up in the wee hours with a lot of pain, and I knew
> I was very subtly in victim/resentment, poor-me that I
> have to deal with this. In the early morning darkness
> and the pain, I didn't see how not to be resentful – what
> did it mean to choose/feel love in this impossible pain
> and limitation. And then I got it, I remembered Marcus'
> teaching, I just said, "Feeling love now, anything goes."
> Love is in control, not me. Choose love and receive what
> is. This moment in the early morning darkness was a
> major step past my constant mental controlling. Love
> no matter what is happening. Love before knowing, love
> before anything, and then stay in love through "what
> goes." I'm still being gentle, doing what I can with my back
> as it is, but I'm not in victim. My heart is open and I am
> not evaluating, judging, and resisting all the time.

It takes a plane ticket to get to Tibet. One travel agent, Joe, was
endlessly patient with this inexperienced traveler. I felt I made endless
phone calls to him. He asked if I wanted to fly in through the Middle
East, Nepal, or China. How would I know? Because of the time changes,
I had to spend an overnight in an airport either flying in or flying home
– which did I want? I finally settled on flying into Nepal through Delhi,
and spending the overnight on the way in. I thought I would be anxious
to just come home once I was headed back, lifetime away though it was.
As I finalized my plane tickets, I wrote in my journal in March 2006:

> Tibet continues to work on me. Practice has been calling
> me lately. And surrender is such a difficult feeling – no
> complaint, I don't know the words, it's just I find myself
> feeling not well, or tired in an odd way, or like I don't
> know how I'll do prostrations, and then I realize it's just
> that I can't control this experience, this process. I either
> do it or I don't, but if I do, it does it its way, not mine. I
> can't do it well. I can only do it.
>
> I have had an awful weekend, and I woke up at 3 am
> realizing that it's because I'm just not kind to myself, and I
> had not been conscious of this. I wonder if masochism will

ever stop being a habit. It doesn't matter, the perception slipped through. It is extraordinarily difficult to accept love. There is so much love available, and I keep setting up requirements for worthiness even when I don't consciously realize I'm doing that. But then I don't feel well, and at some point I see that once again I'm choosing the I'm-just-never-good-enough-for-me pattern, so how good am I ever going to feel with that going on. Nothing new, but the experience of surrendering to love is like being a hillside that is dissolving into a mudslide, like everything I think is important just sloughs off. It's not even important to know what it was, it just slides off into the ocean. And then I feel the terror and the exhilaration of that much love being available, and nothing that I am required to do for it. Practice helps. I can't get this through my mind, my intellect. Only my human heart can bear this much love, and I trust the deeper levels more simply.

Marcus e-mailed me that there was some rioting in Kathmandu, which I would be flying into, and that the American Embassy was closed. He suggested checking a Nepalese newspaper that I can access on-line, and gave me some people I can contact to help me get information. He said, "Your experiences keep on happening and the love is endless." In my heart I thanked him for reminding me it is all about love, and the love is endless. I wrote him some time later:

Dear Marcus, I want to share a clarity arising. Really, what you are teaching is love before love. Love even before choosing love. And the feelings of grief, fear, anger, pain, and joy are qualities of love – that's where density and spirit meet, through feeling. I'm just realizing the immensity of that doorway. Density and spirit meet in feeling in the human heart. It's so enormous to surrender to being human, to feeling. Neurosis/history or energy are easy. Feeling-in-love is something else. It's the only aliveness. I am grateful for you every day.

Blessings

It has long been a mystery why I am surrounded by such profoundly loving friends, all the more amazing since I am socially shy and reclusive. Yet my friends have found me over the years, and have stayed, and sometimes have insisted on being my friends until I could risk knowing that they were there. They have stayed through my silences, loving me as I am. I want to share how so many supported me as I dared to turn my eyes toward Kailash and Tibet.

David has been my friend for over 30 years. He loved me before I consciously knew what love was. I still remember seeing the love in his face, and I was terrified and puzzled: Who would love me? But David did and always has, and sustained this for all the years of our time. And I love him.

In December 2005, David sent me Mary Oliver's poem, *Wild Geese*, saying he was "Thinking of you as you prepare to take your soul journey to Tibet." I answered, saying I would need all of his love, support, and prayers as I approach and enter Tibet, more deeply than I could ever ask or express; that he always showed up in my life, a manifestation of pure love, touching me gently and strengthening me to stay on the path. My feet wander off; they get lost in my head which tells me I am doing something when I am only thinking it, or when I'm really doing something else. But David has just remained present, and has helped me not get lost. I thanked him with my love for sharing and being who he is.

I stayed with another dear friend Emily for nearly a year during a major transition in my life. She took me in, and I learned about being nurtured in a way I had never experienced. Many evenings, over a hot cup of tea, we would just sit, and sometimes talk. My journal from May 2006 notes,

> I said to Emily last night, "If I am the same when I come back from Tibet, shoot me." It just came out of my mouth, and I meant it. It took awhile for me to feel what a cruel thing that was to say! She said, "If you are the same when you come back from Tibet, love you." That's it. Loving me first. To allow love to come and love me. It's all love, endless love. Surrender.

Another friend, Catherine, drove an hour to have lunch with me at my home because she wanted to see me before I left. We are all too busy. Yet she took a rare free morning and gave it to me. My friend Snow made me a little travel kit, little because there is never enough room to pack everything. From her travels, she blessed me with a sewing kit, a tiny pocket knife, a bandaid, a toothpick, and her love.

Tulku Thubten Rinpoche teaches on Vajrayogini, and has touched my heart deeply with his presence and teachings. During one teaching, I asked Tulku Thubten Rinpoche for his blessing for my journey to Mt. Kailash, and for a teaching. As he blessed me, he said there is an inner journey and an outer journey. Go to Kailash and leave behind all my illusions. Leave behind all my concepts and thoughts from all my lifetimes. He said my journey has already begun. There is not much left to surrender. He said that Wisdom is Oneness with Truth is True Nature. He said liberation is to be revealed, not produced. Give up searching. Vajrayogini, Buddha nature, is not outside you. He blessed me. It was a deep and beautiful blessing.

I asked Shenpen Dawa Rinpoche if there was anything in particular I should focus on during prostrations around Mt. Kailash. He said the Seven Line Prayer. I told Marcus, who had encouraged me to speak with Rinpoche, and told him that I did not have the Seven Line Prayer Practice. Marcus said he would get it for me. I waited, but with so many things on his mind, after several weeks, I asked again. Marcus smiled at me and told me to be patient. Later he gave me the practice, and as he handed it to me, he blessed me so powerfully I felt a riptide surge through my whole being, body, mind, and soul.

Realizations

I have worked a great deal, all my life. It is at once a dysfunctional pattern from my family of origin, so ingrained that it is second nature, and it is a vehicle of service, of teaching myself and of giving back the joys and blessings I have been given. I cannot remember when I have taken more than a couple of weeks at a time off from work. The thought of taking a quarter of a year off, no work, no income, was initially impossible for me to consider. Then in turn it was terrifying, guilt-inducing, possible, enticing, and fabulous. As I wrestled with committing to go to Tibet in October 2005, I noted:

> I'm scared of taking three months off for Tibet, and I know I must do that next. It's my next step. I know a lot of things in my life need to change, and I can feel me hanging onto them by my fingernails, even as they fall apart under my hands. I'm so scared of being scared I don't usually let myself feel it, so it's good to feel the fear, even in glimpses.

I began to find that making decisions, and knowing, arose more from my heart than from my intellect.

My mind is serving me less and less. I feel that when I try to understand anything it's just all a mess. And then sometimes from my heart I feel that everything is empty, immediate, pure and empty, and all the mess goes away. I feel safe then, and effortless. And then I try to express something with words and it's all a mess again. Words are impossible.

In January 2006, I wrote of beginning to learn what choice truly is. Through the thickness of my habits, I slowly began to realize that even beneath the automaticity of habit, I am making a choice. I also began to experience that the choices before me were tinier and tinier, yet required more and more effort. Smaller and smaller aspects of my behavior and intention caught my eye and asked what my word was worth. Even in the secrecy of my own mind, the choices became not subtle but stark: Do I complain and whine, do I bargain or engage in magical thinking, or do I keep my word that I accept Tibet's invitation, that I surrender to that invitation with openness and not control, and in every moment and not just when I feel like it? I wrote, "It is not the big things that save my soul."

I wish I could convey the profundity of this experience. I told Marcus in class one day that it seemed that giving your word changes your life. When you give your word, your life is over. This is how I had felt since I committed to Tibet. He asked me if I had ever given my word that deeply before, and that clarified things: I had not. I had not even known it was possible. I had been in two committed relationships. I had given my commitment, the best I knew at those times. But this was qualitatively different. I stood not leaning on the shoulder of Tibet, but solidly in my own shoes, responsible and alone in this choice. And because it was all mine to do with what I chose, there was surrender, an openness to the experience. Not a picture of what it would be like, not an expectation of what it should be like, but a willingness to show up and receive what it was going to be like, because I had said I would. There were no contingencies, no strings, and no clauses. Just me in the moment of my life named Tibet and Khora.

The choice to keep my word was always with me. It was not possible to lie to myself. If I wanted to cheat on prostrations or exercise, it was clearly a choice to cheat. It was not that I didn't really agree to that amount of physical preparation, or that I did not really know I was slacking off. Seeing it so clearly as cheating, rather than blurring the evasion of my word, made all the difference. I was free to do whatever I wanted, cheat or keep my word, but I also knew what I had committed to do. I should say that, perhaps for the first time in my life, this was also not about rigidity. I did not discipline myself to do a certain number of prostrations or time on the ellipsis machine, or practice and prayer. In a life I had survived largely by dogged discipline, this journey was never about discipline. It was about choice, about willingness without knowing what I was agreeing to, about relying on my heart and on divinity, not my intellect, my will, or my image. I wrote,

> Generally constantly upset. The goal is not to feel good, it is to feel. Understanding will never create change. Vitality and choice will. It's not choice to do something, it's choice to be this moment.

My departure date was late July 2006. By mid-May 2006, I was in full swing, striving to prepare while working fulltime and trying to keep all the complexities of modern life in motion. I noted on May 15, 2006,

> I am not prostrating or exercising. I am getting five or six hours of sleep if I'm lucky. But my heart is in Tibet, in love, in worship. I have confidence I will be OK. July feels like tomorrow. Help me.

This effort to live from my heart rather than my knowledge was ongoing. On May 22, 2006, I wrote:

> I can't choose deeper from my head, only from my heart, and I don't – I fumble with that, I want to think the choice instead of be the choice. In my heart, it's not the words; it's the being, it's truth: I do or I do not love me deeper. It's nothing about the words. When I love me deeper from my heart, there's nothing else, no explanation, no reason, just complete commitment at my capacity. No wiggle room.

> It's like Tibet. I give my word not because I know how to do it right or because I know what will happen, but because I will keep my word every moment no matter what every moment looks like. I will keep my word not knowing what it looks like to keep my word as each new moment arises.

No schedule after Tibet. Faith. What am I supposed to do? I don't control that. Faith.

On May 29, 2006, I awoke furious, raging, crying out to divinity:

> Why the fuck did you call me? I feel like I received a call, and I'm packed and dressed and I've got all my stuff together, and I've got special gear and I've been busily preparing – and now, I walk through a door and I'm in a huge space like an airplane hangar, and it's empty, huge and empty, and I'm standing here, a speck in a huge empty void – standing here, wondering, Why the fuck did you call me? What am I doing here? *I can't do this* is all around the edges of my consciousness. Despair is all around the edges of my consciousness.

It took a day or two to calm myself. Finally, I wrote:

> Be still in love. The past returns with love. The past and future have already been loved. My personality won't do this because it will die. Only my love is doing this. There is more love supporting me than I trust, and I am trusting more. Obstacles are not obstacles. They are perfect manifestations to choose yes, no, or victim.

> To accept the dakinis' invitation, I must have been out of my mind, which I was. I was in my heart.

The preparations, the choices, continued.

> June 18, 2006: Doing prostrations with more conscious love today. Doing prostrations still has a great impact on me. I felt irritable, needing to go to bed early. Or are the prostrations just stripping away the lie of how I live? I don't know how to live this life newly. I must choose more love first, and then live differently. I've been trying to do it the other way around.

> June 24, 2006: It is increasingly clear to me that compassion towards me is the fundamental stance, the foundation of all love. I am taking a day off, tonight and tomorrow. I am

taking a day off, because why would I not? Because loving me cannot be obstructive to anything else. Because the point of Tibet, and of every moment, is love, and includes *everything*. I have kept myself separate from my tears. It is time to un-do that separation.

It is the silver I bring, not the tarnish.

"I should be gentle with me today," I wrote. "My quads hurt a lot from prostrations. I am overwhelmed with reading Milarepa's one-pointedness and complete dedication to his liberation. I pray for guidance." At the end of Milarepa's biography, it speaks of his enlightenment and how he became one with Dharmakaya, with beingness, union. I was shocked to feel fear as I read this. I was shocked that my first thought on reading this was that if that ever happened to me, Tracey would cease to exist, would just melt into all beingness – and I reflexively clung to Tracey and resisted the union with being! I was shocked, but there it was, clinging to my personality instead of melting into universal soul. It showed me how attached I am to self, how afraid I am to become one with Wisdom, with Being, with everything, with Love.

And still, one day, the song sang in me:

> Mother Yeshe Tsogyal, my ears are full of Dakini song! Everything only positive in me and in everyone. In life. I am done living as a victim. I am done doing a good job adjusting to what I didn't like and don't want. My heart is open to me. I am raging in my love….Giving up leaving my heart and standing outside myself to check if I'm doing it right!

Marcus' words stayed with me: "The thing to remember is all there is is love….and the love is endless." My own words stayed with me: "My heart is big enough to hold me." See taste touch smell hear blessing emptiness. Everything arises from emptiness. Everything I need, everything I will ever need, arises from emptiness. My refusal of love sustains the repetition of samsara. I am not broken, and I am not afraid.

Leaving Home

The day before I was to leave New Hampshire was amazing. Earlier in the day, I had closed my office and changed my phone message. Onto the next task. My travel agent in Nepal said he had not yet received money that had been wired to him a few days earlier. So I made my fourth trip to the bank. They finally told me the payment for my trip had been received yesterday, although my travel agent the night previously did not indicate he had received it. While the money transfer was good news, I had to wait quite awhile to hear this news at the bank. The bankers had run into customers with whom they were friendly, and were jovially chatting in the middle of the lobby. I was sitting there, waiting to be helped. I heard all about dog breeding and updates on the family, as I waited and waited for the person I needed to talk with. I finally stood up just to be more visible, but their happy chat continued. I am glad to say I was tired but not irritable, even when I found out that I needn't have waited at all since the wire allegedly went through. I was just glad the money had made it to Nepal. I then went to the teller to work out the cash I needed for the trip, spending money and travelers cheques...except that the teller did not know how to do travelers cheques. Another party ensued! She disappeared into the vault, and I heard such jocular chatting. She would emerge from time to time to ask me to repeat denominations and amounts. She thanked me for ordering these so she could "practice" learning how to do this better! She was sweet and just who she was. She finally counted out the various monies, slowly, one by one.

I had brought my cell phone in for repair a few days earlier, but it again stopped working. Then my headlight went out. So after the bank adventure, I had my headlight fixed, and headed to the phone store. As I pulled into the phone store parking lot, I noticed in the window reflection that my other headlight was now out! After much waiting, the phone store gave me a loaner, the best they could do as they had no new phones. As I was driving down the street, hoping I could get back to the car place before they closed, I called the car garage to tell them I was coming. I could hear them but they could not hear me. My phone was defective! So I hurried back to the phone store and got another loaner. I did make it back to the garage, at twenty to five, and they ushered me in.

With each task, I kept saying to myself, *No big deal, done, done, on to the next one,* ticking off each item on the list no matter how many times it took to get it resolved. I kept thinking that the obstacles occur now so they don't occur in Tibet. As I dealt with each task, from office to bank to car to cell phone, I kept thinking, *If I do not live the way I want, I will not die the way I want.*

On July 15, 2006, I left my home. Surprisingly, it was not wrenching. I am usually not good with separations, but aside from some concern for my sweet cats, it was really a simple leave-taking. Connor, my golden retriever, was already settled with the wonderful family who had given him to me many years ago, and I hoped he had a summer of swimming in their pond ahead of him. Liam, my little black cat, was only a year old, and he would not come out the whole morning of preparation. He would not come say good bye. Jesse, my big calico, is much older, and she lay quietly in the middle of the doorway wherever I was packing, just being with me in her own way.

The days before I left, I had wound myself up into a frenzy trying to pack for a trip I did not understand, trying to pack for winter when it was hot summer outside, trying to fit too much into too few duffel bags, not knowing what to take and what to leave. I finally just got an extra suitcase, took everything, and figured I would sort it out before I left for Newark Airport. There was still a seven-day advanced class with Marcus to attend before leaving the country for Nepal. It is very fortunate that I had those days. Each lunch break during class, I would walk into town and pick up cotton swabs or towlettes, purchase a wrist watch, and buy t-shirts at the consignment shop and a wrinkle-resistant skirt to wear to visit the lamas in Nepal. The woman in the consignment shop was an angel. As I calmed down, I was able to focus on what clothes I would probably need, and on each trip to her shop, she pulled out scores of choices to meet the need.

Marcus encouraged me to take a day off from class, and just stay at Dorothy's, my classmate with whom I was staying, and pack. I did not think I would need to do that, but he was right. That day was essential, and a timeless moment that let me organize myself with no pressure and no distractions. Dorothy was at class, I was at her home with a phone, a whole apartment to spread out in, and the quiet to reason my way through my best guess of what I would need in Nepal and Tibet.

> July 18, 2006: I am at Dorothy's, not at class. One day to organize and pack. I am calm. I am in a deep, quiet space. Around me is the void, and I feel my edge dissolving into it and I know I will be very afraid, but for now I rest in my center and appreciate this day in the eye of the hurricane to organize myself at last. Kevin says to roll clothes; it takes much less room packing that way. He's right. Each little sharing is a blessing.

> My travel insurance is still not clear. My insurance agent from New Hampshire and I are e-mailing, calling, but I cannot seem to understand the policy or his explanations. I'm sure

he can't understand me, either. My energy is all screwed up and that becomes the spark that ignites the overwhelm. I am not out of control, but I am ferociously assertive. I seize the phone. This gets straightened out today! It does. I finally lay down for a nap. At times, I get so overwhelmed with all the details, with trying to plan and dress for a trip I don't know. Then I remember where and why I'm going, the prostrations, and my heart becomes still in happiness.

Class

I have studied with Marcus Daniels for eight years. I attend every class I can. Each class changes my life. There are some of us who do an advanced class, where we meet for seven days at a time. Marcus asked the advanced class if we would be open to meeting earlier than usual, so that I would be able to attend class before leaving for Tibet. If we had followed our regular schedule, I would have been in Tibet when the next class met. Everyone very kindly agreed. It meant a lot to me that he asked and that everyone was willing to meet sooner in this arduous work, to adjust their schedules so I could receive their blessing before I left.

It is difficult to describe that day in class when everyone acknowledged my incipient journey and shared their love and support. Marcus allowed me to have a turn at an exercise of owning my good qualities, owning what is good in me. I experienced my ability to stay in my heart, and where I got seduced into leaving my heart for an idea, a fear, or a concept. I experienced how I violate myself by pushing too hard, and I experienced the vast store of love that lives within me. I experienced that it is alright to say out loud my good qualities, something much harder for me to do than to say my faults.

I had purchased some prayer flags. I planned to ask everyone in class to bless these prayer flags, and to take them with me to leave at Drolma La, prayer flags praying in the winds of Tibet for Marcus and my classmates, all of whom I love so much. I had brought my prayer flags to class that day, and a kata, a Tibetan scarf used to mark auspicious occasions, which I wanted Marcus to bless and which I would also leave at Drolma La. Someone in class asked me what the significance of Mt. Kailash was. I had not read much about Western Tibet or Kailash, wanting to experience Tibet first and read about it only afterwards. I was also used to turning to Marcus to explain things. But it was mine to do, and I offered my understanding of Kailash, the home of Shiva for the Hindus, its significance to four major religions, its gift of four major rivers feeding continents around it, its standing as the spiritual center of the universe.

Then the class gave me gifts. They gave me prayer flags which German had purchased, prayer flags to leave in Tibet. There was a card with one hundred eight dollars in it for butter lamps, a lamp for each bead of the mala. In the card, everyone had written a blessing and an encouragement to me. And they gave me a wonderful camera to bring home images of this sacred journey. I suppose I should have expected something like this, but I did not. I was just focused on the gift I wanted to give them, the prayer flags for Tibet. During that class, so much love poured out towards me. Many people in the class expressed not only their love for me, but how they had felt my love for them, had felt my love supporting Marcus and his teachings, supporting class. It is true. I have loved everyone as best I can, but I didn't and don't really think about it. I just do what I can, as they do for me. It was quite beautiful to be bathed in so much love.

Patrick told me that when he first heard I was going to do Khora, he was worried about me, but that now he had confidence in me. Sherri looked at me with eyes I had never seen before, eyes with a mother's love that runs endlessly deep. Many thanked me for ways they had felt loved by me. So much was shared that day. I love and trust these people deeply, but somehow I was reminded how much flows among us all, between us. We do not take each other for granted, and we notice, we receive each other's love. Marcus took us all out for an exotic dinner. Hearts were open and I was blessed in amazing love as they sent me off to Tibet.

The following day was the last day of class, and the day before my departure. On July 22, 2006, I wrote:

> I wake at Dorothy's. Yesterday I faced my good qualities, and I learned that in my open human heart, there is room for truth and lies, and all that matters is love first. My capacity is bigger.

> I think of Class today. I think of leaving for Tibet tomorrow. I feel like a newborn baby. I feel like I've never done one prostration, that I don't even know how. I feel naked and tender and nervous and open. I feel in the Hands of Tibet, willing. I feel the Mountain, welcoming me to the Feast of my Life: my Life is the Feast; I will be devoured piece by piece, while the Hands of Tibet hold me gently. I feel that I am stepping into a sacred consciousness that is so far beyond anything I have touched, and that it is home, and it is welcoming me back. I feel that it is holding some of my good qualities, garments that it is time to again put on.

The Journey

There were many journeys to get to my journey around Mt. Kailash. There was the journey to leave America, encapsulated in leaving my teacher and classmates with whom I risk the exposure of who I really am, devoid of image, defenses, and excuses. There was the journey halfway around this world, through airports, customs, cultures, and rules that were arcane to me. In Nepal I was immersed in a world that was not only new but was also personal. It was not just a matter of finding my way through an airport or from the hotel to the shopping district. It was also meeting my travel agents, figuring out how to telephone friends of Marcus who had offered to be of service to me, and learning how to get around the countryside. I have never hailed a cab in New York or Boston, and here I was haggling over cab fares in Kathmandu to go to places whose locations I did not know!

There was the journey to Tibet itself. While I had not quite grasped this, I would be driving with part of my crew from Kathmandu, Nepal, to the border of Tibet at Zhangmu. These few hours were another immersion, in a Land Cruiser with young men with some English, more or less. Shy or not, I had to introduce myself. I had to learn – everything. When we stopped for breakfast, they had spicy Indian food. While a bathroom in America is both a refuge and a convenience, the bathroom there was a short climb out behind and down from the restaurant to a cellar room with dirt floors and holes to squat over. No toilet paper. When we got to Zhangmu, my crew left me in another small establishment where I was besieged by money changers wanting to change my USD or Rupees for Yuan. Should I deal with them? How much money should I change? It was like being in a street culture, with a swarming, undulating mass of people who knew each other and who swooped down on the transients who came through the border. My guides were off dealing with what they needed to do. I now understand they were getting porters to carry the luggage and supplies across the border to the next Land Cruiser. But then I just felt they had left me in that store in a sea of people some of whom wanted something from me. Then I did not even know that my driver would be heading back to Kathmandu and that I would be adding a new driver and Tibetan guide to my crew.

There was the journey to Kailash itself. The word wilderness does not really have a meaning to anyone who still has the use of a car and a cell phone. I had never really traveled to a wilderness before. That Kailash was in the wilderness of Western Tibet to me meant only that it was more remote and less populated. But I was about to experience wilderness as I had never even conceptualized it. I marveled that my driver knew where to go. We would often drive across a broad plain, and then at some point he would turn right or left, and eventually we would come upon a road. How did he know when to turn? There were rivers: we drove through them, not over them. I did not actually grasp until I was home that the lack of trees there was because we were above tree line, at such a high elevation.

Based on absolutely nothing but my usual good health, I did not really believe that altitude sickness would affect me. I did not really grasp the effect of altitude on my body. I thought that having spent much time jaunting about the Rockies and the Continental Divide with no ill effect meant I was just not sensitive to altitude changes. I entered this journey like a babe in the woods, not realizing how much altitude and elements set the terms of what I faced. I am glad I was so open and naïve. I do not think the experience was controllable, and being so unguarded it really just washed right through me, through every particle of my body, mind, and soul.

And that is just the journey through the natural world. There was the cultural journey. The small towns where we stopped for the night on the five-day pilgrimage to get to Mt. Kailash were a cultural education. They were towns torn between two cultures, Tibetan and Chinese, towns caught in the throes of efforts to modernize, bring in hydroelectric power, build roads and houses. There was also the more personal level of acculturation. Guesthouses were simple structures with no plumbing and generally a naked lightbulb hanging in the room. Beds were plywood platforms with a thin mattress of quilts, and a quilt for cover. There was a thin pillow. Bathrooms were usually across the courtyard. How to tell which were for men and which for women? What is the etiquette: does one greet the woman squatting over the adjacent hole, or does one avert one's eyes? Food was never what I expected, and varied from guesthouses to tea houses. The importance of that thermos of hot water that was in every room gradually became clear to me. There was nothing so important as that precious thermos of hot water! In the guesthouses, there is no running water, no toilet, no sink, no shower. There is no heat, and little electricity. That thermos of warm water was there to sip after a long dusty drive. It was there to wash hands and face and brush teeth. It was there for a spongebath. Once my guide got me two thermoses – oh, abundance! I was able to wash my hair for the first time in weeks. That thermos of water was hearth and hydration and hygiene. It was life.

The journey into this land kept stripping away anything I knew, and never asked me what I might prefer. The journey did not care that I am shy even with Westerners. It just swept me into its loving, vital arms and jostled me into families, friends, factions, and cultures.

Arriving finally at Darchen, the little town at the base of the sacred mountain, deposited me into the arms of Mt. Kailash, where a whole new set of learnings opened up. I had not realized how many journeys it would require to get me to my heart's desire, to journey around Mt. Kailash in prayer, my body on the earth.

*   *   *

July 22, 2006
3:35 pm.

Yesterday, Marcus gave me a turn in class. I thought the task would be to work with my dark side while staying in my heart. It turned out to be working with my good qualities. Am I going to Tibet to face my beauty rather than my flaws?

I am in my room at the Fairfield Inn, Newark International Airport, New Jersey. Dorothy dropped me off after class. My friends gave me so much loving support. Even after class, so many small things continue to support me. The clerk at the check-in desk was quite kind. I asked for late check out tomorrow. She said she'd have to check with her boss, who was handling a big crisis audibly going on at the other counter. But then she took my credit card and had me sign the check-in information, and said she could do 1 pm, and if I called tomorrow, maybe they could allow 2 pm. Her face was so kind, so friendly.

I am in my room, #310. Dorothy is gone. It is the silence that strikes me. All around me there is a deep, enveloping, penetrating silence. The air conditioning behind roars on and rattles away. I hear other guests in and out of their rooms. But all I really hear all around me is a thick silence. The void is greeting me already. I do practice. Toward the end, the space became so thick; it felt like wading through pureed bodies. My belly is nauseous, my stomach, too, but the nausea is deeper in my belly. Thank you.

July 23, 2006

I go to the Airport to check in. I am calm, although I don't know why. I am not an experienced traveler, certainly not internationally. But I am so happy this is beginning, beginning the next level of this journey. I go up to the ticket agent to get my actual tickets from my e-ticket reservations. A young woman seems to think there is a problem, something about my needing a visa for India. I explain I am not going to India; I am only making a connection there to Nepal. She gets her supervisor, a nice, energetic middle-aged man who comes and reviews all the documents. He informs me in a crisp, definitive manner that I will not be able to fly today. He says he is sorry, but he is also glad, because he knows for certain that if he allows me to fly, that the moment I touch down in India, I will be deported since I have no Indian visa. Thus, he explains, it is really best to delay my trip, go to the Indian consulate in New York, and get a visa first. He writes down the number and address of the consulate and hands it to me.

I tell him it is Sunday, the consulate is not open, I have connections and reservations. I ask him what will happen to my connecting flights if my departure gets delayed. He hesitates, as if surprised by this problem, and begins to look at flight schedules. I remember my little statue of Ganesh, the Indian god who removes obstacles and brings pleasure. Ganesh is in my backpack and in my heart. I am praying to Ganesh, and I am not moving along, I am not leaving the ticket desk; I am not getting out of the way for more passengers. If I must delay and go to New York tomorrow, so I shall, but something just does not feel accurate here. So I stand my place in line, quietly asking questions, trying to get clearer answers, because the answers I'm getting are not very clear to me.

The gentleman finally called his supervisor on the phone, and then bustled off to consult with her. The woman at the desk smiled apologetically. She was doing her best to be supportive, and I appreciated it. I smiled back. Many minutes later, the gentleman re-appeared with a handful of papers. He announced that he had learned something today! Truly, good for him, to be open to learning more about the machinations of international borders and permits. Through calls and e-mails and checking regulations, he and his supervisor had determined that as long as I did not set foot out of the transit lounge in Delhi, not even into the Airport, then I could stay there without a visa until my connection for

Nepal boarded. Yes, that was what I had thought. Now it was official. Now he gave me my tickets, and I wandered off to find the gate and settle in for many hours of waiting until my flight was to leave. I thanked Ganesh.

At one point while I had been standing there in line, waiting for all this to be sorted out, my cell phone rang. It was Marcus, just checking in. He was working and was using his break between clients to give me a call. That was wonderful. I shared the excitement of the ticket escapade, and he said what I had thought was true, and what the airport personnel eventually learned, too. One does not need a visa to stay in the transit lounge. We chatted briefly, and he went on to his next client. I am so grateful for his friendship. He is always thoughtful, and this is a momentous moment in my life.

I found my gate. I got a nutritious smoothie. I pulled out my book, by a window, and settled into reading and sipping. Marcus called a couple more times as I waited the several hours before my flight would board. It was good to hear his voice between clients.

5:15 pm.

Marcus calls one more time. He has called me three times today. This is the fourth call, and the tears just arise. I don't know why I'm crying now, but my heart is just brimming over. He is with German before getting a bodywork session for himself. I'm so glad he finally gets a session. He loves me every minute. I love him with all my heart.

It is good to cry. I'm relaxing. It's alright. Love holds me, carries me. Tamdrin, the horse-headed deity, protects me. Garuda, with his enormous wings and fierce beak, flies with me. Vajrayogini, the greatest dakini, the essence of consciousness, watches over me, counsels me. Amitabha is the Buddha who protects and receives all in his heaven. His heart shields me. The ferocious truth of Troma, who devours everything at the point of death, keeps me honest. Ganesh is smiling. Vajrayogini melts into me in silence. I stand up in the teaching and protection of Yeshe Tsogyal, consort of Guru Rinpoche and protectress of Tibet. Guru Rinpoche holds all in his ferocious love. Even though I said I was fine, call after call, Marcus probably kept calling until he could feel I was OK on a deeper level. Such relentless love.

6:45 pm.

One more hour, and it will be close to boarding time. I've been here since 1:15 pm. So many announcements over the loudspeaker, so many flights, so many stand-bys, so many messages. I look out the window and am surprised by the blue sky and fluffy clouds that dissolve into light. Surely it should be night by now. Even more, I am surprised by the Newark skyline. I've heard little unaccented English and many languages among the passengers and the loudpseaker announcers. But I am still in America. I am surprised but comforted to remember I am still here.

There is a long journey ahead. It is alright. I want to go to Mt. Kailash, and I am happy to take the steps to get there, however effortful. The journey to get there is part of the journey of being there. It's all unknown ahead of me. The next hurdle is actually getting on the plane with no Indian visa, again. They told me at the desk, before it was all straightened out, that there was no point in giving me a ticket since they would check again at the gate, and turn me away there. After I get on the plane, there will be more unknown, and more unknown, little sleep, long days, until Tuesday afternoon in Kathmandu. I leave Sunday July 23rd and with the time changes I arrive Tuesday July 25th. Kailash, I am coming.

Patrick said yesterday that when he first learned of my plans to do prostrations around Mt. Kailash, that he was concerned for me. But now, he is not, he has confidence in me. I think that the beautiful terror of what I am undertaking is so great that I am keeping both my fear and my confidence unconscious for now. But I can hear his words, and I am grateful for his confidence.

8:30 pm.

I was just standing against the back wall. There is a huge crowd around Gate 138 for Flight 82 to Delhi, just waiting. There is too little time to settle and read. I've been to the bathroom as many times as I can. So I am leaning against the back wall, waiting for boarding to begin.

A gentle man – and I mean a gentle man – in a small-checkered suit comes up and reaches for my ticket, which is in my hand. Reflexively I tighten my grip on my hard-won ticket. He then asks for my ticket "for a minute." I am surprised, and puzzled. I ask why in a quietly inquiring voice. I am not about to let this ticket out of my hand, after nearly not getting a ticket for today at all! He answered my query: He wanted to upgrade my ticket to first class. I said OK, but still kept an eye on him, even though I had read his official airport badge. He came back and handed me a new ticket, 9L up from 25L, and said, "You are traveling alone?" "Yes." "You will be more comfortable." And then he smiled, like me, a little hesitant. He said sometimes they needed to balance the seating and move people up. At such times, he would look around to see whom he should move, and he could tell I was "a nice person," and "deserving" of this. He told me this twice. He was leaving the plane as I finally entered, and he wished me a good flight again. I thanked him again.

First class is so big; I can't reach my bag under the seat in front of me! Maybe I'll be able to sleep tonight. There's a *menu*....

July 24, 2006
7:50 am.

I am awakening in my first class seat which transforms into a bed. I am not going to Kailash to be a drone, a worker bee. I am going to be a daughter, a blessed daughter. My mother's body was broken. My brother's soul was broken. My sister suffers each day. My nephew has a new baby coming. Class risks living love, loving each other authentically, in a world that crucified Christ for loving. I carry all to Kailash for renewal, for whatever blessings Kailash will bestow.

9:20 am.

I look out the window. Oh my God. I believe we are over Afghanistan. I look down at endless, dry, brown craggy mountains, plateaus ending in sheer cliffs that descend forever. A whole landscape of rough dry terrain. I think of our troops there. There is snow on some of the peaks. We continue flying and I drift off. After awhile, I wake up again. There is an enormous mountain range in front of me. We are flying along it.

I look out a few minutes later. The dry brown land is just as mountainous. There is no relief, but the mountains have grown bigger. Bigger ridges, bigger peaks, deeper and wider valleys. My seat partner asks, "Are they the Hindu Kush? They are coming right up to meet us, 37,000 feet." Row after row of mountains, like the Rockies, but they feel higher. Do I see a small patch of green, and a settlement? And a ways away, another? There is a large river.

The mountains step back. There is a huge wide open plain. Everything is on an enormous scale here. I see a city, a lake. It is greenish against the brown land. More cities now, stretching out, following the spacious valleys. The ground is becoming reddish.

Flying into rain in India. The brilliant sunlight is suddenly thick leaden grey air. I dimly see a cluster of lights below, a city. A touch of blue and orangey yellow between the sandwich of grey above and deepening grey below. As we fly forward, the slice of blue tapers into all grey. Maybe it's not rain. Maybe it's night, even though I just woke up. I think of the first night at the Fairfield Inn after class and before leaving, I just needed to be alone, in the zone, to cry and sleep and veg. To pack and unpack. To suddenly remember something that needed reorganizing. To wander the corridors of my soul. To say good-bye to my life. To remember and move on. I am not a flying arrow, splitting space open and making it wider. I am receptive, receiving all things into my throat and letting them come forth again.

9:00 pm.

India. A few hours of blazing sunlight after I awaken on the plane, and then we land in darkness. I am in the transit lounge, leaving tomorrow at 1:15 pm. I have made it this far. Time to read my novel, *Life of Pi*.

11:00 pm.

Sitting in the transit room in Delhi, India. Another 14 hours to go. Just feeling the chaos. It has been chaos since this journey began. America/Newark Airport didn't feel like America. Newark Airport didn't seem to know I could fly to Nepal through India. Time turned upsidedown. I slept well in first class on the plane...and arrived in India at 9 pm. People – sometimes the same, sometimes new – keep coming up to me here in the transit lounge and explaining that Sahara Airlines will come find me tomorrow and get my luggage and give me my boarding pass. Why do they keep seeking me out and telling me this? Now they begin asking me if I need anything. I think they mean food, but who would need food as late night sets in? Don't people just wait the night for their flight connections? Is this so rare?

Floods of people, mostly young men in their teens and early twenties, keep entering, and then eventually lining up at the exit/customs gates. There is a very occasional Westerner, a more occasional Indian family with children and wife in tow, so patriarchal but so consistent, very few exceptions among the women. The last woman who came and explained to me for the third or fourth time that Sahara now had my bags in the warehouse and would come find me in the morning ended by asking if she could leave now. Why not? It's OK with me, as long as my luggage isn't lost and Sahara knows I'm here. Please go home and rest and have a good night.

Why am I writing all this? My guts are a bit unsettled from Indian/airplane fare and upsidedown circadian rhythm. But I felt Ganesh dancing on the plane, dancing with me. I enjoyed briefly talking with Joe, my seat mate, feeling that electric veteran's energy in him. We chatted about jobs, and he mentioned he had flown those huge cargo planes into LZs, landing zones. I remember working with Vietnam vets who would talk to me about flying into hot zones. Joe was understated, but I knew from the type of aircraft he had piloted that he had had to fly through a lot of shit, a lot of life-threatening shit. Talk to any vet with combat experience. When your job has been life-threatening, everything else is just stuff.

Joe had that laid-back calm presentation with the alertness of a hawk. Nothing missed, pinpoint alert, but no response that wasn't required. He was affable, friendly, but the hawk maintained surveillance. Combat vets are ever-scanning for danger, while the living of life is for those who think safety can be presumed. I liked him a lot, and appreciated him a lot. He asked me where I was headed, and I told him I was taking a three-month sabbatical, going to Tibet, to Kailash. He laughed, and made some comment to the effect that he couldn't get through two weeks of vacation, too restless. Sounds like a vet. I wish him well, and at some point, that he can take, can stand, can enjoy, a long vacation.

So why am I writing all this? Because it vaguely crawls around the edges of my consciousness that I thought that the week before I left home, and the week of class, would be two whole weeks to just rest and acclimate, organize and prepare. I continue to learn that the preparation is every moment of this experience, and that is all there is to it. The chaos is the support. I will not do this because I am rested and oriented. As always, I will do this because I want to. Spirit, help me.

I feel the soft, sultry heat of India, or is it just the enclosed space of the transit lounge?

July 25, 2006
1:30 am.

I am at the day of arrival in Nepal. I'll be airborne in another eight hours, God willing. Napping in between reads of *Life of Pi*. My backpack is a hard pillow but I snooze nonetheless. Snacking on the toffee peanuts, my only nutrition since disembarking. I may form a lifelong attachment to them. I suddenly remember I am flying after lunch; it will be a long time before I am fed. I should ration them. I don't think I care. I am for whatever supports me through the night, even if I eat them all. Back to *Pi*.

3:05 am.

Tired. Hot. Tired. I drink from my water bottle. Water soothes my nerves. Thinking does not help. No help is needed.

4:30 am.

There is something in this journey about who I am. The class all told me what they felt grateful to me for, things I do, that have touched them in some way. I matter. I am not the sound of one hand clapping, and I am the sound of one hand clapping. I continue to engage Marcus' work. Why? Because living love is all there is to do. There is no agenda, there is being love, in my human heart. There is Tracey as love. Who am

I? How can so many in class be grateful to me? Am I visible? Am I real instead of perfect?

The unraveling has begun. These questions, these admissions, this ownership of identity, this commitment to love – experiencing what compassion is – I am experiencing this. I never really understood it, and I knew I didn't get it even though I knew the definition. Now I understand the nakedness without an agenda more deeply than I have before. To love with no agenda is a profound availability, a profound vulnerability.

The thoughts are falling out of my head, my heart is less clenched. I am afraid of this much love. Love is so brilliant it blinds my eyes! I do not need my eyes! This is a monster door. It is so big I get it I lose it I get it I lose it. How does my teacher hold this space, again and again and again? I am exhausted after one moment of holding this space that is infinity, this open-hearted availability in love.

1:38 pm.

Taxiing, to take off for Nepal, twenty minutes late, but we're getting there. However, at this rate, I think we might be taxiing to Nepal! Such a young airport.

I am so tired; I've begun falling asleep whenever I sit down, even if I don't think I'm tired. I have no recollection of take-off at all! The next thing I knew, a stewardess was offering me a beverage, a can of Heineken! I settled for a vegetarian lunch, bless them, it's real food. Sahara Airlines is something else, jocular crew, good food, and Heineken, and lime juice before take-off and candy as we walk in – they are OK! I just moved to an open window seat and I will be able to see Nepal as we arrive, if I'm awake.

6:00 pm.

I am at my hotel, alone. Sonam, my travel agent, met me at the airport. It took a bit to find each other, then to get a visa. He has been so kind. The language is a barrier, but his English pulls us through. He tells me I have one day in Nepal tomorrow. The next day, Thursday, July 27, we leave for Tibet. I thought I had two days and then on to Tibet. I am happy it is just one. There are some things I won't be able to do, such as seek out an important Rinpoche that Marcus told me of for his blessing, but other than that, it's alright. I came here to go to Kailash and receive the blessing of Kailash, not to stop or sightsee. I came here to lay on the earth of Kailash, and I am happy to move toward that.

I re-read the card of love and encouragement that class gave me. Marcus wrote:

Tracey, the center of the spiritual universe already exists
in your human heart. Meet your mirror. Love, Marcus

He's right. This is true. Why do I ever leave my heart? Kailash, take
me home and take me there so deeply that I will change forever, that it
will be – I will be – heart first.

Here I am in Nepal, in the hotel, learning where I need to go for
the bank, for shopping, to find a taxi, to use the phones. I feel my
old habits of timidness and avoidance. Alright, so I do need a little
sleep right now, but despite that, it really is time I ditch this timid-little-
uncertain-overwhelmed presentation I have. I can call friends of Marcus
and talk with Sonam and figure it all out, gently and quietly, but without
the quaking in my boots that says 'Are you *sure* that I'm not a bother?'
Enough, already!

July 26, 2006

It is Wednesday, July 26, 2006. I am eating an enormous breakfast. I
have been so hungry! The language barrier is very thick and difficult.

It's not that I need to *be* a blessing. I already *am* a blessing. My task is
to stop suppressing and withholding this blessing that I am. I don't need
to be more or less than I am. I need to be visibly who I am, because this
is the blessing.

So how much can one fit in a day? There was breakfast – food at last!
Then the bank, lots of forms, lots of gently orchestrated chaos. People
seem a *lot* less tense here than in the States. I did keep trying to explain
I needed smaller denominations while they handed me big bills, but I
guess it all works out.

I came back from the bank, and there was Sonam waiting for me,
needing my passport. I asked about the shopping district, and he gave
me directions. Somehow, as I walked out the very long driveway to the
street, there he was on his motorcycle. He offered to give me a ride to
Tamil, the shopping district, so I hopped on the back. We were moving
before I realized half my thighs were exposed. So much for taking care
to wear long skirts and be sensitive to the culture. And thus I also had
my first ride on the back of a motorcycle, through outrageous traffic,
and arrived safely in Tamil. I browsed and shopped and only bought six
postcards. I had done my best to memorize the way in, and headed back
to the hotel on foot. It was really just one long wall to follow, except I did
miss my turn-off. As things got poorer and less familiar, I finally asked
directions and headed back quite a ways, recognizing things we had

driven by on my way in last night. I got there, hot and sweaty and fine. I splashed water on my face.

My afternoon and evening have been very busy. Marcus introduced me by e-mail to a Rinpoche (a high Buddhist teacher) in Nepal, and I managed to contact him by phone and get to his home to meet him. Marcus put me in touch with another friend, Michael, and Michael so kindly took time to help translate for me. I will always remember Rinpoche's wife's shining face as she asked about Marcus, and about how Rinpoche and she and Michael love and care for Marcus. Through the long afternoon I spent with Rinpoche, struggling through the language barrier before Michael arrived, I felt Rinpoche's deepening kindness toward me, giving me pictures of his lineage, a protection cord and knot, his blessing. I felt his blessing physically enter my being. He expressed his concern for the dangers of prostrating and of Kailash, and he gave me advice. He also gave me permission to do the dakini trail if I finished Khora early. I would like to do that. Generally one must walk Khora around Kailash thirteen times before having permission to walk the dakini trail. I guess doing Khora by prostrations means I don't have to do the thirteen circuits first!

Rinpoche said that he had faith and confidence in me. He had just spent a few hours with me, but we talked deeply, and I was touched that he was willing to receive me, that he felt enough availability and sincerity in me to feel faith and confidence in me. I was surprised. It was something he did not have to say to me, yet he gave me this gift.

As I left Rinpoche's that evening, both Rinpoche and Michael asked me to call when I returned from Tibet. That touched me deeply. They truly care, and they truly get – even more than I do – what this means. I know they get the implications of this more clearly than I do, although I know my longing to be with Kailash is true. My longing is bigger than the fear. It is bigger even than the one thing I have such difficulty with, not-knowing. I want to be at Kailash before I even need to know why or what it means. That's saying something.

July 27, 2006
6:15 am.

It is tomorrow. I have ten minutes to eat breakfast and check out. I just did e-mail. Marcus was there, sending me a teaching:

> Tracey, I am available. I am available to have my true expression by being available. Just as love exists already and my love loves me, availability is available –and I am

available before my moment self-arises so that I can respond to my new moment. All my love – Marcus

I hurry to check out and get to my driver. I meet these new people: a driver, a guide, and a cook. They put me in the front seat, and we set out, heading for the border with Tibet. I am shy and the language barrier is awkward, but the guide has pretty good English and I make an effort to chat and get to know them. Everything is so new to me.

1:15 pm.

We have just cleared the last of the Chinese customs. I feel myself tighten and close as I am immersed again and again in concentrated clusters, crowds of people I don't know, individually or culturally. No need. I can say no without being hidden or xenophobic. I feel my hostility toward the Chinese occupiers as I approach the border. "No Photos" signs are posted. But I also see that the officers in crisp clean shining uniforms are all kids. At the last customs hurdle, some are kids and the rest are sleepy bureaucrats. I know it is not all benign, but I feel myself create another level of problem by my reactivity and hostility. Will I give up my paranoia habit this trip?

At the border, we change drivers, change cars. A Tibetan driver takes over, and a Tibetan guide joins my other two crew members, my cook and guide/sherpa who are also Tibetan but live in Nepal. I have four crew members now. They sit me in the front seat of the Land Cruiser, and we begin the drive to Kailash in Western Tibet. As we begin the drive through Tibet, I can see why it is called the Roof of the World. Will we ever stop going up? When the vehicle stops, it is on an incline. The heights are amazing.

I feel the difference in the land. Driving through the initial kilometers, I find myself thinking that I can now understand nagas, great serpents and water gods. The land is huge, and I can feel that subterranean forces once ruled here. I can feel the depth to which the land is inhabited. Guru Rinpoche came and contained all that so there would be room – physical and spiritual room – for other forces, for Buddhism. The scale of all this is just overwhelming. Magnificent.

3:30 pm.

We arrive at Nyalam. Two young women are there as we unpack the Land Cruiser. One stares and stares at me. I smile and bow. We all unpack and we all haul my duffels and backpack to my room. I find the bathroom. I come back to my room. A minute later, my door carefully opens, and she walks in. She points to the sideboard, stoops down, pulls open two small doors that open like French doors, and shows me cups. She then cleans everything, wiping the decanter of water for washing and drinking, and encourages me to drink. It is hot water! I know my souvenir from Tibet will be a cup with a lid! The warmth is so good.

PS It's finally cold. I mean, I'm <u>cold!</u>

4:30 pm.

Rikjin and Nima, two of my crew, just came to my room with tea and a tray of cookies. Hot milk, black tea, sugar, and cookies! I am famished! They seem apologetic that they will bring dinner here, but I am happy to snuggle into my little room.

I remind myself that I have a habit of holing up, and perhaps should explore this town. I did venture out. I am just back from a walk toward town. It seemed like they weren't used to strangers, although with Eco Tours and this guesthouse, I do not know why. But I felt too many lingering stares. I came back, and was just settling into my novel when tea arrived. A novel with tea, while I try to keep my eyes open.

Driving all day on the journey toward Kailash is surprisingly exhausting. It is not like being in a mixmaster, more like in a bread machine – up, down, back, forth, for eight hours. It is wonderful, but it is a day's work to hang on across the non-roads, the ruts, the rivers, and the mud. The guesthouse is cold, no running water, no heat, a concrete-block building with a bed and a light bulb in each room. I am glad to be acclimating, to be learning what shelter is here. I am grateful for a bed to lie in. God bless Marcus and Dea and their delicious coat they bought me for this journey! It is warm, warm, and warm, and I wrap up in it in my room with my hot tea.

I'd like to give words to a recurring feeling since I began this journey, and it is that there is no turning back. Each half day, each experience, I go deeper, deeper into the heart of what I have come here to do. I don't even know what that means but I feel the inexorable descent, and I could not turn around now if I wanted to. It wouldn't damage something. To turn around now would damage everything.

I read a book given me by Sonam, my travel agent in Nepal. I did not know there are colors with each syllable of the mantra of compassion, Om Mani Padme Hum. Then again, of course I knew that. I just had not put it together. This book is explaining aspects of the tradition I can now bring into consciousness.

7:30 pm.

The more I read and study Sonam's book about Mt. Kailash and the levels of meaning, of essence, that pervade Kailash and the whole Kailash Mandala, the more joyfully and peacefully focused becomes my intention of loving Mt. Kailash through my prostrating Khora.

I am aware, around the edges of my consciousness, that I am a little uncomfortable having my food brought to me in courses and cleared away. As I bring this more clearly to consciousness, I am more comfortable receiving this. It is their kindness, and their job: what is there to resist? *Availability*.

July 28, 2006
3:19 am.

Death is an experience, not a concept. As I approach Mt. Kailash, I can feel myself dying. It is very slow and pronounced, so that I can be available for the experience. I choose to be available.

I ask the dakinis who invited me to stay with me. They are here.

This is a hard journey. Everything about it is hard. The time changes, the flight schedules, the heat in India and Nepal and the cold in Tibet. The horrendous roads. It's not a matter of just driving somewhere. Getting somewhere is an achievement and has a cost. I am willing, but there are no free minutes. Everything is chosen or resisted, and that's that. Bathing is difficult, bathrooms are difficult, and eating is difficult. I happen to look up at my headboard: someone painted and stenciled it beautifully, every inch of it. There is beauty everywhere. I'm not coming to sites. I'm coming to me. There is strength so much deeper than the strength from working out at a gym. Now, I need to rest.

5:30 am.

My plan was to get up and take a sponge bath. My body's plan was to throw up, which I promptly did when I got up. I have a cold, runny nose, brought on by all the temperature changes, I suspect. But I'm going to start some Diamox just in case it's altitude sickness and not just a cold.

One guide came and said we were staying here today because I am sick. I said, "No, I'm not *that* sick," which is true. If I'm going to rest anywhere, it is Darchen, at the foot of my goal, Mt. Kailash. I feel like I am nowhere, and I just have to get somewhere, to Manasarovar or Chiu Monastery or Darchen. We're going.

9:00 am.

We just came through Toling Pass. Cloudy. I threw up twice. It is so beautiful, so expansive. I try to experience it in my human heart.

We were supposed to drive to Lablung and camp, but we continue on to Saga guesthouse because it is so cold at Lablung. It is nearly eight hours of driving to Saga. I throw up the whole day. My guide tells me the driver is happy to pull over if I need to throw up. I tell him that if I had enough warning, I would ask, but I don't. It just rises up in me and I grab the window handle, wind it down, and hang out the window over the door. From that position, I saw two enormous birds on the distant plain. When I recovered, I timidly asked if there are ostrich in Tibet. There are, and I had just seen two!

I learn quickly that each stop of the vehicle is an opportunity not to be wasted. On the first stop, the driver got out and was checking something on the windshield wiper. I turned in my seat to look at my crew, and was startled to see that the backseat was empty. Through the windows I saw everyone relieving themselves some distance from the car. I caught on quickly, hopping out and taking the chance to allow my body to dispense with what it no longer needs. Who knew when we would stop again?

During one "rest stop," I apologized to my guide for throwing up all over the car door. I know it is not my fault, but I feel a need to acknowledge it, and without language or even a nonverbal understanding of the culture, I don't know how to convey this. He waves my comment graciously away and says it is nothing, not to be concerned.

We will spend two days at Saga, because I am sick. It is right to rest here, and I rest. My old unconscious belief arises: "I don't want to suffer. If I do it right, I won't suffer." It is clear to me that that belief will be dying here.

The Brahmaputra River is stunningly beautiful. My bags are being unpacked and all I want to do is sleep. I've set the alarm for a nap as soon as my bags arrive. Heavenly! I keep thinking that if only I felt more, opened my heart more, I wouldn't've been so nauseous for the whole trip. Now I need to rest. I am *so* exhausted.

July 29, 2006

Tashi delek! I told my crew when we arrived at Saga that I was going to sleep. It was 3:20 pm, *no* dinner, maybe water or porridge for breakfast. They urged me to have dinner. I thought they were crazy. They had just watched me throw up for eight hours on an empty stomach: Why would they think I could eat? I told them kindly but in no uncertain terms that I was going to *sleep*. And I did. I worried that if I fell asleep right away, I'd wake up refreshed at 3 am. So I set my alarm for five and was out like a light, just getting up now and then to throw up. At 5:00 am, I went back to sleep, talking to myself about getting over this nausea, but sleeping, sleeping, sleeping, between getting up to throw up or pee.

Throughout the night, I did sort out that I do not believe this is altitude sickness. This is a migraine. I thought if I could just find a shot or a suppository to suppress the nausea, I'd be OK! Then I worried that a small local clinic would not have such things. But surely they must have something to suppress nausea, something other than by-mouth to get it into one's system without being vomited back out. I prayed to Ganesh, I prayed, I nudged at me to feel, I slept and slept and slept.

My crew woke me up at 5:30 this morning, and I happily told them I need a clinic, I need a shot for nausea. I am not sick, I have a migraine (and a slight cold).

I just fell asleep again. I am quite weak. Except for one-eighth of a piece of flatbread and one tablespoon of water which I ate and threw up yesterday, I've had nothing. I think it's the lack of water, not food, that is affecting me. I kept telling myself to sip water through the night, but I just got up to vomit and fell back asleep. I am now happily three-quarters of the way through a small cup of hot water, an achievement! There is a bowl of porridge and I'll risk a bite or two, but it's the water that is my focus. I keep putting my head down to sleep, and I make myself get up again. I can't feel what I need if I am sleeping.

I am so glad my guide changed the itinerary. We were to camp at Lablung, then come to camp at Saga. But we drove straight through to Saga to stay in the guesthouse for two days. Resting at Nyalam would not have worked for me. I was not comfortable there. The town felt unfriendly. It's not that Saga guesthouse is more comfortable. There are many ways that it is not. The bathroom at Nyalam was at the other end of the building, it had to be eighty to one hundred feet! The bathroom here is across the courtyard, outside my building! Both lack hygiene, but Saga really lacks hygiene. The house staffs are friendly at both. But with Saga, eight hours of driving is behind me, I've had time to sort out what is working with me and my health, and to make a plan. And I have slept. In fact, I can't stop sleeping. I am waiting to leave for the clinic now and I keep dozing off. I just made myself get up and clean my body as best I can. I don't want to pee in case they need a urine sample. I don't have many fluids in me. My door doesn't lock, so I've locked my duffels. One does what one can. I've had about a tablespoon of porridge and maybe 12 ounces of hot water, and I haven't thrown up yet. My stomach is still quite delicate. I don't know if I have turned a corner. If I rest all day, will I be able to sleep tonight? It's all I want to do. I'm a little stronger, but not much. I am peaceful, though. I don't even know why, but I am and I have been.

12:30 pm.

I've been sleeping since my visit to the Chinese clinic. Dorjee my guide told me it is Saturday, so the Tibetan Hospital, where I had hoped to go, is closed. The Chinese clinic was silly. After a long wait, a young man took my blood pressure and heart rate and tried to give me Diamox. I explained I have Diamox. So we just went away. They did not charge me for the visit, which was kind.

My tablespoon of porridge and two cups of water have, with a few uncertain moments, stayed down. Rikjin has brought me a bowl of white rice, and I am carefully eating it. My goal is half the bowl, and more water, and one Diamox and one Excedrin. Then a shower, and pack, and rest until supper and until tomorrow.

I notice any upset worsens my nausea. How to be upset and tolerant at the same time. Maybe it's not my job to be tolerant? Just to be who I am? Where is my compassion? Where is my compassion before my manners?

I forget this is only Day 2. No wonder I am still adjusting, "acclimating," to hygiene and patterns and foods and time and weather. It's only Day 2! Oh my gosh! I feel like I've been here forever.

Guru Rinpoche's foot has touched almost every inch of Tibet. As we drove yesterday, I felt the immensity of that statement, the immensity of Guru Rinpoche. Tibet feels like the whole world. Today, waiting for my guides to take me to the clinic, I was waiting outside, and I have never felt so close to the sky.

Everyone to whom I speak of my intention to make this trip, like everyone in class and many other places, looks at me with a mingled expression of love and insanity, except my friend, Maryann. I visited her before I left, and she took my blessing. I was so shocked, but she took my hands into her forehead and received a blessing I didn't know I had to give. She is so beautiful, and in her own way, so unrestrained.

Before I left Nepal, Rinpoche gave me pictures of his lineage. I remember being struck by this, overwhelmed. This is his lineage, it is sacred. I am a stranger to him, I am no one, I am a pilgrim come to attempt something I don't even understand, something I just love. And Oh my God, Rinpoche gave me his lineage. Rinpoche teaches Troma Ngamo, the fierce deity who cuts all attachment. I feel I have been blessed not only by the trust and wisdom of his heart, but I have been invited to touch the hem of Troma Nagmo's world.

I can't do this journey with my heart closed. I can't do this journey in survival mode or in struggle mode. Only in the love that is my heart. Love has no image of me. Love is self arising, and I am self arising, and together we co-create me in the moment.

2:00 pm.

The love of class is supporting me, is opening my heart again, so I am coming back into my body as love. Sleep is becoming less driven. I am weak, but I shall attempt to stand again soon, and shower, then rest and rejoice in love some more. Barbara gave me a beautiful statue of Ganesh which I packed for this journey. He is sitting right next to me. I say I don't know how to get into my heart, that I find myself there or not there, but it doesn't feel volitional. Yet, when I let go of everything else, my heart is where I end up.

July 30, 2006

It is Sunday. Talk about a lesson in non-attachment. The Chinese have changed the name of the town. They are bringing in businesses, and taking the water. To have to live here under such conditions is such a lesson in grief, fear, anger, and pain. Even in this pain, it is heart first before thought, before attachment or psyche.

Leaving for Paryang. I woke up with a second cold. I managed to get down an egg, a piece of dry toast, some water and my Diamox, without throwing up, and I think that's great. Dorjee is still urging me to eat, something about Kailash. I think they are praying for me. They are my crew, and I will gratefully receive all the prayers that are offered. The Land Cruiser is clean. My door is shining white again. Someone has scrubbed my sickness away.

I think of Marcus and class. My heart opens in tears again, and I feel better. I feel Kailash has called me to come to be the feast. The mountain will break me open, devour me, and set me free. We talked about the Troma practice once, and Marcus said, chuckling softly as he walked away, "Remember to cut off your head." I will be a living sky burial. I am learning. It's OK when my heart is open. I love.

In the last class, one good quality I identified in myself was my humanness: "My humanness is beautiful…." Now, already overwhelmed by Tibet, I feel my *teacher* is beautiful, and is a mirror in which I see and receive my own beauty. Receive, Tracey. This is a trip to receive – begin receiving! Stop withholding the abundant blessings all around you! You see them, but you don't rely on them, you don't trust them, you don't let them in. You wave politely at them, and rely on yourself.

9:20 am.

I think as we drive that the fatigue must be from the lesser oxygen. And immediately it arises that perhaps I am feeling how much I have resisted receiving love. I can feel the sins of my lifetime coming to be loved. Love before anything. My heart before anything.

3:10 pm.

Our hearts are not separate.

6:00 pm.

We arrived at Paryang at 4:00. Another guesthouse, but quiet, more rural. It's getting colder. I had some salt tea, and it tasted and felt good. Salt is settling to my stomach. Midday, I began to feel a little stronger, a little normal. Now I just finished a bowl of hot soup and am nibbling on popcorn while I wait for the main course. Stomach seems OK. Burping instead of heaving.

While we sat in the reception area, I asked one crew member why so many houses we saw on the way into town were ruined. I expected him to say the Chinese, but he said the Tibetans. So I asked again later, and he explained the Chinese had built these for the nomads, but nomads can't live together. They need space. He went on about how the Chinese are on a campaign to build every Tibetan a house, it seemed like a two-story house, and he said that Tibetans didn't need houses. The nomads send their kids to a common school but never come near the houses, which are therefore deteriorating. They just live in their original historical tents.

In Paryang, light rain. I awoke after ten hours, needing to pee and now sneezing and congested. All night long, I have dreamed of a liter of cold orange drink! My cook said he could bring me an orange drink in the morning. I drained it again and again in my sleep, looking forward so much to cold fluids! I am so parched.

I get up, dress enough to get to the bathroom across the courtyard, and when I return to bed, I am instantly asleep again! I am surprised at how much I am sleeping. I did have energy to read my novel last night before falling asleep at 7:30. My crew had told me we'd eat at 8:00 am and leave at 9:00 am.

July 31, 2006

It seems like wherever I go, prayers just gather around to support me at Mt. Kailash, from my crew and from people we meet as we travel the distance to Kailash. We stop at tea houses for lunch. These are usually big white nomadic tents. They are comfortable inside, with a stove, seats, and low wooden tables. Sometimes the mistress of the tea house serves a bowl of dried yak meat, or a delicate yak cheese. Often my crew will get tsampa, and I watch while they mix the barley flour with the salt tea into a consistency that looks like pastry dough. Then they eat it with a hearty meat soup to which they add large amounts of very spicy red chilis. I watch but eat the cheese, bread, and at times the boiled egg that Nima, my cook, has packed for lunch. I am grateful not to be throwing up, and feel my stomach dare not risk new foods or seasonings just now.

At lunch, Dorjee was telling the woman who ran the tea shop of my intentions. She said she would pray for me. It almost made me cry. I'm getting tired. I'm so exhausted. I left face cream for her daughter who has some condition. I asked Dorjee to tell the mother that I like her heart and her spirit, and as I added that I will pray for her around Kailash, the mother brushed my words away. I like her very much.

I dreamed last night that Connor, my beloved golden retriever, died. I saw his face so clearly, so beautiful in the water where he lay. A couple of days ago, I dreamed that Jesse, my cat, died. She just lay there on her side, all dried up and curled in, with her eyes closed.

If I get around Kailash, it is not because I was able to do it, but because I was willing to have my heart meet its mirror. There is no ego in the Khora, no fear, no control. There is only willingness of the heart to meet the void. The Khora can only be done because there is that much love within me and that much love outside of me.

5:30 pm.

We arrive at Lake Manasarovar. I can see the base of Mt. Kailash, but the rest is shrouded in clouds. My guide tells me that if I want to do prostrations, they start here, toward Kailash. I am as awkward as any complete novice, but I get down on the ground and begin prostrations. Everything in my body hurts. For whatever reason, after five days in a car over savage roads in an experience that can only be described as a bread-kneading machine, suddenly this afternoon my mid-back hurts so much that I can hardly sit. I do squats and stretches, but my body feels fragile. Prostrating in the dirt road leading toward Manasarovar hurts everything on my front and everything on my back.

I do my prostrations and I take a picture of Manasarovar. It is impossible to capture either the scale or the beauty of this magnificent sacred lake. There are prayer flags I want to hang here.

I hurt so much, and I'm panting just sitting in the car. I want to collapse, to just say I can't do this. But to say that would be to say that my heart is too small for this, and that's a lie. When I think of this, I am strengthened, and I continue.

Tibetans call Mt. Kailash "Kang Rinpoche." The power of Kang Rinpoche is huge. I think of how I do my practices, and how they change my life, but the Tibetans hold a tradition of enormous power, not my tiny little skimming-my-toes-across-the-surface practice. I feel this experience, particularly the prostrations, is going to devour me. A book my travel agent gave me says that there are three sacred mountains in the Himalayas, Kailash, Lapchi, and Tsari. Tibetans speak of Body, Speech, and Mind. Among the three sacred mountains, Kang Rinpoche is Body, sacred Ignorance, and the void. Marcus' teachings on Ignorance keep coming back.

8:00 pm.

It is 8:00 pm. I am exhausted. I am going to sleep. Two more days to acclimate before beginning the de-construction of me through Khora with prostrations. Help me.

August 1, 2006

Tuesday. I can't say too many times that I can't do this. Only my heart can do this. I am broken and weak. My heart is vibrant. It's not that ordinary everyday life is trivial. It's that I go through it with a minimally opened heart. What if I never got to go home? Would I want this much love, this pure?

3:00 pm.

We are camping at Lake Manasarovar, just south of Kailash. I have my own tent and my crew has theirs. I have just napped for two hours. I ate breakfast; this was the first time with no hesitation and with enjoyment. As Dorjee and I left to walk up to Chiu Gompa (monastery), I had just used the latrine tent and wondered if I should again. I was right, I should have but I didn't. Diarrhea starting.

Chiu Gompa has five monks living there. Guru Rinpoche's meditation cave in the gompa is gorgeous. There are images of Guru Rinpoche, Yeshe Tsogyal, and one other consort, I believe. The rangjung or self-manifested footprints of Guru Rinpoche and Yeshe Tsogyal are impressive. But my guide is especially excited about the smooth oval rangjung rock that Guru Rinpoche retrieved from the middle of Lake Manasarovar.

I could see Kang Rinpoche when I awoke. Earlier I had wondered if I should take a picture, but did not. When I awoke just now, there it was again, not covered in clouds.

Dorjee tells different monks we meet of my plans to do Khora with "prayer," which seems to be what they call prostrations. They are casual. No problem, they say, unless there is a lot of snow at Drolma La. I think, *Don't you see me?* I can hardly stand up from lack of oxygen. As one monk talks, I squat to look around the prayer room because I feel like I can't hold myself up and if I don't squat, I will collapse. There is a wall as we chat with another monk, and I am happy to lean against it. Only my heart can do this. I can't.

I deliver letters and books from Rinpoche in Nepal. They are so excited to receive them. There is some initial confusion in finding the monks, but then we find them in the gompa. One letter has gotten put in the wrong envelope and my other two letters are back at my tent. We will get them later and straighten it out. One monk leaves and arrives with katas for Dorjee and me, and bags of incense for us and for Rinpoche. He also gives us bags of a very rare medicine which only the Chiu Gompa monks know how to make from Lake Manasarovar. It is very generous. He says he will pray for my Khora. I tell Dorjee as we leave that there are prayers gathering all around me.

I am just baking in the tent. It is so hot, but I want to rest. I figure out how to open the vents. There is hardly a cross-breeze, but I am grateful for the improvement. I am writing, lying on my side, looking out at Kang Rinpoche. Immense. Commanding. I can't believe how often it crosses my mind that I am back in class and sharing this or that anecdote with everyone. I want to cater a dinner for us all and show pictures and give them bags of the medicine and the incense and love them. The tears come as I name how much I love them and how much they are with me. I think of talking with my beloved sister, and telling Barbara, my outdoorswoman friend, that I figured out how to work the vent in the tent, and sharing with Emily with her round, wide loving eyes, and so many more.

I have never felt a caution not to do this, not to come to Kang Rinpoche. I have never felt any message telling me to re-consider. I feel so weak and frail, yet not for one second have I received anything that said to let this go or even to be tentative about this. As we walked up to Chiu Gompa, Dorjee was saying to go slow, very slow the first day. I said four hours of prostrations the first day. He said OK. He said from Darchen it is smooth, no rocks. Easy. Just go slow. It gets rougher. But he said that after Drolma La, it is all green grass the rest of the way.

As I lay in my tent resting and writing, Nima came and asked about lunch. Suddenly, behind him a monk's robe appeared. When Nima finished, he realized the monk was there and I climbed out of my tent.

He was from Chiu Gompa. He had come to straighten out the letters. He had no English and I thought Nima did well translating. We talked and talked. Finally he asked me what I had to say to him. I was shocked. Why would I have anything to say to him? He's the monk, loving and holding Chiu Gompa. How much courage does it take to be a monk in occupied Tibet? How much passionate spirituality does it take to care for the sacred treasures in Chiu Gompa? What would I have to say to him but to honor him? I told Nima to tell him that I thank him for loving Chiu Gompa and the treasures and rangjung of Guru Rinpoche, and that I thank him for his prayers for my Khora.

Nima said that the monk was distressed that he felt he had nothing to give me, which puzzled me, as he was praying for me, a great gift. But he said that at least he would give me letters for the monasteries on the way around Mt. Kailash where I could stay if I needed to, if it was raining, or if I needed help. I was so surprised. In just the little time from the morning until now, he had done that.

I asked him about the medicine from Lake Manasarovar, and only then realized that in the huge bag of incense he had brought for Rinpoche and me, there was a huge bag of medicine. I was glad I overcame my neurosis about not bothering people and asked how often it should be used. Once a day, he said, and then came the words that this did not seem just to be for sickness but for joy, for wellness. Keep some in your body everyday, he said.

All these supports and blessings are coming to help me, as I move so slowly toward Kang Rinpoche. It is bringing my ego to its knees and my heart to its feet and I haven't even gotten there yet.

I watch the clouds dance around Kang Rinpoche as I write. This same monk just came all the way back down from Chiu Gompa to give me the three notes to three monasteries around Kailash. These must be the letters he mentioned. He came all this way again, and I am winded just standing up to get out of my tent.

Let me tell you, I'm no athlete and I'm not into physical fitness, although I've always had a respect and appreciation for my body. But however sedentary I look, I've always kept up. Maybe it's being the youngest of three, and affiliating more with the active male side of the family, my little legs hurrying to keep up and my younger brain struggling to understand. Whatever its origins, I keep up. But here, in Tibet, I've been on my knees since I got here. I am resilient physically, and when I am sick, which is rare, I heal quickly. Here in Tibet, I am sick every day. What blessings.

6:45 pm.

I finally get myself up and out of my tent. I go for a walk. I meet Dorjee and chat. He has found two fish on the shores of Manasarovar for medicine.

I walk to the meditation cave along the shore of Lake Manasarovar. I am not dragging. I climb up and sit, only slightly winded. I am struck by how beautiful Manasarovar is, in any weather. The rain clouds have been gathering, dark grey and heavy, and still Manasarovar is ringed by azure. I walk back to my tent. I feel OK, just a little nauseous. I am glad to lay down, but I am better than I have been. Kang Rinpoche stands clear against the graying skies, stunning even against the grey.

I have done some malas of prayers. Time to rest in my novel, and re-pack for tomorrow. Tomorrow we reach Darchen, the place where I will begin Khora.

7:50 pm.

It's been a wonderful day. I'm panting a bit again. I haven't done much, just tried to re-pack. It was a great idea, one bag for Darchen, one for the car. But there is no way to do this. Most of what is packed is for Kailash. Even the effort to re-organize is deteriorating, de-constructing, really. Everything is everywhere. I seem to recognize the wanted plastic bag sooner amidst the pile of things in the duffel, but the notion that there is any division between the duffels is fading fast.

The rain has begun. Supper will be late. It's already past my bedtime! But lunch was at 4:00 pm, so I know it will be awhile before supper is here. My cold is re-arising, more sneezing, but I can't say I feel worse. I'm grateful. Walking today, I practiced keeping my heart open in compassion. My attention span is still remarkably short. My capacity is increasing.

August 2, 2006

I do a practice to Guru Rinpoche. It seems absurd to ask Guru Rinpoche to bless and empower me, but I will not ask as a victim or from unworthiness. I will ask from the capacity of my compassion. Guru Rinpoche, if I bring you a thimble, and it is brimming full, it is better than to bring you a wash basin that is mostly empty.

10:45 am.

Camp is broken. I am doing better. My cold is in my chest, too, but breaking up nicely. I carried one duffel and dragged the other to the car, a first. Each is about forty-five pounds. I'm doing better. I want to cry a lot. There is never a reason to not have my heart open. There is never a reason to not ask for Guru Rinpoche's help and support, and to call on Yeshe Tsogyal's wisdom courage.

The only medicine I took this morning is from the Gompa. "Keep it in your body." We collected water from Lake Manasarovar for the feast when I am home. I walked out into the lake, but finally one of the guides took over and collected a good clear bottle full. We stopped on our way out so I could leave prayer flags at Lake Manasarovar, the first I have left from the many I brought with me.

I do not overvalue myself, nor feel that I am special. Yet I see signs greeting me here. The first evening at Manasarovar, I looked at Kailash and when I turned back to the Lake, there was a rainbow greeting me. The dakinis who guard Mt. Kailash, the Senge Dongpa, and Ganesh, visited me in cloud forms that were so clear. Kang Rinpoche showed me himself again and again yesterday, even though there was poor visibility of Kang Rinpoche the day before and the day after. Sometimes it is not visible for days, but he showed himself to me clearly. And there was the monk saying he had nothing to give me, as if I was worthy of an offering. All these signs support my being here.

We left without seeing the cave where Guru Rinpoche had walked through to the other side, leaving this life. I asked a number of times if I could see it before we left, and we agreed. "Forgetting" to see it as we left I understood to mean that I am not spiritually ready for this.

12:55 pm.

Today, driving toward Darchen, we got stuck in a river. The "road" went through the river, and it is of course impossible to see if there are any deep holes. There was one. Generally on the road, everyone just seems to keep going past disabled vehicles. But about three Land Cruisers came by and stopped, and the Japanese tourists all hopped out and began taking pictures of us stranded in the river! Fortunately one Land Cruiser had a wire and a winch, and kindly, generously pulled us free!

So we are at Darchen. I am not so lost as to say I'm disoriented, but I am not so clear where I am. Thank God for Dorjee. We just chatted. He kept telling me that my room, 06, is just for me. A Chinese group was trying to look in. I almost let them, and he diverted them. I wasn't going to give them my room, but he seemed concerned. We walked to the bathrooms. I guess Tibetans don't pee in the night, because it is quite a trek to get there, and if one is sick or in an urgent situation, it is impossible to get there "on time." But at least I know where they are, perhaps a hundred and fifty or two hundred feet behind the guest house.

I've started drinking a liter of water with my electrolytes in it each day. I'm getting used to the taste. I won't throw it up.

The woman at the front desk is having trouble finding the key to my door. This is the third guest house in Darchen that we have stopped at. The first one was the wrong one. The second one was right, but they had given our reservations to someone else from Kathmandu. This one had space. It is very touristy, but to tell you the truth, not as bad as I expected. We'll see how it goes.

Dorjee thought I should start prostrations at 7:00 am tomorrow. I am a morning person, and told him I would prefer to just begin early. Rikjin and Nima will go around the mountain with me. Sounds good to me. I am a little worried about knowing where to begin, how to begin, but they will know. It seems like they are talking about starting somewhere other than Darchen, but this is not clear to me yet. I remember when we drove into Darchen. Nobody said, "This is Darchen." But I thought I saw Kang Rinpoche through the clouds. And I thought, "Oh no. I want to drive another three or four hours to get ready. This is too quick. We're here so early, should I start prostrations this afternoon?"

My breathing is a little better. I am remembering to find my spirit before I expect my lungs to work. Intention. Reading how Guru Rinpoche used mantra, how filled with intention his use of the words was, taught me what intention looks like. I am such a fake. I am glad to see his authenticity, his power, his intention.

Dorjee kept saying my room is just my room, to pray. My own thoughts repeatedly. We are here earlier than I thought, and I want to spend the extra time praying. Not sleeping, not reading, not shopping, not taking pictures. Praying. Tomorrow is the beginning of the end of my life.

4:30 pm.

Resting before practice. I woke up this morning thinking that tomorrow I would be waking up to begin prostrations. I continue to pray for help. I continue to learn intention, and compassion, instead of withholding and unconsciousness.

Two years ago, I left a relationship of over twenty years with someone I had loved with everything in me, my unhealthiness as well as my healthiness. I'll call him Alec. I had two dreams of Alec last night:

Dream One: He asked if I would try again, surely we could make it work. I came back for an evening, and quickly he was absorbed in one of his mood states. I left.

Dream Two: He asked to meet for coffee to talk about us. We met at a local mall, as we once had. I was commenting that he made his pain the center of everything, and it's not that he doesn't have pain, just that everyone has pain, and what else is he going to focus on and develop in himself to bring his gifts to the world? He reached across the small table and slapped me. I immediately stood up, tipping the table and all its contents into him, more like shoving it. He went over backwards in his chair with the table. I picked up my purse, paid the cashier twenty dollars for the coffee and any damage, and left. I guess everything will arise to be digested by this pilgrimage.

5:30 pm.

A thunderstorm has just popped up. The weather changes within any one day here are amazing. It is not just the temperature changes, but the overall weather event. My first feeling is that the gods are angry at the increasing commercialization of Kang Rinpoche. So they should be. As the storm deepens and unfolds, I feel like it is showing me what I am heading off into tomorrow. My ego says this is impossible. My heart says to stand up and kneel down. As it has been through all the preparation, I can't think about this. I can only go and do one prostration at a time.

The first week, when I was so sick, I would dream of that cool orange drink, and of a delicious sandwich on thick bread with waves of fresh crisp lettuce, with cheese or humus, all dripping with dressing or mayo or mustard....or being on the plane going home, first class, and accepting a complimentary white wine but also requesting two large sparkling waters over ice that I guzzle, dreaming of getting home and draining a quart of ginger ale. All those images have stopped. I'm just realizing what a teaching on phenomena they were, what my mind creates to avoid true nature, the beauty of thirst, hunger, nausea, as it is. It fleetingly crossed my mind at the time, but the intense sensory pleasure of these images won. Rather, I chose the phenomena instead of the essence. I am so glad this teaching has come through.

6:35 pm.

My inertia is incredible. I rested for an hour, but did not sleep, a good sign, I think. In class, Beth reminded me repeatedly to choose service, not a driven mission or agenda, as I can tend to get a little persistently focused on something even if it kills me. Her admonition kept running through my head and colliding with Dorjee's "pray, pray, you have a room to pray."

My aversion to dealing with bathrooms is so strong I have just been putting it off. Finally, it is time. I make it through four very friendly Indian tourists who are completely blocking the exit and descend the stairs. I am stunned by the clear, beautiful snow-covered range of mountains, panoramically stretching across the horizon, behind the bathroom building which is at the end of a courtyard at least two hundred feet wide. I turn and the bottom corner of Kang Rinpoche is just visible. I enter the bathroom and I am shocked! Flush toilets! Three stalls: two flush and one traditional squat. But there is water on the floor and filth beyond anything I could imagine. One toilet is empty of water and just has fecal marks on the sides. Clearly it is not functioning. The middle toilet is brimming to the lid with deep brown water and smeared feces everywhere. The water is still running. The traditional squat toilet has feces in it, but I don't have to touch anything, and I squat and pee. I invite my body to take a dump, but it either doesn't need to or won't. The toilet paper dispenser is empty. Used sanitary napkins and toilet paper are piled under it. Outside the stalls there is a sink. I turn it on and it sprays water out over the edge of the sink, all over me and the floor, but not on my hands. Darchen is expanding rapidly, adding rows of new dormitories. How can they have this lack of hygiene? It is all so wrong for Kang Rinpoche. Maybe there are cultures that just never had sanitation?

I am back in my room. I finally learn that lights come on at 10:00 pm, which is about the time it gets dark. There are light switches everywhere in my room, but no electricity is available until 10:00 pm. I've almost finished my liter of electrolytes. Ganesh is watching over me.

Did I mention that someone vomited in the corner of my room? It just dried there, in a kind of *bas relief* puddle. To be honest, my first and continuing response is empathy.

7:15 pm.

I begin practice again. I am realizing that the hygiene issue is helping me lose attachment and to have compassion. We are all as we are, and everything is all as it is. Going deeper, I realize I am like that toilet, all those garbage thoughts and attachments. I could let all phenomena be luminous!

8:05 pm.

I just had a very long talk with Dorjee, Rikjin, and Nima. There are no yaks and no sherpas available, and their respective home offices do not seem responsive to their calls. That means Rikjin and Nima, who are coming around the mountain with me, carry all the gear! We'll have campsites at strategic spots, and hike back and forth from wherever I finish prostrations for that day. I'll also start at Tarboche, since they can drive supplies to the first campsite near Chuku Gompa. That means I'll do the last two days from Darchen to Tarboche at the end. Dorjee asked me where I wanted to start, although clearly he thought Tarboche because of the lack of yaks/sherpas. I said that if starting there did not stain my effort, it was fine with me. We agreed I would do the Darchen-Tarboche link at the end. I think that will be hard, but there is a lifetime between me and that, and I just need to begin. He keeps telling me to go slow, the first day slow, and then we'll see how my body is after that.

I will now attempt to pack only what I need into one duffel, to minimize what they have to carry around the mountain. I'm upset. My emotions are calm, but the nausea has kicked in.

9:02 pm.

Finally I realize, Oh, I forgot to sing! I just start to sing, and this is bringing me back to my adult, to my heart, where all is well. This is all so much. I am kind with me. It is all so much. Not too much.

10:20 pm.

OK, crises resolved. Mine resolved with singing, but Dorjee just came and said he talked to his friend who just came from Drolma La and reported that there is <u>no</u> snow. He looks so relieved! So now, I sleep. Bless me.

Khora with Prostrations

August 3, 2006. Day 1

7 am. Tossing and turning for an hour, sorting things through in my thoughts. I am so afraid. I am so afraid to set my foot on Mt. Kailash. Why did they invite me? I don't want this much vitality, this much ability, this much blessing. All my life, I've just wanted to be left alone and to be ordinary, and now, I come and accept an invitation like this. It's not going around the mountain. I think I can do that if I choose to. It's that if I go around the mountain, it never stops. There's no escape from all this love. There's no escape, and that's what terrifies me. MotherFather Kailash, receive me, teach me in the way I need to be taught. Despite my ignorance, despite my blindness, I have come to you. I have come. I have come to receive your blessing and your teaching and your empowerment. I have come to love you. I have come to love me.

"I am available before my moment self-arises so that I can respond to my new moment." The moment won't go away. This is not about whether I'm eating enough, or whether I'm sick. It's about whether I live in my human heart or wander around lost in repetition, lost in thinking, in the joys and scars of my history. I can live in my past or I can live available to the unbroken moment now. Given that choice, who wouldn't choose love? But choosing love means letting go of everything, and receiving everything. Choosing love means complete freedom. It means complete devastation. It means the loss of how I want things to be and the engagement of how things are, experiencing life on life's terms, with joy.

Why am I here? This is not the kind of thing I do. I help *other* people do greater things, live kinder hearts. That's what I do: I help other people *see who they are.* <u>*Why did you invite me?*</u> I don't want to know me. I love this, and I hate this. For the first time, I get it: I *love* hate. My love is holding the love and the hate. How can I love the hate in the world when I don't love the hate in me? But I haven't gone deeper. I'm walking right around the edges of it. Here I am, in front of an open door marked *Void,* and I'm holding onto my history and my personality.

My crew was so sweet. Dorjee and I had agreed, and agreed with everyone, that it was best for me to start early, and we would be in the Land Cruiser at 9 am. Despite this, we left one and a half hours late. Dorjee, Jigme, and I sat in the Land Cruiser a little before 9:00. Nine o'clock came and went. We sat, and sat, and sat. At times, they got out and went looking for the other two, but to no avail. They came back, and we sat some more. Rikjin and Nima had disappeared, and there was nothing to do but wait. Dorjee and Jigme seemed a bit perturbed, but they were just gone and there was nothing that could be done about it. I was more in a cultural dilemma: should I be stern when they got back to convey this should not be a pattern? Or should I stay with the understanding that everything is just as it should be?

I didn't know exactly where they went, but when they arrived, they hopped in like not a thing was amiss. Everyone began talking pleasantly and laughing, and we drove off. When we got to Tarboche, I began to understand. They had gone to make a celebration for the beginning of my Khora. When we got out of the Land Cruiser at Tarboche, I was just looking around. Dorjee and I decided I would begin prostrations at the fireplace there. He said that way I would know exactly where I began, so I would know exactly where to return to. I would know I had indeed gone all the way to where I had begun. I was glad to have this small certainty, this concrete landmark.

My thoughts were on getting my apron and hand clogs on, and figuring out how to begin, when Jigme pulled out incense to light in the fireplace. Nima and Rikjin had been AWOL to get other celebratory materials. Nima pulled out Cokes for each of us. Everyone shook their Coke, spraying it in celebration, drinking what we could, and then setting the cans down on the ground. Then each of them gave me a kata! I couldn't believe it. These young men who didn't know me at all, gathering around me to send me off around Kailash with their blessings. I was deeply, deeply touched.

Dorjee then explained: three prostrations to the East, three to the South, three to the West, then one to the North and just keep going. I'm not sure of the sequence of directions. I kept explaining I wanted a picture of the first prostration, and Dorjee kept putting the camera away after photographing the celebration. I put the apron on, over my head and tied around my waist. It is a big, heavy apron. I felt shy garbing myself thus, like I was putting on a tennis outfit for Wimbledon without knowing if I really knew how to play tennis. But everyone was very interested in this project. I stood for a moment, preparing, and Rikjin asked about my hands. I had forgotten to take out my clogs from my backpack. In a way, everyone was dressing me, everyone was preparing for Khora through me. Then Rikjin asked about gloves. I had left these in my backpack, as it was not cold at the moment, but then thought he would know if it would become cold, so I'd best put them on. So I got them out of my backpack, and we *all* put the hand clogs on again over the gloves, adjusting and re-adjusting the Velcro straps. At last, it was time for the picture, and suddenly Rikjin was in front of me, dancing around like a photographer, snapping shots. It was all happening around me: I was in the center of the unfolding of this beginning. There was nothing for me to direct or orchestrate, it was unfolding around me in its own energy.

We agreed on a whistle in case I got lost, something the travel agent had suggested. We worked out how to attach it at the back of my apron so I was not always coming down onto it with each prostration. I thought Rikjin would be checking in with me, bringing fluids, and I pointed out my electrolyte bottle, thinking he would be carrying it for me.

Just as I was about to begin the first prostration of my Khora, there was a rock slide on the mountain facing us. My crew immediately oriented to it. I could hear it, but not see it. I was just was not used to the scale of Tibet, expecting to see a huge side of a mountain sliding. I expect it was a big enough slide, but the mountains are so high that a slide is on a part of the mountainside. It took me a moment to focus in on the sound, and to find the part of the rocks that were giving way. I felt it was a sign from the dakinis, that they were blessing my endeavor, encouraging me, welcoming me to this task.

Then everyone but Dorjee left to set up camp for the night at some point ahead because the car was needed elsewhere, and this was the only campsite to which we could drive. The rest of the sites around the mountain would be accessible only on foot and Rikjin and Nima would carry everything each time until we got back to Darchen. Dorjee walked up the little rise in front of me, and set my water bottle with the electrolytes in it on the top of the rise, and then disappeared over it. I wondered what I would do with the bottle when I got there, as I had not anticipated carrying anything. But there was nothing to do but begin. I just let it all be what it was, and began the first prostration, self conscious, uncertain of just how one was supposed to do all this, yet doing what I knew, what I could, what I did. There was only me to rely on, so I let the prostration come through me, figuring if I was doing it wrong somehow, someone would tell me. I remember many, many days later, really, weeks later, a party of young people passed me as I was prostrating, and one young Tibetan with a big cowboy hat stopped, set down his water bottle, and grabbed my wrists as I was prostrating. He pulled my arms straight out in front of me. With sign language, he was quite adamant that I was not to bring my hands together as I stretched out on the ground, but to stretch them out straight ahead. He instructed me several times, in no uncertain terms, then picked up his water bottle and went on ahead with his group. In their own way, everyone was part of this Khora, and teachings were there for me even when I didn't know I needed them.

I prostrated up that first little hill at Tarboche, next to the huge flagpole and the myriad prayer flags adorning that site. The hem of my skirt kept catching on my hiking boot. I finally decided to tie a knot in my hem to shorten my skirt. That worked. I took the gloves off because they were too hot. I got to the water bottle, and tied it to my waist with the rawhide string which had wrapped the apron in a bundle for carrying. I got to the top of the little hill, and Dorjee was standing there. He smiled, and commented that I looked good coming up from the prostrations. He seemed a bit surprised but quite pleased. I am sure these beautiful guides, who see so many tourists and so many kinds of people, had no idea whether I had ever done a prostration in my life. They had no idea what to expect in watching me undertake this. I think they had courage to reserve judgment and just support me, with the Cokes and katas and incense, before they had seen so much as one prostration.

At the top of the rise, Dorjee stopped to talk with me while I adjusted my knee pads which were slipping as ever. He said this is his seventy-ninth trip to Kailash, and he has never had a trip like it. He said he and the crew have never felt this way. It was hard to catch all the details as he spoke, but they seem happy and excited to be on this trip with me. I kept worrying that they might be disappointed, having a "group" of one, which surely meant less money in tips. But this never came up, and throughout the trip, again and again their joy at accompanying me on this magnificent journey came through, a journey whose magnificence I only barely glimpsed. It was Day 1, and already Dorjee was saying they were so happy to be on this journey with me. They were feeling something special about this journey.

Dorjee continued that last night, big burley Jigme, our wonderful driver, asked them, "Where's the missus?" I laughed inside, not thinking of myself as a "missus." Dorjee said I was praying. He said that this somehow affected Jigme, which I didn't really understand because Jigme would break out into a mantra when the roads were *really* impossible, so I felt that prayer was just a part of his life, as it seems to be for everyone here. Yet something about me was touching him in some deep way. I just listened.

It was time then to continue prostrations. I began again, and he stopped me, pointing me in the opposite direction. This had been my biggest fear, that I would lose the Khora path and head off in some wrong direction, and here it was! Everyone had said, and believe me, I had asked many people, that you can't lose the Khora path, there is just one path, and it is clear. But here it was. I had lost it right at the beginning. But this turned out not to be so. Dorjee was directing me to prostrate around the stupa. Like so much about this culture and this tradition, I did not know that Khora was begun in this way. I was grateful for his guidance. He then pointed toward the tents in the distance. "Camp." He kept pointing to a dark tent beyond the white tents, explaining that was where camp would be. I guess he understood what I did not at that point, that what you can see from a distance quickly disappears as you approach the horizon. I didn't know it then, but it would be a long time, and an exciting search, before I found those dark tents! Then Dorjee left. He left me with much mutual gratitude. I prostrated around the stupa, and then began the path around Kailash.

All day, as I prostrated in blazing clear skies and hot sun, I could feel Marcus holding the vajra tent, the blessed, protected space, around me. Dea kept showing up – all day! I could feel her power and her beauty, and to have her and Marcus "accompany" my first day was an unexpected blessing. Well, I knew Marcus would be here, but to feel them loving me together, each in their own ways, was amazing.

The first day seemed a hundred years long. I met so many people. People kept stopping me, looking at my hand clogs, asking me questions, touching my apron, asking where I was from. I was videotaped, and given candy. I tried to return the favor with a half-dollar piece to one woman as a memento from America but she seemed very offended. It became a long, long interaction with a group of mostly women, and two or three very old ones. I felt so refreshed after encountering them, despite all the mix ups and errors in communication, despite my hesitancy to just receive their gift without trying to re-pay them.

I learned that when I say Om Ah Hum, I can receive the empowerment of each syllable. I can just say them as sounds, or I can feel the power in those syllables. What a revelation.

I learned that no matter what, a mantra goes with the prostrations, it's better that way, whole, no matter how tired or uncertain I am. I tried two prostrations silently, and they were empty, incomplete. I learned that the mantra will come to me. Sometimes I would choose a mantra, and it would fall out of my head, words I had said hundreds of time would fall out of my head, and a different mantra would arise, would teach me what I was to be saying in that moment.

A ten-year-old boy walked toward me with his father, thumbs up, encouraging me. Two young women called from a distance words that were clearly encouragement. People stopped and just watched as I prostrated past them. I always said Tashi Delek and Namaste. But I was also aware that somewhere I gave up some of my space to what I thought they needed, caretaking instead of living my moment.

A monk I met said through a translator that some days ago he had a dream that a dakini was coming into Tibet from Nepal. It seems the night he referred to was the night before I crossed the Nepal border into Tibet. He said he feels I am a reincarnation of someone; I couldn't follow all the Tibetan as the translator had an accent, but he was very joyful as he spoke to me. It was almost like a song was bursting from him. I listened, and then I tried to explain to him that I didn't know what to do with what he was saying to me. I didn't know what it meant if I was a reincarnation of a dakini. I am just Tracey, just a Western woman who has come here out of love for Tibet and Kailash, come here to lay on the ground of Kailash and be blessed, to attempt prostrations but not knowing anything, really. I did not know what his dream meant, what dakini meant. He said something very nice. He said, "I know you don't know. But I know." I appreciated his acceptance that his experience was his experience. He was not putting anything on me, not expecting anything of me. Then he gave me his prayer medallion. I had never seen one like it, and it seemed very special to him. I was very touched that he gave it to me as a protection for my journey around the mountain. By the time I learned it had been given to him by his teacher, it was too late. He would not take it back. I felt this huge gift, this offering to accompany me around this magnificent and supreme mountain.

10:00 pm.

Dinner is done. I am finally done for today. I finished at 4:15 pm – five hours of prostrations for my first day. It took me an hour to find the tent. That was an adventure! I had only planned to do three and a half hours or so, as Dorjee and Rikjin suggested, starting slowly. But I thought my tents were just beyond the white tea tents, and not being used to the scale of Tibet, where everything is higher and farther than it seems, I kept going a little farther, and a little farther. Finally, though, it was clear that I was not going to make it to the white tents. It was not even an option to push myself, to violate my body and override the sense that I was done for the day.

I worried about setting up a cairn. I was on an open plain, and how would I find a little pile of rocks in the morning? But I made my cairn, did my best to locate natural landmarks around it, and set off walking for the white tents. Somehow, I thought our deep blue tents would be right behind them. Not so. I went into every tent there, looking for my crew, expecting to see them having tea, really, expecting to see them looking for, waiting for me. Not so. It was 6:00 pm. Would they miss me? Didn't they think it was a bit late? Apparently not! But oddly, I was not worried or frightened. I was just lost. No one spoke a word of English. In a long "conversation" with the people inside the tea tent, it was clear that they had no idea what I was asking about, tents and my crew, but they were offering me a couch to sleep on and tea to drink. I had no money, and did not understand what they would expect, and I wanted to find my tent and sleep there. So I declined. Finally I understood something one woman turned and said to another, "Hakomasong." "I don't understand." Hakomasong! I had learned that phrase sitting in Newark Airport! I heard it! I explained, "Hakomasong, Hakomasong," and they laughed, but we still didn't understand each other! So I thanked them, and wandered out of the tent.

I had checked every tent and every person I could find there. Logically, my camp could not be where I had come from, or I hopefully would have seen it in passing. So I began walking ahead, beyond where I had stopped on the Khora path. As I walked, small hills obscured distant objects, so I felt I was walking blind. I could see no distant landmark. Perhaps there was nothing I was walking toward. When I stopped, there was thunder, the prodrome of an intense storm gathering in the valley. Now, I noticed a very dark cloud mass, air mass, really, coming down the valley that I was walking up. A storm was gathering. It looked like a significant storm, but what was there to do? I kept walking. I walked for awhile, still wearing my apron and knee pads. Finally, a Land Cruiser approached.

I flagged it down, only to discover it was filled with a Japanese party who spoke no English. But we were all good humored about the attempt to communicate, and through sign language, I got some useful information. In response to my questions, they seemed to indicate that there were tents up ahead, and I felt that was as good a sign as any that they might be my tents. So I thanked them and kept walking in the direction I was going. Finally, over one rise, I saw the tents. I walked and walked, and finally I saw my guys, Rikjin and Nima. They greeted me like I was strolling in after a half hour walk. They apparently had no concern about my being lost or delayed. I was tired and happy. I am not much of a talker at the best of times, so we chatted briefly, but I mostly just wanted to get my gear and shoes off, and relax in my tent. They brought me refreshment as I settled into my tent, my wonderful little tent.

All in all, I feel I finished the day in false bliss. What a great learning. I got seduced into my personality. Class will be glad to hear, however, that I am developing a limit. I have a tendency to set my sights on something, and go on relentlessly, without thought to fatigue, reality, or anything but what I have set my sights on. But that was not how my first day of prostrations went. On that first day, Rikjin had commented that he thought I could make the tents before the end of the day, and I tried, but it became clear to me that while I would have liked to get to such a clear, neat landmark, I needed to stop for the day. I felt in having a limit that my little girl, who has no boundary, who will take on anything and not quit, was beginning to die and the woman was beginning to live. It is very shaky. It's beginning. Yet, looking back, that remained true for each day. Amazingly, after a lifetime of ignoring the messages of my body, of fatigue, of physical feeling of any kind, never on Khora did it even occur to me to push myself. I did each day fully, and each day was hard, hard all day, some days harder than others. But I never pushed myself to do something that was not in me, freely, joyfully, out of devotion. I did Khora with prostrations as the prayer it is, not as a discipline or mastery, but only out of what I had inside me at any moment.

When I finally found the camp, I was so blissed out and exhausted that I just rested amid glowing thoughts. "If this is the only day of prostrations I do, I am joyful!" I frankly didn't know if I could do another day of prostrations, or how many more days. As the high of the day settled back down to earth, I felt some other impression inside me that said I had come to open or re-open something. It was not about feeling high or low. It was about showing up each moment.

The vitality to show up before my moment is showing itself to me, acting from vitality instead of effort. I hurt and I'm exhausted, and it is perfect and I'm happy. But somewhere the space from which I am choosing this journey is not clean. I am seeing, slowly, through my pride and my errors, this truth. I will wake up into tomorrow for more learning.

August 4, 2006. Day 2

I awaken, and it takes me a considerable period of time to sort out whether I am awake, or whether the nightmare which coiled around me through the night was truly a dream or is actually real. In retrospect, it has been a night of wrestling, I think, with whether I really want to do this. The nightmare seemed to last the whole night. I dreamed a flash flood came through and wiped out every tent but mine. I was completely alone.

For some reason, I could hear my classmate Beth's voice as she grabbed what was left of her stuff and began hiking out with other survivors. I didn't go, which just made me feel even more stupid. I huddled in the darkness, disoriented, not sure if any of my gear was still there. I finally, physically, not in the dream but in real time got up and went outside my tent to look around. I did this twice. I looked at my clock: 1:14 am at the first foray out, and 1:27 am at the second. I could see nothing either time, not even Rikjin and Nima's tent. Looking back, I must have been in a hypnogogic state, physically awake and moving, but mentally still in the dream state, like a sleepwalker. I went out a third time at around 4:30 am to see if anything was left after the flood. Leaving my tent was an act of courage for me rather than being paralyzed with fear or retreating to denial. I was still in the dream state, not sure if the dream was real and we had had a flood which wiped everything out, or if I had been dreaming and all was well. Still, I found the courage to go out and face whatever was out there. Finally, I did see their tent.

I am finally awakening fully now, with a phrase from one of the practices in my head, "Not to do evil, always to do good, this has been shown to us...." I don't know why that prayer makes me cry. I awake realizing I need to do practice before I leave to continue Khora. It will probably be 11:00 am before I start prostrations. Will I still feel this vulnerable, this open once I stand up, outside my tent? Whether I do or not, I know I need to do the practices before I leave for Khora. The tears come again. I don't know why, I just know it's good for me to let the tears come at this point.

I don't know what I'm doing. I don't know why I'm here. I know my prayer is to make it through Drolma La. I don't know what I can do. I am bathed in not-knowing. Ignorance is my blessing.

I talk to class constantly in my head. They are my lifeline. Tibet is an entirely different playing field. The scale, yes, but also the depth. It is not to be messed with. If I were the Chinese, I would go home. The forces that simply move here everyday are so enormous. They are not to be messed with.

I am just unzipping my tent to again go to the bathroom and true daylight is out there. The theme song from *The Poseidon Adventure* rings out in my head. "There's got to be a morning after...." It's both freeing and real. I can't stop crying.

9:31 am.

When I pray to Guru Rinpoche, he is so close.

9:55 am.

I was just finishing practice in my tent, and I noticed a very poor and normal looking Tibetan motioning to me. I looked up and waved, but he kept motioning. He wanted me to come out, so I put my shoes on and came out. That seemed to be all he wanted. We bowed to each other. He walked back to his two companions, looking back once or twice.

It is chillier today. As I prepare to leave, I decide to bring my sunhat because I see blue sky breaking through. My regular dress included a shirt and hiking pants over undergarments and socks and hiking boots, a long skirt, and my leather apron. I wore knee protectors until about the last nine days or so. I wore wooden clogs on my hands, and gloves when it was cold. I had two hats of different warmth, pullover fleeces, and a cold-weather, hi-tech jacket when needed. Today, I put on a warmer, lined fleece pullover, and immediately feel better. There is a constant cool wind and many rain clouds still.

4:35 pm.

Home after prostrations. My goal was three hours, with the hope of making it to camp. I made camp in five hours. The last five or ten minutes, rain began, big fat drops, then hail, now a downpour. The weather has been kind to me.

It is hard to begin each day – each day?...this is Day 2! But it was hard, and the night of nightmares didn't make it any easier. It strikes me as I say this that a night of good sleep is false enthusiasm. Everything just is what it is, tired or rested; it is my choice to show up fully in love. "Because I am available before my new moment self-arises, I can respond to my new moment."

After lunch today, as I began prostrations again, Patrick's words came through, "I have confidence in you," and that I have a "very strong heart." Time to receive this blessing. I could feel Marcus and Dea circling around me throughout the day, like large love birds keeping an eye on me and loving me. Then Patrick's words came, and Dea's voice, "Receive." And I felt that I have always loved me secretly, and I began to feel the split: Why not love me openly, deeper and deeper? Receiving my love, my parents' love, my sister's love, my brother's love, Alec's love, class's love, life's love. Receive. There is just the tiniest crack opening between inner and outer, between love loving me and me loving me. This old masochism, this old unquestioning self-rejection, this unquestioning self-hatred and unworthiness is coming to be received with love, rather than letting it direct my repetitive choices to be unkind with myself while trying to be kind with everyone else.

Generally, Rikjin or Nima walk out to find me on the Khora trail after about three hours and bring me lunch and more liquids. Rikjin came today. Over lunch, I asked if the bird circling overhead was a vulture. He told me it was, and that there are two kinds of vultures here, those that eat bones and those that eat meat. This one, which had a white head and white underbody, eats bones. It carries them way up high, drops them to break them open – clever! – and then comes down to eat. The scale here is so enormous. They look like pigeons circling, but their wingspan is about five feet.

Then there was Milarepa's Soup. Yesterday's dinner was white rice with Milarepa's Soup. Milarepa refused to leave his meditation cave until reaching enlightenment. When he ran out of food, he began eating the nettles which are plentiful here. He ate so many nettles, he developed a slight greenish tinge to his skin, but he kept his word and remained in his practice until he achieved enlightenment. Nima made Milarepa's Soup from all the nettles here for my dinner. It is still difficult for me to eat. Each spoonful is small and tentative to see if my stomach will go along with it. Everyone is, of course, urging me to eat, as am I myself. But I'm doing the best that I can. I wondered if I'd ever get through that bowl of thick green soup, carefully taking half a teaspoon at a time. Then suddenly I looked down, and the "waterline" of the soup was way down! I thought, this is just like trying to get anywhere on Khora. I prostrate and prostrate and prostrate and I go such tiny distances. And then suddenly I've actually gotten somewhere. Not through will, not through big steps, but through staying with each tiny moment as it is.

5:19 pm.

Two monks just stopped by. They wanted to see the tent. Fortunately Nima arrived, everyone chatted, and they went on their way.

As I continued, I felt today that each day is what it is. I have no concept of finishing this or not finishing this. I don't feel it is in my hands. My perception is that I am going *painfully* slowly, and there is nothing I can do about this. I have no problem with that. I seem to rest a lot, standing between prostrations, at times sitting. I am doing this the way that I can, not the way that I should or that fits some picture or obligation. I'm not trying. I'm listening to my body and to my heart, and I'm listening to the teachings that come through, and that's all I know. Each day feels like an elevator shaft. It's a huge vertical column of spacetime, not connected to the day before or the day after, but with the infinity of that day in it.

This dakini stuff, being spoken of as if I am a dakini, is really upsetting me. It's lucky I don't have to do anything. What could I possibly do? That would really overwhelm me, and the very idea itself is pretty overwhelming.

I didn't see Kang Rinpoche at all today.

6:38 pm.

I've just been resting, and the bells kept ringing, and I finally said, yes, the horses. There is a small herd of horses grazing around our tents. It is time to take some pictures of this beautiful campsite. It was then that I realized that I cannot find my beautiful camera. I've been through all my gear twice. The only possibility is that it got left in the truck at Tarboche. That's not much better. Who has the truck? My memory is that I unpacked it in my tent. Is that a wish or a memory? Camera gone. Impermanence.

7:18 pm.

You know, I feel suffused with spirituality, like I have eaten too much. Kindness. Rest. Emptyhead.

8:31 pm.

Something's going on. I feel upset. The thunderstorm outside just makes me feel more trapped. I am zipped into my tent. I can hear some animal trying to get in. Good thinking, it's very wet out there. I'd try to get in, too. It is occurring to me that what I'm upset about is the spiritual stuff, people telling me I'm a reincarnation, a dakini.

8:45 pm.

Dinner arrives. I ask Nima if he knows if my camera got left in the truck. He answers immediately that he has it; do I want him to bring it? It is still raining. I say no, no need right now. I am just so relieved that it is still here.

It gets clearer to me. What upset me were two things: when I thought my camera was lost, I would not be able to share pictures with my precious classmates. And I would not be able to photograph rangjung Amitabha when I get to the monastery. I am starting to cry again. I'm coming apart. The old supports of familiarity are falling away. It's not the camera. It's the impermanence becoming more real. Everything that orients me, the sense of control, is gone. Each day is just get up and prostrate. I don't know where I'm going. I don't know how long. On the trail, I don't know where I am. I don't know if I'll get there. I don't know to what end. I don't know what will happen if I do this. Dear Lord, the Chinese are out of their minds to mess with this place. Milarepa crosses my mind. The ordeal to break you down, to open you, open you to what you came here for to begin with. I don't want an ordinary life, so what's my problem? Only Day 2 and I am starting to come apart. I am grateful. It's what I came for.

Even while I'm starting to come apart, there are signs of stabilization. I figured out how to use my Petzel light and I've been reading my novel all afternoon. I am eating easier, at least tonight.

August 5, 2006. Day 3

I wake up to the bells. I wake up afraid. I wake up thanking the dakinis for being so gentle with me. I wake up slightly closer to more capacity, to my roar, my zest. I wake up with the door of diamond light.

It has stopped raining. I am grateful as I don't know if I am ready for a day of prostrating in the raging storm. Everything is so unknown. How to stay warm. How to be not too warm. How to not get lost. When to start. When to stop. There are no answers. Love holds me and I hold me, and together we figure it out. Marcus answers my question in class and the teaching returns to me: "Love has no image of me, and I have no image of me, and together we self-arise my new moment."

The little foal got herself all tangled up in one of the outhouse guide wires. She got herself out again. I was in the outhouse tent, taking my time with my body, and suddenly this tiny little muzzle was nuzzling the side of the tent, just a few times. So sweet.

My cold is still in my chest. My sinuses are draining less. I wake up with headaches, but that's my spiritual resistance. I keep remembering that the blessings are there to be *received*. I do practice and expect it to transform me. *I* have to *receive* it. The blessing is right there, the empowerment is right there, but it won't come unless I accept it, receive it. It's right there.

9:34 am.

There is perhaps a tiny quality of surrender. I am quite tired, but I'm not depressed, I'm not resentful, and I'm not inert. I still head into the day blind, looking into the unknown. I am so grateful there are other pilgrims walking this path. The complete aloneness on Khora would be difficult. The dakinis are giving me just what I can handle and no more.

I see the golden groundhogs, and tell Rikjin I did not know Tibet had groundhogs. He says they are marmot. They are so beautiful. I spend time watching them scurry in and out of their burrows. There are many around our campsite. Our campsite sits at the foot of a mountainside, but then everything in Tibet is in relation to a mountain. A waterfall hurls itself down this mountain, cascading to the edge of our campsite. The beauty is overwhelming. Horses, marmot, waterfall, how could we find a campsite so beautiful?

6:35 pm.

Five hours of prostrations today. I could not do five and a half. Five hours and a half-hour walk back to camp. Some people gave me money, and I'm asking Rikjin to teach me how to say "butter lamps." I want them to know I will light butter lamps with the money. A young man gave me a kata. After two hours of just resting and sleeping after getting back to camp, I am still just wiped. Headache. I hope I have enough Excedrin for the trip.

It is hard to get going after stopping, in the morning and after lunch. I am surprised I get anywhere at all. I just follow the mantra that comes into my mind, and keep going. Lots of stops today for yaks and parties on horses. Huge herds came by. I move over to the very side of the Khora path, and let them pass. The yaks are so beautiful. They seem gentle, but I don't really know them. I know a horse won't step on me, but I don't know how yaks feel about things in their path.

Once I get started again, after an hour maybe, I'm OK. I feel like I'm going *very* slowly. I have no control over anything, speed, number of hours. I am just doing what I'm doing. I felt today that it's all love. Each time my body touches earth, I am loving and being loved. I felt the dakinis for awhile. I asked Guru Rinpoche to open my heart in this wonderful place.

8:00 pm.

Nima went into Darchen for supplies. He is still not back. The evening rains have begun. I had asked Rikjin what season this is, summer? No, he said. Monsoon. In Nepal, June-July is monsoon. In Tibet, it is August. I am so grateful the rains come at night so far, although I know they may not always be so. I am relying on the dakinis to guide me. I don't know what to do or why. I just get up in the morning and open my heart. They are kind but clear. This journey is not a Hallmark moment. It is real. It is true.

Walking back to camp today, I was struck by how chipper everyone's walk was and how slow mine was. I'm generally a fast walker, but I don't think my pace is going to change here. I'm happy. I'm peaceful. And my body is simply not moving any faster.

Rikjin showed me the trench he dug around my tent to divert water last night – how kind! I vaguely remember dreaming something about some sound outside. So it was him I heard. He must have gotten soaked. He said his and Nima's tent leaked and they got quite wet.

On Day 1, a blessing from my time on Easter Island was present, in being in such hot sun and tolerating it well. I could never bear the elements very well until Easter Island. There, I was immersed in them, and without trying, came to peace with them. My physical self came to peace with the ways of the physical world, and now I can be in sun without an instant, days-long headache.

I am learning to let my knees dry out at lunch, loosening the pads, opening my zip-up pant legs and letting air move through.

9:38 pm.

The first clear thought that I need to let go of class arises. Stop chatting with them and sharing with them. Just be here.

I believe my next cold is starting.

So many people today asked me where I was from, mostly Indians, some Chinese, Tibetans. They seemed surprised and pleased that an American would undertake a spiritual journey.

Somehow, it has gotten to be 10:20 pm. The rains are passing. My teeth are brushed, the breakfast-at-9:00-am request is in, and the dishes from dinner are returned. I sing myself a Strauss waltz, and my whole insides smile. I reflect on my effort to put intention into my body, and it's like dragging a greyhound bus down the road. When I act from my heart, there is no effort and it simply is what it is. Time to sleep peacefully.

August 6, 2006. Day 4

Storming all night. Nightmare-like dreams again, having to get up in my dream state and go through everything to see what had not washed away in the dream-storm. I laugh as I write this. The symbolism is so obvious! Once I am truly awake, I look to figure out what to wear to do prostrations in the rain and wind. I am trying to know if I should take the day off or not.

I had set the alarm for 6:30 am. I managed to get up by 7:10 am. I'm actually doing better. No stirring from Nima yet. It's 7:58 am. Rain has stopped but it is very cloudy. I am tired, etc, etc, but ready to walk back to my site and continue.

At some point this morning in the growing wakefulness, the thought of "I'm just Tracey, being more of Tracey" was rattling through, and I realized that's a diversion. Tracey is nothing. She's not bad, she's just inconsequential. Tracey has to die. I have lived much of my life from

Tracey. She's not enough to live this life from. I have made her first and my human heart second, actually my spiritual heart first, Tracey second, and my human heart third, and that does not work for me. My spiritual heart will always love me, but my human heart runs the show, and Tracey is a form that comes and goes.

8:20 am.

Downpours. There is joy in my heart. These beings, Amitabha, Vajrasattva, all of them, are so much love! And they are here! Loving us! All creation is love, it's all love, one manifestation after another. So much love. I am love.

9:30 am.

Nima is very late with breakfast, but the light is up. I come out of my tent, and there is snow on top of the rocks! It is hauntingly beautiful, the jagged peaks of the low hills newly dusted with pure white.

6:29 pm.

I've been home for an hour. My feet are tucked into my sleeping bag. I've just encouraged myself to get up and put my soaking shirt, hat, and wet jacket in various places where they might dry. There were showers on and off all day. Nothing much really. Lots before and when I left to walk to my starting place, but not after. But heading home, I walked back up the river valley that I'm following, right into a storm with cold driving rain. I must have looked a sight when I got home. Rikjin teased me by asking who I was, and Nima just stared. I had my white fleece cap on under my hood, and my canvas hat in front of me, partly because I could not disentangle the hat strap from the hood, my braid, and the leather apron I had slung over my shoulder, so there it just hung on my chest.

I prostrated for five hours. When I stopped, it seemed like I had gone too far. When I finally picked up my apron, got my knee protectors off, took a pee, and made a cairn to mark where I stopped, I could hardly stand with tiredness and belly pain. One of the energy bars I ate had dried fruit in it. I won't be eating that again. I think my intestines did not like it.

When I headed home, it took me ten to fifteen minutes to get back to where Rikjin brought lunch, which meant it had taken two hours of prostrations to do what I walked in ten to fifteen minutes! That can't be, even though it was uphill, but my brain was too tired to find the error in the calculations. Overall, it took me about an hour to get home, which means I'm on track, half hour yesterday, one hour today; I must be covering some ground.

It's hard. Spiritual admission is not cheap. I still don't know where I am, or what I am capable of. It was very hard to get started. I started at 10:55 this morning, too late for me. With an hour's walk to get to the starting place, plus breaking camp tomorrow, I don't know how I'll get any prostrations done tomorrow. Of course, there's nothing to get done.

There were very few people (and yaks) today. I must say I appreciated the silence. It was a hard day, and I liked being with the day. I must also say that just the right amount of people came, and I was surprised how buoyed up I felt after some. One woman actually asked permission to film me doing prostrations. She's the only one who has asked. And then she asked my name, and I asked hers. She was from India.

Two young women from Taiwan stopped, one in particular had so many questions, and the other one was quiet but attentive and kind. The one with questions asked if I was a Buddhist. I paused and said, "I'm everything." "That's a good sentence," she said. She asked another question: pointing to the ground, "Is it painful?"

"No."

"Peaceful?"

"Yes."

When they were getting ready to move ahead, the quiet one expressed distress that they had nothing to give me. She had offered water and crackers, but I was still supplied. I told her they had given me something, their kindness, and they seemed quite moved at this. But I meant it. They weren't dissecting me for information. They were truly interested.

A young man from Holland joined us for lunch. One in his party was American, and he was saying that he had made a comment about American politics, and while not a fearful person, he became quite afraid at the American's reaction. I commented that there were a lot of very difficult things about America right now, a lot not to like right now. There was a silence, and I wondered if I had been too strong in my words. He described the American's response as a fist pounding down on a table. I noted it sounded rather fascist. Maybe that was going too far.

Walking home, I sang a waltz again. I could feel something jammed up inside, more than just tired and hurting. I wondered, I am going so slowly, but there seems nothing to be done about it. I wondered, if I don't finish in the twenty-five days allowed, should I just go to Lhasa. The answer kept coming so clearly, *Finish Kailash. Stay with the earth of Kailash until the circuit is completed.*

I felt, too, my fear, as I get closer and closer to Drira Phuk Gompa, higher up and ready to begin the approach to Drolma La, I feel the space thicken and deepen, and I feel fear. Even now, the tears start. I don't know what that is, why Drolma La affects me so much. Marcus teaches that fear is a quality of love. Love is present.

I injured myself today. This morning, I came down on a rock which connected with my last left rib. Not too bad. Sore. Mostly the coughing bothers it.

I was prostrating along the river. At one point, some yak herders and traders on their return trip from yesterday called and waved. I looked over, and one young herder was giving me a vigorous thumbs up. I recognized him from yesterday. It made me laugh! And it touched me, so much support from these people. I am a foreigner in their land, attempting something so sacred to them, and they encourage me. I do not take this for granted. I take it as permission, as empowerment.

9:30 pm.

Downpours for the past two hours. I feel suppressed. Fear is what awakens most. I can't believe Nima and Rikjin have to *carry* camp to south of Drira Phuk tomorrow. I hope the weather is good. They estimate three trips. I would actually find that more difficult than prostrations. Hiking is harder for me because I still can't breathe. The slowness of prostrations allows me to pant my way along. Walking is too fast, I can't breathe quickly enough to get enough oxygen.

August 7, 2006. Day 5

It's so hard to keep track of time. I backtrack to make sure I'm on the right day. Heavy rains all night. A brief respite this morning. I try to dry some clothes in the wind. I take a few pictures before breaking camp, but now there is a steady rain again. It's very cold. I am hopeful there is a break behind this set of rain, maybe a clearing moving up the valley. I don't know how Rikjin and Nima will move everything today. I am packed, sleeping bag back in the stuff sack, pillow stuffed, too. Duffel and backpack all set to move.

I woke at 7 am with my alarm. I remembered Marcus' teaching that we wake up the way we want to. I feel some very deep-down reactions to doing this Khora. Fear is the closest real thing I can find. My mind cannot seem to find a picture of who I'm supposed to be, and I don't seem to want to function unless I know how I'm supposed to be doing it.

I remembered Dea's message, "Bring home the joy." I remembered that I accepted this invitation from the dakinis, and I don't know how to do this. I just don't want to lie. I don't want to fake this journey. I don't know anything and each prostration has to come from my heart, not my knowledge, not my mastery. Not from comfort nor from suffering, but from one taste. And then, whatever the dakinis want me for will do itself. I am ignorant, but that monk at Chiu Gompa knew something about me, about the calling for me to come here. I could feel his holiness and his perception.

10:15 am.

It's pouring slightly less. It's very cold. I'm going to finish packing and go. Practice helped a lot. It's all the same.

7:55 pm.

The body is a wonderful thing. It self-generates heat. I am gratefully in my sleeping bag, fully dressed because I am so cold. But I am warming, loving the whole body, the body at rest as well as the body praying and prostrating. Love is the whole body.

So much was in today. I finally left camp in the soaking rain. I got back to my cairn around 11:35 am or so, and by the time I got all suited up, I began prostrations at noon. I must say I enjoyed the walk in, one, one and a half hours. I took pictures of many things along the way. I figured I'd probably only be able to do three hours of prostrations since I was starting so late. So I let go of my agenda, my efficiency, and stopped to photograph waterfalls and eagles as I walked back to my cairn.

I had the insight about body as sacred when resting as well as when busy. A little Tibetan girl, maybe eight years old, ran by with a group, and stopped to watch me prostrate. The next thing I knew, she's ahead of me and bouncing down to the ground and then up again, without losing a beat, prostrating along the path. Really, bouncing down to the ground, and bouncing up somehow, and then down again, effortless, quick, rhythmic. She seemed to be having a joyful time. Now that's how it should be done, so nimbly! She kept smiling at me. She had all kinds of braids, waving and flying about as she bounced from ground to sky, until she went out of sight ahead on the trail.

Rikjin and Nima brought lunch, along with heavy packs they were carrying to the next site. It was 2 pm. Two other guys joined us, and that was fine. I'm so exhausted it's hard to write. When I began today, it was the first time I began with enthusiasm or joy or centeredness, I don't know what to call it. I felt like I was finally answering the dakinis' invitation. I sustained that for a good hour, took a liquids and snack break, and continued, more tired. I was quite tired when Rikjin and Nima arrived with lunch.

Two other guys had joined us. When all four prepared to move on, two young men on horseback arrived. One kept inviting me into the saddle, which I assumed was because I was a woman. For me, I couldn't figure out what he did not realize about what I was doing. Clearly, I would not be taking any rides. Finally they followed Rikjin and Nima, and I began prostrations again. Less than half an hour later, Rikjin and Nima came quickly back down the path with the two men with horses. Rikjin said they had rented the two horses for three hundred yuan. Sounded good to me.

All afternoon, I kept waiting for them to return and pass me. Surely horses and men on foot go faster than me prostrating. But they didn't come. I prostrated for four hours, still expecting them to come along at any moment, and didn't think I could do much more. I did tackle a very treacherous curve around the cliff above the river. I prostrated into the uphill slant away from the embankment because the path was so narrow and tilted. I was moving through a huge flock of sheep. The shepherd had sat with me when I had taken a break. We "chatted" as best we could with no common language. When I was struggling around the embankment, he came again and seemed to be telling me that he used a path above. I told him I was waiting for two horses. He seemed to intimate that sleeping arrangements/tents/horses were back the other way. I finally just thanked him and continued. I wanted to get around that embankment before stopping for the day if possible. To be truthful, I did not have any extra energy to explore a possible alternative path. For what it would cost me in oxygen and energy to climb up the embankment to see the path he was indicating above, I might just as well continue on the path I was on. There was no guarantee there was a safer or clearer path above, and I could not risk wasting energy looking for an easier way. I didn't care about an easier way, and I was happy making my way slowly around the embankment. It was quite a task. If I had fallen, I would have gotten bruised but probably not seriously hurt. The embankment dropped off sharply to a delta-like plain leading into the river itself. But I clung into the path, my body at a twenty or thirty degree angle into the hillside so I would not roll off the edge onto the rocky delta below. The shepherd did not understand why I did not follow him, but I couldn't help that.

I did manage to get around that embankment, around the "corner" which I could not see beyond until I rounded it. In front of me was the river in its delta. I began prostrating through some of the river delta that needed crossing, but I did not do much. All those small, smooth rocks look easier than they are. Mostly I was concerned why Rikjin and Nima had not come by, and especially if they were setting up camp behind me, and whether they would come to find me. I stopped after five hours, tidied up, un-geared, and then climbed the nearest highest hill to see what I could see. I kept going up and forward on this high hill, until I saw the horses. But the two men there did not seem to be Rikjin and Nima. They waved for me to come down. When I got there, they "said" in sign language that Rikjin and Nima were walking from the old camp.

They offered me food and liquids. I just wanted to sit. They were very interested in my leather apron, clogs, and knee pads. One made it very clear that once I had returned to Darchen, he would like to buy the apron. I made it very clear it was not for sale. He did prostrations with the hand clogs. It was very clear he knows how to do them. I guess all Tibetans just know these rituals and mantras that are all new and magical to me. His friend just wanted to try everything on, and I intervened so he did not accidentally damage anything. They struck me as nice but basically a couple of wheeler-dealers. When I took a picture of one of the horses, one was terribly interested in my camera, and wanted to take a picture of me. I made it clear I did not want that.

Rikjin and Nima finally arrived. There was more talk among the four, and then they began loading up the horses and themselves. From this, I surmised that we were not at our campsite. We began to walk. I don't know if it is possible that we walked one and a half hours. It felt that way. The huge flock of sheep followed us. I waved at the shepherd as we slowly moved out of his pastureland.

As we walked, we were moving around the base of a very beautiful mountain. Could it be Kailash? I felt stupid not knowing, but at some point it was easy for me to confuse lesser mountains of the range with Kang Rinpoche itself. At one point, I asked Rikjin what that mountain was. He said the west face of Kailash. I had thought it was too near to be Kailash, it felt like I could reach out and touch it as we walked around its base. It's the first time in three days I've seen the mountain. Breathtaking.

We finally got to the campsite. It looks like a tea house where herders also bring their herds. There were four little kids, and the two year old girl just fixed onto me, staring. Finally she came over. Then three of them came over, just touching, pulling on my scarf, wanting to go in my pockets. I did not let them since I had learned at the last guesthouse that I really needed a better understanding of the culture and language to manage children. Being friendly with children there meant to them that they could just come in and out of my room, and it was difficult to re-establish a boundary. Different cultures. I don't know their culture, and don't speak their language, and they just kept coming and exploring and opening and touching, at the guesthouse and here. So I learned to have some boundaries. I was friendly, I hope, but set limits.

Today, I must have trekked three extra hours, and done five hours of prostrations. Oh! Amazing for me. During the day, I began just continuing my prostrations if horses were coming or yaks with handlers, instead of stopping and waiting on the side of the trail. I knew horses would not step on me, and yaks seemed to prefer their own lane, too.

August 8, 2006. Day 6

Yesterday was just too much. Dinner was at 11 pm. Poor Rikjin and Nima. I was just freezing, standing there while they negotiated the camp site and paid for the horses. Finally they put up my tent, and then went back for another trip to move the last of camp! Then they put up their tent. I don't know how they did all that in the cold and wet. I let myself sleep in this morning, and even now I am waking up slowly. I thought of Connor, my golden retriever. He is so far away. Everything is so far away. This place is a different plane. I hope to do some prostrations today, to begin to work my way up to this new place. It feels like a place I have to earn.

I lay here in my tent. The tent seems smaller and narrower. Cream-colored fluffy inner fabric, with a half-circle on each side, zipped doors, one to get out. Laying here, I feel like I'm in a coffin. I just feel filled with grief. I feel like I'm crashing into a depression, although I know this is not a depression. This is the hardest thing I've ever done in my life. It is so hard. Watching my mother die was not harder than this. Well, I came to die. What do I expect?

I begin to feel the difference of the short-lived gratification of discharging my nervous system and the infinity of staying in my human heart no matter what is coming up.

5:56 pm.

Back at camp. I did five hours, much to my surprise. I was so tired from yesterday that I figured three hours would be fine for today. I don't know if I'm on track, if I am keeping up with my schedule. Nima brought lunch today. It was good to chat with him. He said camp is two to three kilometers from Drira Phuk, and Drira Phuk is a four-hour walk from Drolma La. It all seems very far away. I hope to make camp tomorrow. A humble goal.

Nima also shared a little about himself, how he has done this for five years, and does not work in the winter so he can study. He could not manage school, so he hires a private tutor. I think he struggles with what we would call learning disabilities. Nima tells me that books and notepads are so very expensive. Everyone is so poor in Simikot where he comes from. His parents are farmers, but do not make enough to make ends meet. Periodically he'll send them something from Kathmandu, some clothes, and they are so excited and proud to receive something from him. I admire Nima so much for not quitting on his education. I try to explain learning disabilities and night school and tutors in America.

When I am back in my tent, Rikjin brings my noodle soup and asks if I need more liquids. With supper, I say. I'm fine now. His face is shining. So much light.

Have I mentioned the noodle soup? At our very first campsite, they offered to bring me some hot noodle soup when I returned from prostrating that first day. It has become such a treat! The most delicious thing in the world is my bowl of noodle soup when I get my boots off and lay my body down in my little tent. I keep a piece of cheese from my lunch to crumble into my soup, where it gets soft and stringy. Ecstasy. Haute cuisine.

This morning it was fifty degrees. When I got back it was seventy-three degrees. Now, at 7:48 pm, it is fifty-nine and dropping. I was sure it would take me one and a half hours to walk back this morning. I feel the edges of discouragement closer. One more level to surrender. The reasons do not matter. Discouragement is just a control issue. It actually took me forty to forty-five minutes. I forgot that where we started walking from was way before I ended prostrations, probably one and a quarter hours. I had forgotten that I actually prostrated beyond where I backtracked to find my guides.

Today the morning was hard. I was so tired. I felt better with lunch. Today I felt the most clear that I have felt, in my open human heart, and no thinking. Just here. Dakinis are self-manifesting beings of love. Why would there be thought? There is no reason for love. Love is. Today I felt the beginning of grieving my mother without feeling that I let her down or she let me down.

From three o'clock on today, prostrations were difficult because of the amount of traffic. Two huge yak herds came through, and a number of Indian parties on horseback. One little Tibetan girl asked me for food. I gave her the leftover cheese from lunch and the remaining piece of chocolate from a bar some trekkers had shared.

One time it got hilarious. There was a Tibetan guide leading an Indian gentleman on horseback. In the party, there was also a great amount of supplies as well as other people. This guide stopped instead of passing me. When he realized I was doing prostrations, he became very urgent about something, but he didn't speak English. He kept pointing to sacks behind the saddle where the Indian gentleman was sitting. I thought he wanted me to ride if he moved those. But the more I explained I was doing prostrations, the more urgent he became. Clearly, our efforts at sign language were not connecting, so I finally just thanked him and resumed prostrations. By this time, there was quite a crowd because he was blocking the path and more parties were unable to get by him.

At one point, he just pulled the sacks off the horses and began opening them. He began showing me all kinds of foods, supplies, even toilet paper. At this moment, a Tibetan who spoke excellent English came to the front of what was now a crowd who was watching all this, and explained that this man wanted to give me something. I explained I could not carry it. It seems that then he wanted to leave supplies for me at the tea shop ahead. As we conversed, I told him I had a guide and cook in the blue tents ahead, and he then suggested leaving it for me at my campsite with my crew. This option seemed to calm him. I told him the shape of our tents, and Rikjin and Nima's names, thanked him again, and went on with my prostrations.

At one point during this whole melee, he actually made the Indian gentleman dismount! I don't know if it was so I could ride or to get some supplies. It was hilarious! He literally chased the Indian from the back of the horse. The poor gentleman was very calm through it all, and did dismount. I saw them awhile later down the path working on getting him re-mounted. The Tibetan was so supportive of my devotion in doing prostrations that it seemed that he could not offer me enough, even the horse that someone else was riding on.

Many people gave me food today: an apple, a pear, a box of fancy cookies, more candies, offers of flat bread.

I have just been resting since I'm back, in and out of sleep for an hour. I made myself get up and use the latrine. Now I'm writing some more, but mostly I could just lie here and stare and sleep. Catching up from yesterday, I think.

Temperature is dropping quickly, it's fifty-five. Did I say it began to rain just as I was leaving this morning? It rained all the way back to my starting point. Then it was a pretty nice day. It got pretty cold and windy half way through. There was a spectacular moment of Kailash with no clouds and a huge bird just floating right next to it.

I was sitting on the side of the Khora path, stopping for lunch. Three Tibetans going by seemed to have never seen a boiled egg. They just stood and stared while I peeled my lunch.

John, a wonderful man in New Hampshire, insisted I take a small roll of JFK half-dollars to give to the Tibetan people. That was what I attempted to give the women who gave me candy on the first day, and who seemed so offended by this. Today, I left the first fifty cent JFK piece with a prayer that John, who wanted to send an American gift to the Tibetan people, may know how good he is before he dies. I left it at the first gate to the west face of Kailash.

I think my colds are better. Still coughing, partly from that, partly from dust. Started Arnica today to see if it would help my rib.

August 9, 2006. Day 7

Dinner came at 10:30 pm last night. I was asleep. Even reading my novel was too much. I tried to read, just for variety, but I became nauseous, which let me know I was pushing. When my energy is gone, I will get nauseous if I push forward anyway. So I just rested. I ate what I could, very good food, just too late for me to eat. There was a downpour all night. I kept waking up from 1:00 am to 6:00 am, thinking it was time to get up. I kept dreaming of cleaning myself, maybe using three whole handiwipes to really get clean! I felt my sticky skin, mostly on my legs. I finally got up at 7:30 am. The rain had stopped. It's 8:45 am, and now, it's begun again. More snow last night! So beautiful, gracing the rocks.

I am bleary this morning. I remember Marcus saying, "You wake up like you want." I spill my cup of hot water. I am still coughing but the pain in my side feels a little more resilient.

I begin to think of Drira Phuk, the second of the three monasteries I will pass on the Khora path I am following around Mt. Kailash. Maybe I'll reach that by tomorrow. Tomorrow is one-third of my allotted days to get around the mountain. I don't have to think of Drolma La. Could I possibly reach Drolma La? How big is it to traverse? This is a timeless unbelievable journey, going nowhere, taking everything. It's true: only my heart supports me. Only the space in my human heart guides me. I am not presumptuous enough to assume I can finish this journey. But I cannot bear to think I won't. I cannot leave Tibet the same. If Kailash is unfinished, I am unfinished, looking at a door, but still on the same side of it.

Everything hurts this morning. As I sit with it, I think it's what it feels like when ego dies a little more. Nothing's a problem. There's nothing to do. My human heart is clear. But my personality and my physical form hurt. All there is is devotion. Whether I'm in Tibet or the United States, whether I'm prostrating or cooking, whether I'm learning or enjoying mastery: there is only devotion.

3:30 pm.

Four and a half hours. I drag myself through every prostration today. I have gotten beyond the tea shop. I don't know why it's so hard for me to go through populated areas. My heart just calms right down when I'm alone in the wilderness. The prostrations are not any easier. I'm just calmer. I had lunch at my tent today because I was so close to it. At lunch, I finally caught up to where camp is pitched. Then I continued on and attempted to get to a cairn outside of town. I really didn't feel well today. I did get to the cairn beyond town, but there were times I thought I would literally fall over. I stopped today because I really could not do more. I am so slow.

Some young people at the edge of this little settlement around the tea shop stopped me, wanting to show me a special rock and a rangjung image of the Buddha. The image wasn't clear to me, and they felt too pushy. They did not feel like people who lived here, more like people passing through, although they may very well have been residents. The whole town had an unsettled feeling to me, and I just wanted to get through it, focusing on my task, not on their efforts to draw me into seeing the local attractions.

Nima says the path is easier once you get below Drolma La. He said that an Indian and Korean party turned back at Drolma La and came back through here today. Apparently they are particularly sensitive to the cold, and could not handle the pass at Drolma La, which is at an altitude of 18,500 feet. It is cold now, even here.

After I stopped and I was sitting resting so that I would be able to walk back to camp, four little birds came within twelve inches of me. So sweet. They didn't want their pictures taken, though. A European man walking by commented on how close they came. And this magnificent eagle flew down to the river. I took a couple of pictures. I don't know if they will come out. But the eagle was unbelievably huge and graceful. I later saw it gliding up around the mountain top. That's what I saw yesterday gliding around Kailash.

A cold wet wind began to blow as I walked back to camp. The nightly rain coming in, so I thought. I reached my tent just as the hail began to get serious. I felt so badly for the parties that had hiked past me, as they would still be out there in the storm. It turned out to be a furious storm, huge winds, rain, and hail. All I wanted to do was get un-geared and get warm in my sleeping bag. I couldn't summon the strength to go to the bathroom first. I felt so ill. I was just laying there, like a beached whale, when a pair of sneakered toes showed up at my tent. It wasn't Nima. It was Kelsang! He had brought gifts: three bottles of water, three cans of

Coke, stones from Lake Manasarovar, and a hard-cover book on Tibet. It was pouring and hailing, but he came to find me. These guides are just amazing. Weather seems inconsequential to them, as does altitude. They just run up and down hills, and I am panting from the effort of sitting up. Kelsang told me he just wanted me to know he had received the letter from his brother that I had brought to Tibet and sent along to him through one of the guides. Kelsang is leading a Khora with one of my crew who is not with me as I go around the mountain, and he sent word that he also wants to see me. I sent my hello to him. I don't know how these guides do it. They must be soaked and I'm sure cold, but energetic and joyful. What a sweet young man. I noticed that with all my crew, there is joyfulness. Even when they were grumpy, which is exceedingly rare, there is no edgy or neurotic overlay to it, and there is a definite core of resilience and happiness through it all.

Tonight, more diarrhea. I worry that my body is just tired. It has felt the same everyday except for today, and except for the fear I feel as I approach Drolma La. Should I take a day off? Would that help? The panting hasn't changed. I still pant through every day. The altitude is not higher yet, but I am not breathing better. I have not acclimated, I guess.

I came home early today to rest, and I am resting. I hope I sleep tonight.

8:18 pm.

I don't know. And I perceive. Rest in ignorance and live in perception.

August 10, 2006. Day 8
8:30 am.

I went to bed around 3:30 to 4:00 pm and I've been there since except for supper and pee breaks. I can't tell how I feel yet. I hope my strength is coming back to me. *More* snow on the mountains! It stormed all night.

I feel my fear as I head toward Drolma La. In many ways, I feel immobilized, like I could just camp here forever. Not go toward Drolma La, not go home. So much more dying to do, I guess.

I just looked in my little mirror. I look awful. I actually have a bag under my right eye.

There is a glimmer of joy as I sip my black tea with milk and proceed through the morning chores, gearing up for the day. Applying sunscreen is next.

9:23 am.

It's hard for me to distinguish if I just want a day off or if I want to run away. If I run away, there is nowhere to go. I can't go home. I can't go to work. I will have broken my word at a level I can't live with, and that I can't lie about. My task is to tolerate the unknown and trust my heart, rely on my human heart. There is nothing my nervous system or my force of will has to offer to this effort. Where my ability to show up for this Khora comes from is so far beyond nervous system or will.

You know, I am beginning to admit that I don't like camping. Never have. A couple days are fine. But day after day of discomfort, always crawling around in a space too small for me: I just don't like it. It has its charms, though. Yesterday, I was just lying in my sleeping bag, and this big soft fuzzy sheep muzzle appeared, then another one, grazing around the edges of my tent's outer shell. A few chews on the guide wires and the shepherd moved them on.

10:30 am.

A light steady cold rain. I head out.

8:42 pm.

Nima just brought dinner early again, bless him! Cold dahl and hot rice, but I don't care about food. I ate almost all of it. My focus is on staying warm and sleeping.

The little boy who visited with Nima and me two days ago just came over with his mother and younger brother. They just unzipped my tent and came right in! They apparently were curious about my clock and tent, so the family came to see. This has happened to me many times since I've been here. People are curious, and just walk up, walk in, and look at length. There is no intrusion intended. It just seems to be the way the culture is.

I am amazed I got five hours of prostrations in. I have no concept of distance. A very nice woman returning from Drolma La stopped to talk. She said Drira Phuk was great, but once she began climbing to the pass, the breathing was too difficult. It seems a lot of people are having trouble with the pass for one reason or another. I can't even see Drira Phuk yet. I was so touched talking with that woman. I would guess she was in her sixties. Her voice was so soft, and so was mine. We just talked about how hard it was to breathe, and she said I was doing so much more. I said I was very blessed, and almost couldn't hold back the tears. There was such a kindness about her.

I gave more food away, to a young shepherd. I spent much of the afternoon prostrating through his yak lands. I wonder what he would have eaten if I hadn't had anything. He seemed very poor. A man offered me his gloves today. I showed him I had mine in my pocket. People are so incredibly generous to me.

My body continues to turn everything in the daytime into gas. It's painful to prostrate on a bloated belly. I changed what I had for lunch today, but there was no real effect on my digestion.

There are these little tan and brown fluffy birds that keep finding me, yesterday and today. They come right up to me. I have no food. But this is the second day they have surrounded me. And there was this eagle hunting along the river many times today! So magnificent, she just wheels on the wind current.

Rikjin spent two days in Darchen. He went to procure a propane tank and a yak, but there is no yak to be had. I don't know how they are going to move tomorrow. I don't think it is physically possible. Tomorrow is moving day again, moving camp again. I'm going to try to get up a little earlier, but I seem to have no motivation to push myself. Rikjin said my face looked puffy when I got back, maybe from all day in a cold wind with rain on and off. Only a little rain, though. I felt cared for by Kang Rinpoche. When it was time to walk back, there was a cold rain, but nothing like yesterday, and there have only been showers on and off. I've been sleeping since I got back. I'm so exhausted. It's a forty-five minute walk back in tomorrow to my starting place, all uphill. I plan to take my camera, since I won't be walking back again as camp will be moved for the night.

I miss home. I miss being clean. There is something deep inside me, changing about how to be at home. This is the first I have felt that.

It was amazing to realize that I could see the western edge of Kang Rinpoche all day! It was like he was walking with me in this effort. Nima said in Drira Phuk I'll be able to see the northwest face. I just felt so encouraged to be so close to the very being I have come to love.

I'm glad I've taken the effort to write. I don't know if I'm just tireder, or lonelier. I really miss all my crew's spiritual support and I feel badly about saying that. It's not their job to support me spiritually. Every morning, and each morning so far, it has surprised me that there are really no choices. Yes, I could take the day off. But then there's the mountain, there is what I came to Tibet for. I guess in a way it surprises me that I have chosen this. And yet I know I have, and not for one second have I ever had a second thought. Everything is hard. I am not complaining. I am trying to take care of my body with sunscreen and rest and food. My body just keeps peeing and peeing. It is so difficult to get in and out of the tent. I'm staying mostly dressed tonight so I can make it as simple as possible. I try to limit fluids, but I've been peeing more today anyway. I am cold, no complaint, just cold all day, even while prostrating. My knees and wrists are holding up, and my feet. And my spirit, which has come to be broken open. What does that mean? More love. Such happy trekkers I meet. How can anyone be happy trekking this land with these huge spaces, where everything is always going up, and such thin air? I guess the same way I am happy prostrating it.

This is all about love. This is all about compassion. This is all about dispelling illusion. This is all about receiving the love that is always already there. This is all about breaking down illusionary walls. I could feel today when prostrating that each obstacle, whether it's the weather or crossing a river delta again, is a blessing. It is exactly as it should be. I remain afraid of Drolma La.

Pet Clark has come to sing to me in my head: *It's A Sign of the Times.*

August 11, 2006. Day 9

A slow start today. Maybe a slow day. I think when I reach Drira Phuk Monastery I need a day off before beginning the climb to Drolma La. It's cold, although it's only forty-six degrees. The rains didn't begin until midnight, rain and sleet. I had to go out twice, once for diarrhea, but I made it. Some little lamb was lost in the storm, and that poor dog that is always tied outdoors went from barking to howling to whining to whimpering. All in all, I slept well. I awake with my cough, less, I think. My face and hands are puffy. I don't know what that means. It is hard to break camp. That's one reason I am going so slow. I figure it will feel like forever until there is a tent to retreat to and to roll out my sleeping bag in. Both moves have been difficult. Maybe this one won't be.

I awake with my eyes doing iridescent figure-ground reversals. The phenomenon is passing. Maybe there was just too much light too soon.

9:50 am.

There is no accomplishment here. There is truth. There is no goal, no triumph, no 'I did it.' There is only I am, what's next, what's the next moment.

10:50 am.

I am falling apart. My weakness is love. My strength is love. Only agenda will un-do me. Love will un-do me with love.

A couple of days ago I realized for the first time that the abuse in my history was an experience, an opportunity as all experience is, not a victimization. It changes everything to realize this.

11:15 am.

I'm shaking. There is joy in my bones. Everything above my bones is shaking. Everything is made of light. Everything.

8:48 pm.

Got back to camp a little before 8:00 pm. I would guess it was a fifty-minute walk, the same as the last two times we've moved camp. And as usual, although they always tell me how easy it will be to see the camp, I couldn't find them. Rikjin pointed at a blue tent beyond the white tents where they would be. So I began my prostrations, and I finished up to a point I wanted. It was such a crazy day. I felt so ill this morning I didn't know what I would be able to do. Yet I also felt an opening of the Om Ah Hung, and for a day now, that all is light is more and more compelling as a fundamental reality. All is love. Lunch never arrived because of the great difficulty of moving. Nima and Rikjin stopped on the way, and I said no lunch was fine because I wasn't hungry, which was true.

It was an odd day of a lot of alone time and a lot of fervent pilgrims. Many Indians seemed so touched by the prostrations. Two in particular just came unglued. The taller one burst into tears. Both of them insisted on kissing my shoes. They wanted me to touch their heads. They finally went on ahead. I feel they had good hearts and were truly sincere in their pilgrimage.

Then a Rinpoche with his entourage passed and then stopped. His interpreter seemed to be Japanese and spoke flawless English. He said he had done prostrations nine years ago from Lhasa to Shanghai. It had taken him a year and he did not use knee pads. He gave the interpreter two booklets, and then Rinpoche asked my name, and asked me to write it down. His name was in the sadhana, the booklets. He asked my age – fifty-six – and said, "Just go slowly." He wanted pictures of us. He wanted to give me food and supplies but I didn't need them and had no way to carry them. He wanted to give me a sadhana, a practice, dedicated to Chenrezeig. His interpreter showed me the two booklets, one with Rinpoche's seal and one without. He pointed this out repeatedly, and insisted on giving me the one with Rinpoche's seal on it because that was "for the holy one." He gave me an enormous kata, and did not put it over my neck, but said to put it down the front of my coat and told me not to lose it. Rinpoche was warm and encouraging and kind, but he never smiled. They all left finally. I didn't think to have my picture taken with him with my camera. Maybe I'll see him again.

The two Indian pilgrims had finally gone on when the Rinpoche came and stopped. His stopping created quite a scene, and the Indians stopped, looking back to watch. When they saw Rinpoche having pictures taken of him and me, they came back after he left and wanted pictures with me, too. It was alright with me, but a bit overwhelming. They were very sincere; I could feel their hearts and their faith. Why they singled me out, even before the Rinpoche, I do not know. I guess it is the prostrations. I guess most people just don't do this.

The reason I didn't think to have my picture taken with Rinpoche was because I was just overwhelmed with the whole event. Indian pilgrims kissing my shoes, a Rinpoche telling me I'm a holy one, taking pictures, acknowledging me. I'm just a humble Western woman doing prostrations at Mt. Kailash. I'm not a dakini; I'm not a holy one. It is difficult to receive all this.

Later, a Japanese man with his daughter insisted on giving me some very rich food, and some flat bread. He just kept telling his daughter (who translated) of my "goodness." I asked her to thank him for his goodness.

A young woman brought "lunch" around 5:30 pm. She said Rikjin and Nima were about an hour behind me. Her English was pretty good. She is a guide, too, and knows all four of my crew. She kept saying how she admired me. I couldn't figure out what the issue was. Maybe because I'm a middle-aged Westerner doing this?

Anyway, I set my sights on a large rock near the white tents as a stopping place. I had been moving so slowly all day, but I got there. I actually did an extra hour and a half because I knew there was no camp to go to, so why not do whatever I had within me. There was nowhere to rest anyway. Finally, I un-geared and headed toward the blue tent in the distance. I must also say that this is the first day in seven days where I haven't left wet or returned wet. When the sun was out, I was hot. When it was not, I was cool. It's impossible to dress for this.

The blue tent was very very far away, over very rough terrain. I thought that tomorrow would be a difficult day, prostrating across these rivers and rocky pastures. It will be very slow going. There was a group of about twelve pilgrims heading in the same direction, toward the guesthouse at Drira Phuk. One Tibetan woman who was trailing behind that party looked so poor. I gave her my food. Then I headed away from the group. They followed the river bed, and I began to climb. *Finally*, after much effort climbing and climbing, I got to the blue tent. A very nice family of three lived there, and offered me food and sleep. Clearly, this was not the blue tent I was seeking! We communicated as best we could, and I thanked them for their offer of hospitality, and kept going, wondering if I could have looked past our blue tents in my focus on this one. But

I couldn't see any behind me, so I decided to climb to the next level, moving like a snail. I was rewarded for this effort. There was my little round tent, some distance away, up. There was Drira Phuk gompa, and more white tents. And there were horses grazing all around the tent land. It took some time to ford the rushing stream between me and the ground where the tents were pitched, but when I got to the little round tent, it had our stuff and my backpack in it, and soon I was in it, too.

So many impressions. Home is where the horse is. I can hear their bells, and occasionally soft whineying or snorting as they graze around the tent. I asked for some washing water, feeling that I should clean up before beginning Drolma La, although I feel it will take me two days to prostrate there. If it had not required getting out of my tent to cancel the order for a basin of warm water, I would have. My great ideas of bathing and washing a few clothes faded fast, and I just wanted to rest. But when Rikjin brought the water, it was *warm!* Oh, to immerse my hands in warm water! What a feeling! To wash my face, and a few areas of my body, lovingly. Then I washed out my two handkerchiefs, since between meltdowns and congestion, they get a lot of use. I do not believe I'll touch warm water again until Darchen. Nima says there is a shower there. But it was wondrous. Now it's cold outside again, the temperature is only fifty-eight, but it dropped ten degrees in about a quarter hour. There is a constant wind blowing through my tent.

Tonight is a good reminder of impermanence. I am happy, tired, my eyes are sore from the sunlight, and I feel like my home is so far away I shall never see or feel it again. Tomorrow will be arduous, not easy, and Drolma La is coming closer. It's time to sleep, and everything's OK.

August 12, 2006. Day 10

Every campsite is a new lifetime. I awaken feeling maybe I'm adjusting to camping. The little fluffy bird has come to say good morning already. I am mostly calm. Going back to my cairn and heading for Drira Phuk gompa: that is my next goal.

There is a slight stir within me. It's only about more love, more love in this human experience. Love is truth. Truth never hurts. It opens, which can feel like pain but that kind of pain brings more life. Truth is always truth about both inner and outer. So my truth in this moment about you must be grounded in my truth in this moment about me. You can call that taking responsibility for who I am and what I want in this moment, or you can call it something else, but there it is.

How can I do prostrations with more love? 'Don't forget to cut off your head.' How can I be the living compassion, not be compassionate, but be compassion?...only without trying, with surrender that love is loving me, and I am loving me, and there is nothing else to do. Stay in my heart. There is an inner earthquake. My outer is feeling unaccountably fine. My inner is shaking apart.

At this moment I could sink into a depression or I could go out and love.

8:30 pm.

Six hours of prostrations today. When Nima and Rikjin met me for lunch, we got to talking about how much time it will take to finish Khora. Rikjin thinks I'll need four days to do Drolma La. We talked about my itinerary after I leave Kailash, which cities to cut if I need extra time here, and he mentioned that Dorjee, Nima, and Jigme and I could decide since he has to go back to Lhasa on September 5 to do another Khora trip. I said that made me sad. He said it made him sad, too, and that touched me. I can't really tell how I am for them to be around, but it seemed he would sincerely miss me.

But something in the conversation fired me up, to try harder, longer. The ground and rivers were arduous today, rocky, muddy, and a lot of climbing. I am so tired, no energy, but after lunch, I just got back in the saddle, as it were. I did six hours. I'm going to try for that each day. I even made it a little past camp, so no half-hour to hour walk to my starting point tomorrow.

Tomorrow starts hard, a huge gully with white water and rocks, and two twelve-inch bridges to get across. After that, who knows? Five thousand feet of elevation to Drolma La. Rikjin says the ascent is not as bad as the descent.

I was hot all day. I'm going to risk dressing cooler tomorrow. Rain last night, but not in the morning or all day. It must have been mid-seventies or more.

And thankfully, today no one told me I was a holy person, although many were clearly touched by the spiritual and/or arduous aspects of the journey.

Why am I doing this? Because I was invited. But it is taking me past what I can control.

9:47 pm.

I find myself reminding myself to keep the play, the pleasure, the joy of circumambulating this great mountain. I don't know if I can complete it. I ask the dakinis for advice tonight. But it can never be a mission, only a service. With vitality!

August 13, 2006. Day 11

I woke up happier, with joyfulness. My little birdlets are around, chatting. One just popped under the tent flap. There was a huge rain storm around 3:30 am. I had to pee a lot. I can't say I got more sleep. I just kept thinking that dakinis are self-manifested beings of love and joy, so how could they want me to make this a mission and suffer?

My eyes are weird again. Maybe I should try different glasses. It's like the light and color fields reverse, and everything is glowing, iridescent. I want to worry about crossing that gorge ahead of me. I shouldn't worry. I should just do what I can. Peace and joy fill my heart.

It's never a cosmology that you should have. It's you, your human heart. What happens when one's cosmology is secondary to one's heart? What does life and culture and expression look like then? How can the center of the spiritual universe exist in my human heart? How can we be that much beauty? With our humanness, not in spite of it? Seeing the true essence in all phenomena, no separation, no judgment. It's all love when I love deeply enough. How could I fail anything if I don't finish Kailash? It's not my job for someone else. If it is, the dakinis will let me know, and I will do my best. There is something gentler about me today.

Did I mention that yesterday, I heard some livestock behind me? I looked, and it was a large herd of yak. The next thing I knew, I was prostrating along in the center of a grazing herd of yak. It all went well. Eventually they grazed faster than I prostrated, and they left me behind.

8:10 pm.

I did six hours today. Lunch did not come for five hours so I just kept going. The terrain has been so hard yesterday and today, rocks and rivers and mud and riverbeds. It was really a relief to begin the climb to Drolma La. It is inconceivably steep. I became afraid crossing the river on the stone and log bridge. I almost fell once. I had to come back across it at the end of the day to get to camp. I revised my strategy, and did OK coming back across. The bridges are really just logs held together with coat hanger wire segmented by piles of rocks. It is like walking on a log, not a plank, and at times is very narrow. White water rushes beneath. It demands balance, and not looking down.

It began to sleet lightly when my six hours were up. All day it was cool, and I was glad I had not dressed down. It is pouring now, and has been for a few hours. It's so cold! Only forty-eight degrees, a pretty average temperature since I've been here, but just so cold tonight! I may sleep with my socks on.

I realized today that the mornings are hard. I don't think, so I don't form the words, but in the background is discouragement at my slowness, despair at being able to complete this, and how hard this is physically. I remain surprised that I even get anywhere. Yet I do. I am just letting everything be, not thinking, not being positive or succumbing to negative. Every moment really is new, it's never the same morning, or evening. To be fair, while my nervous system is obviously there a lot, this afternoon as I was struggling upward, I felt such quiet joy. The joy pops through, too. I have let go of completion in favor of joy and faith. I never was the one running this show, and I never will be.

It was a forty minute walk back to camp. Not bad, light sleet. I got in my sleeping bag as usual. I'm not warm yet! But I've been reading my novel for one and a half hours, not sleeping. Just here. Just living.

My rib is improving. Still coughing. More diarrhea. Still panting but I think my endurance is better. Rikjin did not think I would need more Diamox as we climb. I'll trust that.

August 14, 2006. Day 12

Such a night, up for hours, in and out to pee. The blessing was the moonlight! And after that, the starlight! Kailash reflected in the night lights is hauntingly beautiful.

9:30 am.

Very hard to get moving, mostly because it's so cold. Sleet has started again. Should I dress warmer? Will it all turn hot in two hours? It's a day of climbing, climbing toward Drolma La. A horse whineyed most of the night, and still is. It's camp moving day again. There is a full-fledged sleet storm now.

10:20 am.

The harder it gets, the more I need to rely on the love in my human heart. It gets harder every day. I don't even know what I'm doing here. Now I'm having a meltdown, and I don't even know what it's coming from. I can't see through the tears. If I am that much beauty, of Kailash, then there is joy. If I am deficient, there is suffering. Oh! Is that where the joy comes from? Everything is all here, constantly, and my love is indestructible. Nothing can ever happen that destroys my love. It's exhausting to open to unconditional, unlimited love.

6:06 pm.

I've been resting for an hour, and plan to continue that all night.

Rikjin and Nima just left for the last trip to move camp. I don't know how they do it. Their tent isn't even up. Cold rain just started. Otherwise it has been a beautiful day. There are less and less people the higher we climb.

I had no energy today, from the beginning to the end. Out of kindness, I stopped a little after I reached camp. I just did four hours, and I dragged myself through every minute. It became so clear today that this entire journey has to be about loving me. It can't be about success, or permission, or approval, or anyone else. It's about my relationship to myself. I will ask for guidance, but no one can make it OK to love me as I am in any moment. So I've just been living with that all day. Now I am resting, hoping it will strengthen me, but most of all because that's what I need to do. Thunder is beginning.

10:00 pm.

My heart is spacious enough for truth, not for good deeds or efforts, for truth.

Waiting and waiting for dinner. Nima insisted on cooking. I feel a dying beginning and I want to spend some time with it. But I am waiting, waiting, because I know the dinner that he really wants to make for me will arrive.

My image is beginning to die. Having *any* image, of what I should do or what anything should look like, that is the image that is beginning to die. The disintegration of image leaves me loving me before I can be available for anyone else to love me, before I can receive any other love. What is loving me? No judgment. Tracey is beginning to emerge from behind the image, the shoulds. I don't know what the journey around Mt. Kailash is supposed to look like, because *there is no answer to that.* To put an image of what this journey should look like before what my heart feels is a violation. There is no right way to do this. There is only my heart in the moment, my heart before the moment so I can choose my response. Love is not about knowing the right thing. Love is about remaining present in giving/receiving love, love without separation. Love is about never leaving love.

Dinner was great.

August 15, 2006. Day 13

8:55 am.

Though Khora is not a goal, it is an experience. Perhaps that is why it never becomes easier. It is always a teacher. It is never about the lesson, which could be mastered, but about the teacher, which is always present in the new moment. The Khora is a teacher, not a goal. I'm beginning to not know where this Khora is taking me. That's a good sign.

New hand clogs today. The strap on one is wearing.

I have been prostrating through a cemetery. The cemetery is a mountainside. The Tibetans sometimes use "sky burial," where body parts are left outdoors to be devoured naturally. I look for body parts as I prostrate through the land and rocks of the cemetery. Rinpoche warned me about the wild dogs that are getting hungrier, and to be especially careful in the cemeteries, not to be alone there. But all the wild dogs I have seen and met have been remarkably gentle. One has been sleeping a few feet away from the back of my tent, not pushing, not begging. Just staying close, curled up on the ground through the night. I have found no body parts in the cemetery. I don't understand. Lots of pieces of clothing, but I thought the bodies were cut up and left there as well. I'll have to ask about that.

But bodies and clothing aside, this cemetery is so steep, going straight up a hillside that is a small mountain. The path dissolves into boulders and narrow winding turns. The cemetery/hillside is endlessly high, an amazing incline. I did six hours today. It was unbelievable, climbing, climbing, climbing that cemetery. There was cold rain in the air. Sleet storms came on and off throughout the afternoon. I finally made it to the top of the hillside, through the cemetery. Once on top, I headed for what looked like a rock gate. I hoped to be able to see Drolma La ahead through that. But I didn't find out if I would see it. A thunderstorm/hailstorm descended, and I kept going thinking I would just stop at that gate. But when the ground was quite white with sleet, I thought it was best to head for home. So tomorrow I'll find my little cairn and see what is beyond that gate. Probably more valley before I can see anything.

I kept throwing up this morning. I can only assume it means we are gaining altitude, because I feel fine otherwise.

I met that same man in the cemetery. He insisted on giving me more food, and was worried about my coat. How to explain it is water-repellent? I think he is a lama, but I don't know. He is just very kind each time we meet. After all his worry about my coat, when it finally came time to go home in the intense hailstorm, I couldn't get the zipper to work! I at least velcroed it shut and headed back through the sleet.

Tomorrow is a big day, if I make it through to Drolma La Pass. I have saved Kelsang's Cokes, and I have the prayer flags from class. It brings tears to my eyes. I hope I can get up in time to get a little clean, to pack, and to see my guide before he leaves.

People were kind today. Some just left me alone. Others were deeply moved. By the afternoon, traffic had quieted, and the scale of Tibet just stood all around me as I managed through each prostration. When I headed back, I couldn't find the tents. I didn't panic, but it was curious to see them from a distance, but then to be wandering and wandering along the many interweaving paths through the cemetery and along the river, and not to see camp. I kept strategizing until I found it.

9:44 pm.

Rikjin just brought dinner. I've been in and out of sleep since I got back at around 6:00 pm. No latrine tent at our camp this time, just our two living tents. I am managing. I am happy to manage without a formal latrine. I don't think my crew needs one more thing to have to do after carrying all our gear from campsite to campsite.

So now I know why I've waited for this late hour to write. Just after Rikjin zipped me back in with my dinner tray to preserve what little warmth there is, the tent unzipped and there is Dorjee! He's going back to Drira Phuk in the morning, so I will see him again. We chatted briefly. All is well. And then just after he zipped me in again, unzip! He handed me a special altitude sickness medicine, something to use just until I am through Drolma La Pass. He just beams out thoughtfulness.

Rikjin said he thought I had been away longer today. I am making an effort to do more, plus yesterday was so very hard; I did much less so he may feel the contrast. Where is my faith in the midst of the physical struggle? I want to feel the vajra in my forehead, throat, and heart, but all I do is pant my way through the next prostration. I want to feel empowered, and all I feel is humble. Nothing in this is being controlled by me. I am happy to be here, but even confidence feels like arrogance. I am here as a guest of great beings who have done great things. I am the maid who is grateful to mop the floor after the important meetings. I am blessed to even know that great beings exist. I am a wind-up tinker toy in the company of angels. I think of what Guru Rinpoche does with a mantra. He takes words and makes them diamonds. I take diamonds and make them glass. Still, I accepted the invitation. I showed up. I don't have a picture. I do have my fear. There is good in all that. What is the next level of spiritual power, the "signs characteristic of development"? What does it feel like to live that? Good night, sweet beings who read this and sweet beings who watch with me in the night.

August 16, 2006. Day 14
9:20 am.

Wow, I am pretty depressed today. I'm awake, dragging through the many morning chores. It's colder, forty-five degrees, but that's just one thing. This is the day I shall at least approach Drolma La, my goal. I may even begin it, so why be depressed? Don't I want release from a year of karma? They say that circumambulating Mt. Kailash washes away the karma of a year. Somewhere, I probably don't want that. Too much love, too kind. That needs to change. Oh, to receive that much forgiveness, and truly receive it!

11:00 pm.

I will make an effort to write. I am exhausted beyond words. It took me about forty-five minutes to walk back through the cemetery mountain and the river bed to camp last night. I walked in a driving hail storm. It took me an hour and thirty-five minutes to walk back *up* this morning. I was so exhausted when I finally got back to my starting place. I did five hours anyway. I tried for six, but I was so spent. The terrain was so difficult. Rikjin and Nima were moving camp, three trips up and down that mountain! I don't know how they did it. When Rikjin finally found me, effortfully striving to just get to the start of the Drolma La trail, he just commented, "You lost the trail." Trail! Pile after pile of boulder landslides. I don't know how anyone finds the trail (but they do). I did not see a trail. I went for the hypotenuse between the campsite and the path ascending to Drolma La. I ended up in an enormous boulder slide amidst a small pond, prostrating my way across boulders and water. When Rikjin showed me the trail and I walked back, even parts of that were rock slides with water running through. How does he know the trail? Still, now I am oriented for tomorrow.

Nima tells me we are camping here two nights. That means that one way or another, I make the climb up to Drolma La twice, prostrating up once, and then walking back up the next day to continue. I am cold now. It is ten degrees warmer than this morning. I am cold because I am tired, not because of the weather.

Dorjee is so full of excitement. He said before he left this morning that he checked with Rikjin about how my body was holding up, and they said fine, which is true. Even I am surprised but grateful. Dorjee also gave me some high-powered altitude sickness medication, for today's and tomorrow's climbs to Drolma La. I only started throwing up again yesterday, climbing the cemetery mountain. Maybe I mentioned that to Nima when he brought dinner. I have re-started the Diamox, and used Dorjee's medicine as well. He mixed it with water for me before he left.

He also brought up whether I would finish the Khora, and I said I was wondering, too. He said it was important. He said people in Darchen are talking about someone doing the Khora. He said I should not prostrate down from Drolma La, that it would give me a headache, but to count how many prostrations I would do, and we would do them at Samye or Chimpu. This is essentially the same advice that Rinpoche gave me. Dorjee seems to think we can manage my schedule to allow me time to finish Khora. Maybe that's one reason I tried so hard to get close to Drolma La today. There is not infinite time, just what my travel agent guessed that I would need to get around the mountain. But I am doing all I can. All I can. Heart first. And I am not at Drolma La yet. I still don't know what will happen with the Khora. It doesn't belong to anyone but me, yet it seems to belong to everyone in an exciting way. Dorjee mentioned something about a Buddha, meaning me. His words were flying past, but the main idea was that people were excited. I don't quite get it. After all, Tibetans do this all the time.

I met two monks today, who gave me yak butter cheese. They would have stayed to watch me prostrate, but I was just gearing up and it became clear it would take several more minutes to get all my things arranged, so they went on. I met a Tibetan family with a pre-adolescent girl, and she fished out a big roll of cookies from their pack and conveyed their excitement. There is so much love here.

I am peeing constantly, at least every two hours when asleep and when awake sometimes more frequently. I feel fine. It's just curious. I am anxious to get back down to where there is oxygen.

I am so cold and so weary. I am going to sleep now.

August 17, 2006. Day 15

My clock re-set itself. It says 1/1, Tuesday, 9:45 pm. I'll deal with that when I am back tonight. Drolma La seems hopeless. The day gives hope. There is brightness outside my tent.

9:50 am.

Today is such an odd mixture of despair and excitement. I can't do this, and such joy is arising for no reason. I tried so hard to get to the starting point of the path to Drolma La yesterday, but I couldn't. I just got mired in that boulder field. I could see the path from far away. It just goes up. It looks like it goes up for a thousand feet, although I don't know. Maybe it's seven hundred. Maybe it's more than a thousand. But it is steep, just up, a line on the hillside in the distance going up.

It's not about the psychological lift of starting at the path to Drolma La today. It's not about a lift or enthusiasm. I can't do this, and I can't do it twice, make the climb again to Drolma La because camp is behind me. I don't want people around, yet they will come if they come. None of this is on my terms. I am joyful. I will do practice, eat, and go see what experience comes, and what I do with that experience. Such an odd place as I begin my day.

> Joyful thoughts arise from deep within.
> May all beings be freed by this my gift!
> –Yeshe Tsogyal

10:14 am.

I am touching the point where it is getting harder to let go of the love of completion of this task than it is to hold onto it. I can't bear to think of not finishing this one long prayer around Mt. Kailash.

8:45 pm.

I've been home for half an hour. Nima has brought me my soup and promised an early dinner, after which I promise you the Tibetan sun may be up until 10:00 pm, but my eyelids will be sealed shut. The soup is re-energizing me a bit. I prostrated for five and three-quarters hours today, utterly spent and trying to figure out how much energy I'd need to get home, to walk back to my tent. I remain aware that I need to always have enough energy to get myself home after the day. To my amazement, it took me forty-five minutes at a *very slow* pace to walk home. There is a young man who makes mani stones on the hillside. I passed him this morning, and we waved as he continued his work. This evening, as I returned, he offered me a hot dinner, then tsampa, a Tibetan staple which combines barley flour and salt tea. I kept thanking him but pointing to my campsite. The woman yak herder stopped me and asked if I prostrated. I said yes. She was so nice. I wished I'd had more language to tell her how beautiful she is.

Prostrating up that steep path that I have been looking at for days now, I had the thought that if I could just get to the top of it, I would see Drolma La, I would see the prayer flags and Milarepa's great stone. I did finally get to the top of that steep path. It flattened out into a very small area, like the landing on a staircase, and I could see that it was just the first leg of the climb. I climbed over the top edge of that path, only to see the path continue – up! Tibet is amazing. I took a breath and just kept going.

Over lunch Nima told me a monk from Toling was prostrating, and wanted to meet me. He was going fast. As I was walking back, there he was, beautiful and strong in his prostrations. We chatted a bit, and I wished him well the best I could, and then went on. After a minute or two, I turned and he turned, too. I waved. He waved. Then a few minutes later I met a woman prostrating. She has tennis shoes on her hands, and was humble and vigorous in her prostrations. We chatted a little, but I felt a heartfelt connection to her. I hope everyone in the countryside has been as interested and generous with them as they have been with me.

Nima and I sat at lunch, looking across an enormous chasm at the mountains rising up on the other side. I asked him if there were avalanches there in the winter, and he said yes.

I feel like I will never reach Drolma La. I kept prostrating, the climb is endless and steep. I could see the Pass finally. I went as far as I could, but I knew it was still too far to reach today. I stopped within sight of it. There is an enormous rock field between it and me. I think I have found the path across, but I don't really know. I climbed and climbed and climbed all day and then finally to see it! More rocks and climbing. Tomorrow, I feel it will take me two hours to walk back to where I stopped, if not more, and I'll arrive exhausted to begin my day. Will I reach Drolma La tomorrow? How wide is the Pass? Will I make it across and be able to begin my descent? It all seems so impossibly out of my reach. Rikjin is off getting three yaks, *yes*. He'd *better*. It's absurd for Nima and Rikjin to carry all this stuff over Drolma La.

I have a fantasy that the terrain after the descent from Drolma La is manageable, not constant rivers and rockfalls. I feel like a misfit all dressed up for someone else's culture. Yet I am devoted, every day, the mantras and prostrations all day. I am devoted. I'm just so western, and we are so attached to thoughts and other phenomena. How do I bring more goodness in the world? I know, *Be it*. And now, *Be it deeper and wider*. Set that up by loving me with more honesty and more tenderness. People can either be honest or kind, but are rarely both.

This circumambulation is my prayer and my offering. All the not-good-enough voices are around the edges of my awareness, but the only voice of truth is that this is my prayer, my offering.

August 18, 2006. Day 16

I wake up to snow. I can't see how many inches are on the ground. It's like hail or sleet. I can hear it on the tent, now that Nima has shaken off the tent, which was sagging inward. I sleep a little longer. I could sleep all day. I am so tired. I wonder what this means. I won't be able to find the trail to Drolma La if the ground is covered. I think if we were one day ahead of schedule, we'd be having the storm from the other side of Drolma La. I think that it's all love and that my response is joy and love, even if I do not do one more foot of prostrations. This is not my design. I'm just here to keep my human heart open, doing this moment, willingly. Did I mention yesterday when I began the climb to Drolma La, more correctly, when I left camp, that I was so scared that my knees were like jelly? I don't know what it is about Drolma La.

9:00 pm.

I am so cold. My handy travel clock died, even with new batteries, so no temperature read. It took me two hours to climb back to my starting point. I just can't climb in this air. Rikjin was so sweet. He had found three horses to rent, and he offered to stay with me as Nima and the three horses went ahead. I said no. He did anyway. I was just sitting close to the bottom of the first steep trail up to the Pass. I just can't walk in this air, and every few minutes if not sooner I have to sit. Rikjin suddenly appeared at my shoulder. I guess he had bounded back down the trail. He offered to carry my apron for me. Carrying anything at all is too much for me, especially when I am ascending. I let him. I nearly started to cry. It was hard to receive the kindness and generosity, but that's one old tape I came here to put a bigger dent in.

After two hours, I finally got back to my starting place, at the far edge of the boulder field, with the prayer flags of Drolma La calling to me from the other edge. I wandered off to find a rock to squat behind and let my body do what it needed to do before I was wrapped in my apron, coat, hat, and gloves. Then I began. I climbed, prostrating, losing one trail, finding the trail, just heading toward the top. The trail seems so clear from a distance, but at nose-length, it disappears. Rikjin would appear and point it out as I was about to lose it again. He was so understated, and so talented. We had light sleet as I climbed, a continuation from waking up in the snow. I have to say again what a blessing Rikjin was. The trail ascending to Drolma La is quite treacherous, and it does disappear through fields of boulders. Rikjin would disappear, then re-appear. He was keeping a tactful eye on me, and would point out the trail only when I was about to get myself stuck somewhere, heading off to some blind alley.

I got there. I got to Drolma La. Oh my, I got to Drolma La! We drank Coke and sprayed Coke to celebrate, and he began a mantra. My hands were numb with cold, but I hung the prayer flags from class, fumbling with numb fingers, and even now it makes me cry. Then I hung Marcus' kata, and Nima's last kata that he had been so urgent that I have. Drolma La was not what I had imagined. Nothing has been. It was gray, cold, and sleeting with varying visibility. We finished the prayer flags and katas. They felt more like acknowledgements than celebrations. My heart was so open to class and how much I love them all, and how much they love me. Then I went back to prostrating, looking at the flags and katas as I prostrated by them, heading across the short, flat top of the pass, heading toward the descent. I got to the edge of the pass. Before starting my descent, I made sure I had touched a portion of Drolma, Milarepa's rock.

While we were there, Rikjin spoke a little about Drolma La, the place of Tara. He said White Tara and Green Tara can leap to Lhasa from here. It seemed to be a special place to him. I asked him the difference between White Tara and Green Tara, but he said what everyone else I have asked says: really, it is all the same. Another guide told me that Yeshe Tsogyal was an incarnation of Green Tara: it is all the same.

As I reached the edge of the pass, looking down at an incredibly steep, winding path, at any moment I expected Rikjin to tell me to start counting prostrations and walk down the steep trail, but he didn't. I asked at one point as I started the descent, "Shall I keep going?" He said yes. So I did. A Tibetan woman doing prostrations was close behind me. I kept catching the hem of my skirt on my heel, and she saw me trying to adjust the knot I tied to shorten my skirt. She came over and did something with the back of my skirt. No words, she just took a handful of material and adjusted something. I thanked her and we continued. After awhile I pulled aside so she could go past me, as I was going my regular slow pace. I watched how she did prostrations as she moved ahead.

From that height, as I came around one corner on that descent, Rikjin showed me the sacred lakes of Shiva and Parvati, his consort. The color was one I had never seen. Such beauty.

I kept going on the best I could. I continued for maybe three to three and a half hours. I didn't watch time today except for starting and stopping. Rikjin finally came and suggested twenty minutes more, then to count as Dorjee had said, since we had an hour walk back to camp and it would be hard to walk back in tomorrow. I should count prostrations so I could do them at Samye. So that's what we did.

When I finally stopped prostrations and prepared for the hike to our new campsite ahead, I insisted on carrying my soaked apron, although Rikjin offered. He was still carrying my backpack as part of moving camp. I felt that was heavy enough for him to carry. He led the way but walked very slowly out of kindness for me, and I guess out of the reality that I seem to have one speed in Tibet, panting along. It took us two hours to get to camp. The descent was stunning. Every time I thought we had leveled out, I was suddenly descending another rock slide or sharply twisting spiraling rock staircase. I did not fall, slip, or hurt myself, which given the terrain and my level of exhaustion, I think is a testament to me. I have tried to care for myself as well as I can, not unconsciously or immaturely. I am very aware how easy it would be to throw out a knee or ankle and so sabotage Khora. It is not my intention to find an escape from this privilege, but to remain willing and available for as long as the mountain will have me.

When we got to a huge rock fairly close to the nomad camp, Rikjin said to start there tomorrow. I was surprised. Camp was still beyond a rock slide, and I mean a wide field piled high with boulders. Camp was still much muddy, boulder-strewn, river-soaked ground away. I had thought I would be starting from camp. But I agreed. I had not come here to avoid anything. In the two-hour walk down, I counted eight malas of prostrations for Samye/Chimpu.

Nima was so sweet and kind. After bringing me an immediate cup of hot tea, he then brought my noodle soup as I was unpacking my mattress, sleeping bag, and what-not. He saw my soaked apron and scarf in the corner of my tent, picked it up and laughingly said it felt like fifteen pounds. No laugh about that! I have no idea what it weighed, but it surely was not the four pounds when it was dry. He offered to dry it in their tent. I thanked him.

I still can't think about finishing this. Every day is in charge of itself. My job is to show up with a good heart. The night rains are pounding on the tent, and pounding the river into a roar. We are very close to the river. I am so cold, I must tuck in. Sweet dreams.

August 19, 2006. Day 17

I wake up empty, utterly spent. It's a good empty, light and clear. It's cold, but with my clock gone, I don't know how cold. There was lightening in the night. I awoke and saw it, but heard no thunder.

7:45 pm.

The evening winds and rain begin. I went out today. I couldn't face crossing another rock slide tomorrow, so I decided to attempt it today. It took me one and a half hours to walk back to my starting point, which attests to my exhaustion. It was difficult terrain, but not that far in terms of distance. I met the one I think is a Bon lama. He was kind as usual. I began again by the mani stone with writing on two sides close to the rock with prayer flags. And I proceeded. I found a path, and that was amazing. There were few people, and that was helpful. The ones that passed were kind and encouraging. Every time I thought I had lost the path, a traveler showed up and there was the path again!

At one point, I was finally nearing the rockslide, a massive tumble of boulders spilling over the hillside all the way down to the stream. I didn't know the best course through it, upper, middle, or lower. Suddenly more travelers appeared. I must have looked like a giant marmot. As they entered the boulders, I paused in my prostrations, and stood straight up, alertly watching where they turned with this boulder, and with that. Stock still, I watched three or four parties enter from various points, but there was a general consensus on how to get through the rocks. Having taken in their strategies, I stopped being a marmot and went back to my prostrations. Finally, I, too, entered the rockslide. There was still nothing clear. Boulders at a distance and boulders up close are different. But I found a path that began and ended, taking me through. I got half-way with prostrations, but then the path was so steep, narrow, and muddy that it truly wasn't either safe or possible to prostrate. I counted the last half-way to do at Samye. That makes eight and a half malas now. I hope there is time. It feels very special to be able to do them there.

When I got back to the tent, two young women who had passed, chatted with, and encouraged me, were chatting with Nima and Rikjin. I told Nima I was prostrating to the tent and stopping. Most of the day had been a cold light rain with occasional snowflakes mixed in. But I was so spent from Drolma La yesterday. While I knew I just needed a rest, I also knew I had to have that rockslide behind me. I accomplished that, and prostrated across the soaking wet field to my tent. Everything except my socks and shirt were soaked, so everything weighed much more. Most of all, I just needed some time to rest.

Dorjee had said it was all green once I reached the other side of Drolma La. Well, yes, it is green, but I discovered, prostrating to my tent, that the green was from a field saturated in the run-off water coming from the mountainsides, running down toward the river. The land looked green, but it was actually composed of little hillocks, little green mounds around which coursed rivulets of water making their way toward the river. Hillocks are not flat. I think he was trying to encourage me, although I don't remember being discouraged. One more experience!

Rikjin brought my soup almost immediately while I was still trying to get my soaking shoes off. I got my soaking skirt and soaking knee protectors off. My pants were wet in places.

I'm still not doing much better with receiving. Receiving cannot be done by the personality or the image. Receiving can only be done by the open human heart. When I try to take it in, it has been going to my victim (poor me) or my image (wonderful me). In my open human heart, I don't manipulate the receiving in those ways. It is the love all around me showing up. I find today as I rest that I am still troubled by all this attention I've gotten. Why? Tibetans do this more often and better than I. Celebrate them! I am worried about Darchen. Will there be a fuss? Like when I started in Tarboche? What troubles me? It is all what it is, and I am not the designer, so be at peace.

Even writing is tiring. I hope more rest tonight will refresh my tempo. My heart remains joyful that I am here, in this amazing mystery of what I'm doing. I would like to proceed tomorrow with some physical energy to go with the happiness in my heart. I just keep thinking of Dorjee saying that after Drolma La, "It's all green, it's all green." He didn't mention the rockslide, nor that the green is often one to two inches under water, punctuated with ten- to twelve-inch high hillocks that the water drains around on its way to the river. Sometimes Dorjee's sense of "all green" is just hilarious.

8:40 pm.

Love is truth. Open heart is refuge. Any act of kindness is universal. Psychology/personality is illusion. History is illusion.

August 20, 2006. Day 18
8:50 am.

Violent thunder storms all night. Violent dreams of Alec the first part of the night. He was violent, and I was violent. I didn't start it, but I wasn't willing to permit it. Blood everywhere, but I had had enough of the collusion, of working around things that should not have been happening in the relationship. I couldn't make the dreams stop, and finally wondered if my vitality were awakening as I refused to be a victim. Second part of the night: long sweet dream about traveling in Tibet with a wedding party to a wedding. In and out of Western and Tibetan scenes. My sister was there. We were sampling desserts at some huge buffet, fun girl-stuff but not immature.

I got up in the middle of the night to put my copies of the practices I had brought with me anywhere I could find that was drier. Some things are wetter this morning than they were last night!

9:35 am.

Nima is slow this morning. I finally dressed to go out and see if I could have breakfast a little earlier. Now I know why I was so cold. It snowed last night! The tent is covered and the ground is spotty. Nima was just coming out.

8:25 pm.

Got back at 6:00 pm. Did six hours and a forty-five minute walk back. Quiet day, waved to the "usual" lama. Met nice people. One woman seemed to be with her older mother. The woman kept laughing, so lightly. Both talked with me. I have no clue what they said, but I did my best. The mother touched me lightly on the arm as they passed, a beautiful touch. They literally seemed to dance across the rocks of the river and continue on their way. Where do these Tibetan people get their radiance? It is a hard, blazing radiance. Not all. But more than I've ever seen anywhere. Another young man, I think he was Japanese, walked briskly by, but turned and gave me a firm thumbs up. An Austrian woman was leading a group that stretched out across the path. We chatted. When I told her I was American, she said, "It figures. Americans are tough." Then she gave me three white concentrated sugar squares for the journey. I don't know if I looked about to fall apart, or it was just a recognition that what I was doing was "tough." Many kind and wonderful people. There was one group of young people who kept giggling, one man with his two school-aged children, smiling shyly. Two people just wanted to know the time.

I think I must be getting tired. It's hard to maintain concentration during practice in the morning. We're moving camp, and Nima and I agreed I need to get an earlier start anyway because it is so hard for me to get back to where I left off. Even though I had so much extra rest yesterday, when I got back, I still could've gone right to sleep for the night.

Regarding my body, I should say that if ever there was a bunny take-off, it was today. I started right outside of camp, and maintained a good pace with no rest in between each prostration for an hour to an hour and a quarter, right through the swamps and hillocks and rocks and water. I thought I did the best I have. By the end of the day, my heart is the same joyfulness but I'm generally in geriatric tortoise class as far as speed of movement goes.

When I got back tonight, I told Rikjin I had made it a ways past the river. He said tomorrow I'd really do well. I said I thought I had done well today! I saw the East face of Kailash, a real treat, and such beauty in the landscape, flowers and wildlife. I don't know how this will all be. I'm doing all I can. It's not my agenda, it's the dakinis'.

My critic attacked once today. Rikjin told me that the Tibetan woman doing prostrations had already passed. That's no surprise. Sometime later, though, as I was prostrating, that critical voice started comparing my prostrations, energy, ability, whatever, to hers. I'm not going there. I think she's a shining light, and I love who it is that I am.

Both Rikjin and Nima have commented on the weather. Apparently, it is not usually this wet. I have no reference, so I'm just loving it as Tibet, or as what I need. Today went from hot to chilly to cloudy to hot sun all afternoon in a very short space of time. At the end of the afternoon, a moderately severe hailstorm broke out as I was trying to fold my apron. Part of it had actually dried! But the hail soaked it again. On the walk back, at least my skirt dried (almost) in the wind. I have one dry item that I didn't have before!

Please help me to remain in my heart with consciousness, to do what you are asking of me, and to be truthful. I just keep standing up into the next thing.

August 21, 2006. Day 19

Another wonderful horrendous night. Dreams of/remembering Alec's sexual refusal of me, and sexual blame of me. This information is not new, but the hurt, the grief of that was new. I never realized I had never grieved his sexual cruelty. Last night, I grieved deeply; I just let it be there whatever way it wanted to be there. The grief felt like an act of love for me. I wasn't going to tell myself I was doing the grief wrong. So I grieved. Then the grief turned to rage. Not revenge. Rage. It felt like I was beginning to pull the arrows out. Pieces of past abuse, my issues, pieces of Alec's issues flashed by, fitting together. It was not an act of intellectualization; it was an act of self-love. It said, "This was all your choice. It was not all your fault. It didn't happen because you're bad or disgusting or unworthy. It happened because you made your choices looking through the lens of history and not through the lens of your heart, your beautiful human heart that is here to experience and feel. Your beautiful human heart that is here to live your life and no one else's. And you don't have to keep drawing your conclusions and having your perceptions through what the lens of history tells you. Your heart is open and clear."

Before I went to sleep, there was a shouting in my head, "You can't let love in through your personality. There are all kinds of triggers that get set off, 'I don't deserve this, I refuse this, I resist this, it's too late,' on and on. Love has to come in through the undamaged, whole, feeling human heart."

8:40 am.

Before starting practice, I think of Pema at the Gompa. I think, "He is very holy," and burst into tears. What am I doing in this world? I think Ganesh is laughing at me, just to keep my perspective.

There's a line in the practice to Guru Rinpoche, "...May you receive these offerings with love...." Why would Guru Rinpoche need my love? He doesn't need it. All existence needs it. It's all love, and until I claim my loving human heart and open it, the universe is incomplete. Every moment. Every situation. Every level.

9:54 pm.

Fifty-one degrees. I knew the temperature because my clock is back! I just knew if I tried new batteries one more time it would work, and it does. I did six hours today. Nima and Rikjin moved camp again. They just got in with the last trip. Nima got me off to an early start today so I had an hour to hike to my starting point and gear up, and six hours to prostrate. I met them at one point in their back and forth trips, and we chatted very pleasantly. Rikjin and I made jokes about my apron giving me strength training. It is so heavy, being saturated with water from prostrating on the wet ground and through the streams! The day I began the ascent to Drolma La, I remember hearing a very loud ruckus in Nima's tent. A Tibetan woman seemed to have stormed in, and there was some very noisy communication going on. She finally left. Today, I asked Nima what that had been about. Apparently, the woman who barged into his tent before Drolma La did so because she saw my apron. Nima did not seem to think it was a noisy encounter. It's still not clear to me what the issue was. She was prostrating, too.

It's been another good and challenging day. The first three hours I prostrated in a cold rain. Everything but my socks and shirt and hat (thanks to my hood) was soaked, and stayed soaked all day. The last half hour, rain began again, in a driving cold wind that I was heading into. It was a hard day, through river after river, mud, hillocks, and rocks. The trails all went in the same direction, but some went up, and some followed the river. There was a yak center, maybe a tea shop, and I didn't feel like going through the middle of that, so I kept to the river. It was very hard for me to navigate, or to know if I was wasting time skirting the tea shop. It turned out I was right on track for our tent.

There were very few people today. One young man made a point to come over to where I was (he was taking the up trail, I the down) and gave me three candies with a smile. He was very kind. It was raining and raining.

Yesterday was my mother's birthday. She's been dead a very long time. But I do believe that yesterday was the first time I was able to wish her an open-hearted Happy Birthday, not from neediness, not from obligation, not from caretaking, but just because she gave me the experience of herself as my mother, and the opportunity to enter life through her.

I could wish her Happy Birthday sincerely for who she was, not what I wanted her to be, and really just love her as she was.

The rain is pouring again.

I gave up my knee pads today. My right knee started to fuss yesterday. I don't know why, but it seems happier without the padding. My right hamstrings are fussy, too, but overall we seem to be holding up.

August 22, 2006. Day 20
7:40 am.

For some reason I wake up softer this morning. I'm awake before Nima. I begin the morning ablutions. It's not too cold, fifty-five degrees Fahrenheit. Nothing particular on my mind. Just a moment in being. I'll do my Amitabha practice.

8:06 am.

I can't leave this Khora undone! I've tried to be so open to whatever is, whatever will be. I'm not strong, I'm not fast, if I could go any faster or longer, I would. I can't control this. But I can't bear not to finish this Khora. It would feel like a gap in the fabric, and like I would be wandering forever in that gap, unfinished. Like I had let go of what I was told to hold onto, my one little thread, and I let go of it.

When people would ask me about my intention to do Khora with prostrations, I would just say, "It is my heart's desire to do this." Yes, I was terrified and I was frightened, but that didn't seem important to say. When I said it was my heart's desire, it was almost like I could hear myself saying it, like I was a little embarrassed to feel so deeply about this task. I am slow, I am weak, and from my human heart, I want to finish this. How open will my heart have to be to hold me if I don't finish this? I feel Guru Rinpoche and the dakinis closer. They are just there, closer. They are always with me, I know.

9:30 am.

I can't seem to stop crying this morning. My brother is in my awareness; my father is up, too. I am up. There was nothing wrong with the terror and the abuse in my family except that I left my heart during it. I left me instead of staying in my heart through it all.

7:34 pm.

Seven hours today, plus a one-hour walk back. I am exhausted, but not sleeping, just resting. And I walked back with no rest stops, slow but steady. Small signs that I am strengthening slowly.

I've been resting for about an hour. My apron was about half dry by three o'clock, and then the hailstorm hit. It wasn't dry anymore. But other than that storm, which probably lasted half an hour, the weather was beautiful today, and I got back to camp with an almost-dry apron, a dry skirt, and dry pants, a first in I don't know how many days. Even things inside my tent that have been wet for days dried. It's sprinkling and thundering now, but the dry air was a great gift. I hope it holds for tomorrow. We're moving again, and it is so hard on Rikjin and Nima when the weather is difficult on top of everything else.

This morning, I only did my Amitabha practice. Amitabha is the Buddha who holds the Western Buddhafield, the paradise which receives all: all are welcome there. Adding any other practice this morning would have felt obligatory, not what my heart felt. I talked with everyone else about that, all the other beings on whom I rely, just so they would know I honor them constantly. But there was something important about the Amitabha practice calling, everything welcome in the Western Blissfield, all creatures having an advocate and a home, all things transformed into Amitabha's Blissfield.

It's pouring now with huge thunder and lightening, and yes, the ground is turning white with hail.

As I was walking home, it occurred to me that I do want to know more about dakinis, I do want to open to that level of service if that is what is within me. This is the first tiniest step of not being so afraid of them. I think the way for that opening was prepared earlier by the thought of all these people who are arising for me, relatives and non-relatives, all these foci of trauma. In all these experiences, all this history, the only thing that needed changing was more kindness from me. Know who they are, love them as they are, get out of the battle to make them fit some picture I have of who they are supposed to be in my life. It's who *I* am supposed to be in my life. Kindness in loving them as they are, instead of resentment and suppression that they are who they are. I saw that so clearly with my father's death. I'm seeing it so clearly in just loving my sister, in just loving me: I, too, just am who I am. I can love me as I am, every moment, and go from there.

Very few people today. The Bon lama came by again. I guess his practice is to do Khora every day. He was kind as usual. He seemed to be talking about my wet apron with his colleague.

Then I ran into three young women. They saw me pick up a rock after watching me prostrate, and then one pointed to my hair, a braid that always falls forward as I prostrate. We chatted about this through sign language, me indicating it's just what it does. She took matters into her own hands, seized the purple tie I had in my hair, and re-secured my braid in one of the most creative uses of that purple tie that I've ever seen. It was all very sweet, girl stuff. There are things I just like about the way men are, and this was one of the things I just like about women. Hair is one of our domains, and we have permission to touch each other and adjust this or that. Like the woman prostrating on Drolma La who saw my hem get caught on my heel, and just seized the moment. I don't know what she did back there, but it's what women do for each other, tidying and re-arranging and fixing. We were women across cultures. There was no barrier.

I had energy today. Not that there weren't periods of snail's pace and fatigue – there were many. And by the end of seven hours, I was moving very slowly. Yet there was a joy and an ownership that I have not had. I know it's related to the meltdowns this morning, the heartbreak of the thought of not completing the Khora. I was changed by owning that it matters to me, that I deeply want this, in the deepest fiber of my being.

8:45 pm.

Two hours of jelly legs this morning. I am just emptied. I don't think it's just the extra hour of prostrations. I think it has to do with opening my human heart more, less judgment, more love. I also found my voice more today. The mantras were audible much of the time. I'm coming forward. I'm opening my throat a little more.

August 23, 2006. Day 21
5:26 am.

I can't sleep. What a night. I'll try writing in hopes I can catch a little more sleep. I don't know what went on between midnight and two a.m. I wouldn't be surprised if Rikjin and Nima told me they came to my tent to help me settle down. I don't think they did, but that's how surreal it all is. I couldn't sleep. I felt like I was thrashing in my sleeping bag and my tent, like I could thrash them to pieces. It got so warm outside, I finally took off my microfleece, to just cool down a bit. But my feet were pushing against whatever at one end of the tent, and my head and shoulders were bumping into whatever at the other end of the tent. Of course I was peeing every hour, and continued to. Finally it felt like someone helped me straighten out the sleeping bag and tent, and just calm down. Then I was very calm, very peaceful. I believe what happened is I have opened my heart another notch, opened it where I didn't even know it was closed. Like yesterday, when I realized I am open to learning more about the dakinis, and being that if that is who I am.

Somewhere during the night, I also opened my heart to being in a relationship when it arises. That's huge. But the other big thing is, I'm not so afraid. My heart is touched to become available, and I'm excited about whatever experiences that will bring. But I'm not afraid. Usually I would approach everything through the door of fear.

So why can't I sleep now? I don't know. Tomorrow is moving day again, lots to do when I officially awaken. I don't know if Nima will bring breakfast early. I've got an hour's walk back, I may attempt seven hours of prostrations again. I want to do this, from my human heart.

5:30 pm.

Let me say at the beginning that what I am about to recount, the story of today, is a happy story. I had an awful night. I got myself together and walked back to my starting point. At 11:00 a.m., I began prostrations. Rikjin and Nima stopped by on their first trip moving camp. We chatted. I asked why people seemed to give me so much food and support for prostrating, and did they give that to Tibetans, too? Rikjin said yes, although I haven't observed that. Rikjin also mentioned that I should notice where the trail split and went down toward the river. I asked if I should be prostrating more toward the river. He said yes, and tried to explain that the tent, that is, camp, would be on my left, the trail on my right, and that I couldn't miss it. I always worry when people say things like I can't miss it. They left then to make more trips to move camp, and I continued prostrating. It was a difficult morning for me. I was upset from the night, and I knew there was something emotional jamming my system, something about the dakinis. At times the tears would well up, and then someone would stop to talk to me. I felt like I just needed to have a good cry, but it was not to be.

I didn't feel well physically, either. I nearly threw up breakfast, probably the upset from the night. But I just kept prostrating. The terrain was very difficult, narrow, steep, up and down, rocky. People were kind. I had a gentle encounter with a group of yaks on a hairpin turn around a ravine. They seem so timid. I was on the hairpin when I saw them coming around right behind me. I pushed as far as I could to the side of the trail. I was on the edge of a ravine with nothing but the drop-off behind me, trying to get out of the path so the yaks could pass. However, it, or I guess I, seemed disconcerting to one yak that stopped and would not pass me on the trail. Watching the small caravan of yaks backed up, I also remembered that when they pass, some have big baskets on their sides, laden with goods, which could inadvertently push me over the edge of the ravine if they bumped me in passing. So I adjusted my position up the side of the edge to be more visually out of the yak's way. That seemed to help, and he or she timidly moved forward and passed me.

After four hours of prostrations, thinking around each bend, over each hill, that there would be the tent, there was still no tent. It was three o'clock. I thought I should discontinue prostrations and search for the tent and find Rikjin and Nima. So I did, reluctantly, as I was finally feeling OK physically and would have been happy to continue at least two more hours, maybe more. However, reality is reality, and I had looked high and low for the tent, to no avail, and couldn't believe the tent was beyond where I was. I forgot how long prostrating takes and how fast they walk, that they could easily have pitched the tent much farther ahead if I thought in walking time instead of prostrating time. So I un-geared, and began slowly back down the trail I had been prostrating along. I climbed the hillside and perched on a big, high rock to be visible and to surveil the trail for the old campsite. There were false alarms. I spotted people wearing similar colors to Rikjin and Nima, but the people coming down the trail were not Nima and Rikjin. The yellow parka and turquoise shirt belonged to someone else. I moved further forward on the trail, looking for where the path intersects and heads toward the river, looking for my tent. Nothing. I kept moving forward on the trail, toward the beginning of it, hoping I would intersect them as they came along with the next installment of moving camp. I figured if I got closer to where the trail begins, there was less chance of missing them or getting past the turn-off to the tent that I was unable to find.

After about an hour of searching for them, a storm started to gather up the valley. I could only hope it would be short. It did gather, and it was a beauty of a storm. It came at us. I wanted to keep walking forward as the hail began, hoping to meet Rikjin and Nima on their last trip from the old campsite, before they took that turn off that I couldn't find. Walking forward put me walking into the storm, which was a sleet storm that was clearly gathering force rather than just passing through. There was magnificent thunder and lightening, strong winds, rain, and increasing size of hail.

I struggled to get my gloves out, my hood up under my hat, my hat secured, vents on my jacket closed, jacket arms velcroed tight at the wrist. I didn't know if I was in for a wait of hours, all night, or something shorter. I was not afraid, which was interesting even to me. I truly felt there was a good chance that I would be spending the night on the mountain, out in the open, huddled by whatever shelter I could find. I couldn't find my camp, and I couldn't find my guides. In this storm, how would they find me? I thought that it really has not been that cold at night, it's not like I would be in danger of freezing to death. It would just be a night of waiting until morning, as comfortably as I could.

Amid these thoughts as I struggled forward into the winds, an elderly monk came by, going in the other direction, and insisted that I hole up in a rock shelter that put my back to the storm. I thanked him, but wanted to go forward to hopefully meet Rikjin and Nima on the path. However, the old monk would have none of it, and pointed again at the little cubby of rocks. He was tiny and frail, but he clearly was not about to let me step back onto the trail. I understood what he meant, and lacking the means to argue, and mostly feeling that he was giving me a gift, an act of kindness, giving me shelter in this furious storm, I settled myself into the rocks and thanked him, and he went on his way. I didn't know how he kept his umbrella intact as he walked forward in the wind!

So there I sat, huddled in, watching the passers-by – and suddenly, there was Rikjin's face under a soaking wet hood in a line of three people. It was Rikjin and Nima, and another man who just happened to be on the trail. I greeted Rikjin, and he made a space for me in front of him, Nima in the lead and the other gentleman somewhere. No slow, panting walking from me. I resolved to keep up with Nima. Truthfully, I think he slowed down a little and I speeded up a little, but we proceeded. Some ways up the trail, we passed the old monk, huddled into a rock niche with his umbrella. I waved and thanked him again. I wondered if he had given me a shelter he was searching out for himself. I think he did.

Unbelievably in the darkness and driving rain and hail, Nima sprinted along the path, along the ravine, along the narrow steep rocks I had struggled over for the day. He passed where I had stopped. I had a fleeting thought that I should have continued, but I knew that was wrong. When we finally got to the place to turn off toward the campsite, it was very clear that I would never have seen the "turn off" of the trail down to the river. It was down, and it was long, and it took a long time before I could see the tent, planted in the midst of a large plain alongside the river. I might have prostrated right past it, in which case Rikjin and Nima would never have come upon me, as they took the turn-off. So I was grateful I had given up an hour or two of prostrations to be found by my team. Bless them!

The sleet continued, roaring, pelting. Partway down the hill, I encouraged Rikjin to go ahead of me, and in a flash he and Nima were way, way ahead of me. But I could see them, and the tent. The rain continued to deluge us. I assume Nima and Rikjin put up their tent in the furious storm. I got in my tent, and slowly set up my air mattress, sleeping bag, pillow, and so forth. Before I got in the tent, I chatted with Nima, asking if he was cooking tonight, because I didn't care about food.

I asked further, for tomorrow, if he would bring tea and milk, and an egg sandwich. No porridge tomorrow. I know it's good for me, but I just didn't care. I don't like porridge, and I wanted to get up, get ready, and then start walking however far back down the river it would be to my stopping place. I'm tired, time is very very short, I gave up precious time today (good decision, lots of grace), and I just want to prostrate. I don't care about eating. I was going to tackle washing and getting clean, but that will be deferred another day while we all recover from the storm. I just want to get up tomorrow and prostrate.

It has been six hours of sleet/rain storm and it was still storming when I went to sleep.

I did see a giant marmot today. I wish I had taken a picture. I was up high on one of the cliffs, the trail snaking along the edge as usual. And there was a wider area, with a large stone and prayer flags. Before I stopped to look for my team, I just stood there for a moment, reflecting on what I should do, gazing out at the valley and terrain far in front of me. Then I saw it: a huge boulder, it must have been at least three or four feet high, planted on the ground. Next to it, standing on its hind legs at alert, was a marmot. I mean, a *marmot*. It was as tall as the rock. I thought my eyes must be playing tricks, so I looked and looked. I looked at the rock. It was huge, and the marmot stood as tall as that boulder. It had to be at least three feet tall. A giant marmot! Later, I told Rikjin what I had seen, and he said yes, they do grow that big. I didn't believe him. I thought, what kind of burrow does that marmot live in? How large a tunnel does it have? And where does that tunnel connect? It would be an underground aqueduct system for an animal that size! Impossible! What an amazing sight!

August 24, 2006. Day 22
8:20 am.

I am remembering now, when I prayed to Yeshe Tsogyal during prostrations yesterday, I was so afraid she would answer. I still am, but I'm asking.

9:06 am.

I can't stop crying. Nothing's wrong. My heart is opening. What will I do without my judgment? What will I do without my self-importance? I'll be more joyful, and I'll be more available to love.

Ganesh is with me all the time on this journey. Beautiful Ganesh.

8:24 pm.

I must be acclimating. I have bathed, a full sponge bath, the second one since Khora began. I have re-combed my hair, two braids instead of one. It may not sound like much, but I've been waiting to do that for weeks since I've had no energy. I've washed out a few pieces of clothing. I drank three liters of liquids today, which seems like what it should be, but I've been drinking much less. Of course, it was a warm day, but I don't think that's the determining factor. I prostrated for eight hours, and made Zutrul Phuk Gompa, the third and last monastery on the outer circuit around Kailash. I'll pass it first thing tomorrow, and head to Darchen. I walked back again slowly but without a rest break. I still breathe shallow and fast, panting through everything. I struggle with the exertion of the prostrations. But I'd say all around, I'm doing better.

It was the first day since the first two days of Khora that I returned to camp not soaking wet. I left soaking wet, and the clothes dried as I walked. But there was no significant rain during the day or walking home. I'm trying to dry out my duffel. My knapsack seems dry.

Very few people today. The ones that passed were kind, and their support helped. A shepherdess so timidly followed and followed me as I skirted her pasture and flock, and then finally came and offered me two pieces of bubble gum. She was so pure, so unassuming and sincere.

Walking back, I met Rikjin. Dorjee had sent a supply package that had to be picked up. Rikjin teased me that he'd catch up with me on his way back, implying that I walked so slowly that he would walk to where I just left, pick up the package, and still overtake me on the way back. It wouldn't surprise me, but as it turned out, he didn't (almost, but not quite).

Then I met a guide leading a gentleman and the guide stopped and said Dorjee had sent a package, and delivered the whole message again. I told him I knew, I had already seen Rikjin. But then he went on that he offered me much support on the Khora, and much encouragement. He continued that he felt what a spiritual thing it was, and that he could not do it because he was not physically strong, but that he truly hoped I would be able to continue. By this time, the gentleman he was guiding had walked some ways on! I don't know if I was listening to Dorjee's voice or this young man's own spiritual yearnings. I was touched by his sharing and his kindness. I told him that in his own support and feelings about this Khora, that he was doing it with me.

By the end of the day, I had quieted my nervous system. My prayers to Yeshe Tsogyal were humble and trusting. I am available to be taught. Love does not come to overwhelm me, and I am more willing to be available as the adult woman that I am instead of the child with the childhood patterns.

I asked Rikjin a personal question today, and said he did not have to answer, but how did he know so many mantras. He said it was his own spiritual belief. Then he talked of how from Drolma La Pass, Tara (Drolma), White and Green, could fly to Lhasa! I didn't fully understand this, but I could see the spirituality alive in Rikjin's heart as he spoke of this.

9:43 pm.

Trying to sleep, but spending time integrating. Through this experience, I am slowly giving up being afraid of who I am. There is never better or worse, there is just being who I am. "The spiritual center of the universe already exists in your human heart. Meet your mirror," said my teacher, blessing me as I departed on this journey. Am I willing to rely on my human heart to that extent? I am opening to what that means.

August 25, 2006. Day 23
8:17 am.

Last night at 10:25 pm, brilliant lightening split the sky and thunder echoed up and down the valley. Then the torrential downpours came. I just hoped Nima was not walking here from Darchen. The lightening was so brilliant it illuminated everything, even with my eyes closed. Ah, Tibet, not one whole day without a display of your power.

I am tired but up and moving. I don't know if we are moving camp today. I am just trying to get me ready, and I'll deal with that later. Needless to say, no clothing dried last night. It will dry in time.

8:44 am.

I do have strong faith. Not because I am worthy or unworthy, but because I choose to have strong faith. Guru Rinpoche doesn't become one with my heart and love me because I'm worthy. He does it because I am here. *All* beings. It's just me. There's nothing to earn, nothing to become. It's more to stop rejecting and suppressing who I am. The love is already waiting for me.

8:23 pm.

I've been resting about an hour, getting warm, just resting. It was moving day. Rikjin and Nima had, of course, one more trip to make to the new campsite. I hope they had minimal rain. It's been pouring here. It just stopped a few minutes ago.

Where do I begin to write about today? A very difficult day punctuated with kindness and light. I made it from Zutrul Phuk Gompa to camp, which was an amazing accomplishment. I felt like I had lead all over my body, all over my soul. It would be too dramatic to say I felt miserable all day, but only because I refused to sink into it. Mid-afternoon, a really crashing depression invited me in. I wouldn't go, but every prostration, every step, every moment was just so labored, so hard.

I kept going, looking for the tent that would show me where the new camp was. My body is beginning to hurt. My right foot is on fire. My right knee is fussy. When it first started acting up a few days ago, I stopped wearing the knee protectors, and that seemed to help. But my left Achilles started getting very fussy today, along with my right foot, and my right knee.

I was continuing on my way, a short ways from Zutrul Phuk. A man who looked Chinese suddenly ran from his group, maybe a hundred yards away, and gave me one hundred yuan, amid much bowing and honoring. I was very touched by his feeling and offering, and told him I would light butter lamps with it. He ran back to his group.

Quite a ways from Zutrul Phuk, a woman with a French accent came over from her group, some distance away. She said she would only interrupt my task briefly, but that she had to give me something. It was dutsi from the Dalai Lama, given to her Rinpoche, then to her. It seemed important for her to let me know it was almost directly from the Dalai Lama. She poured some into my hand. She was crying, saying that what I was doing was so special and important. I cried, too. I told her I was just doing what I could, nothing special. She grabbed me, and hugged me, and kissed me, and I hugged and kissed her. Then she ran back to her group. I guess she saw me trying to figure out where to put the dutsi, since I had no container. She called out and asked if I wanted some more, and I said no. I finally put it in my hat, and wrapped it tightly so I wouldn't lose it.

People bless me this way, over and over again on this Khora. Stopping, crying with me, touching me, honoring this task. They are seeing more than I see. I just see the next prostration, like my next bite of food, nourishing me, cleansing my bones. Like a vulture who drops me from on high to break me open, and let the river water run through me, washing my broken bones, as my soul dances forward this Khora, this mystery, one prostration more.

Awhile later, Rikjin and Nima came by with their first load. I asked if they were going to rest or keep going, and Rikjin said keep going, which reflects how tired and harried they were. Usually, they always like to visit, I think to support me and because their pace is naturally slower and more social than my Yankee temperament. But not today. So I asked them to pause a moment, unwrapped my hat, and offered them the dutsi as they stood there with their heavy packs. They were so touched, so reverent. Rikjin took only one piece, and I encouraged both to take two. Rikjin commented he could feel the spiritual energy it provided as they continued their heavy journey. I was so glad to be able to share this with them.

I just kept going. I had my peanut butter sandwich for lunch, took a picture of another beautiful waterfall, put new film in my wonderful camera, and kept going. My energy never rose. Not resting, not eating or drinking, nothing. It was just an effort every moment. There seemed to be hours of no people, and I enjoyed the deep, expansive silence. Some people came by occasionally, kind, offering food and encouragement. That helped a little.

I just kept going. Rikjin and I had talked about where the camp was. I wasn't sure if he said after the bridge or after the ridge. I knew he had mentioned we had to cross a river, and I was hoping that my energy would at least hold out to get me across the river, wherever it was. I found it, shortly after some monks and people gave me food and kindness. There it was, another stone and log bridge. I did prostrations before for the portions of the bridge that I would be unable to prostrate on. It was very steep down into the river bed, and back up again. Then there was an area that was wide, flat land leading up to a climb, but still a wide flat smooth area. I felt how hard all the rocks and narrow winding rocky paths had been all day. Here was open, smooth land. A luxury!

I would have thought my pace would have picked up just because the land was so easy, but it didn't. I dragged myself through each prostration, saying the mantra. Then I began to prostrate up the hill. I was about halfway up when a party stopped. There was a very avid gentleman and apparently his elderly father. There were some other people who I think were a separate party, but they joined the gathering he was creating by stopping to talk with me. He asked where I was from, and I asked where he was from – Indonesia, living in Singapore. He said he was surprised, he had thought I was a local. I said no, locals moved much faster, but the humor was lost on him. He asked how long I had been doing Khora. I said this was Day 23. He couldn't get over that. He said it had rained every day. I said every day but maybe three. He asked if it was my first time in Tibet. I said yes. He was doing his third Khora. He kept going back to how amazed he was that this was Day 23, with all the rain. Today's afternoon rain had actually just eased up, thunderstorms, light but steady, soaking rain, a little sleet. He just kept staring at me and asking how I did it.

I guess what struck me about the whole encounter is that it gave me a reality check. From my perspective, I'm just doing Khora with prostrations the best I can. I can feel I'm getting tired, but there's nothing to be done about that except pray for the strength and support to complete this Khora. But his reaction to twenty-three days of doing this, in the rain, with maybe another three or four ahead of me, was a very different reaction than mine. He was a very sweet man. His father was, too. I should've asked him why he keeps returning to do Khora.

It was hard prostrating with my Achilles burning. I didn't want to damage it so that I couldn't complete this Khora. I tried to get down on the ground without using my left foot and heel. It was difficult coming down so many steep and rocky trails. It was maybe the hardest day I've had, and I guess that's saying something. But the trails on the hills were narrow and completely rocky. At times I prostrated into the side of the hill because the trail was too steep to lay on without falling off and down the embankment.

At one point, a large group of Tibetans stopped me. They wanted to give me something to drink. I showed them I had no way to carry it, but thanked them anyway. The woman who seemed to be the leader of the group seemed unable to get over what I was doing. She didn't speak English, and I didn't speak Tibetan, but from the facial expressions, she just seemed reluctant to move on and let me get back to prostrating because she felt it was just all too much. I happened to look back at the valley I had just come out of. It was filled with a rainbow. Since the discussion/food thing wasn't going anywhere, I began to take out my camera. I had just prostrated through the rain, sleet, and thunderstorms of that valley, and the rainbow was subtle but beautiful. But with all the interruptions from the group and their disbelief regarding the prostrations, and my not wanting to be impolite and just focus on my camera, I feel the rainbow had mostly faded by the time I took the picture. We'll see.

Later, two women were passing, and stopped to talk. We actually had quite a spirited conversation. What I could surmise was that they wanted to give me a bag of food (yak cheese, some crumbly mixture), and if I didn't want it, they were going to give it to a dog who was hanging around. I thought giving it to the dog was a terrific idea, and we haggled back and forth over this choice – me or the dog – back and forth quite a bit. Finally it was agreed upon that the dog got the bag. They opened the bag, rolling back the top edges so it stayed open, set it in the path, and went merrily on their way. The dog was just beginning to check out the bag when I went back to prostrating down a very steep trail. Maybe a quarter of an hour later, he appeared with a very nice white dusting all around his muzzle and looking like he had had a good meal. It made me happy. He had had some good Tibetan food.

An older woman whom I had originally met with her daughter passed again. She is so beautiful. It was so good to see her beauty.

This morning before I left, Rikjin said that Dorjee had sent a message about finishing Khora. Dorjee will be here tomorrow to talk about finishing Khora. My heart was excited to hear what he had to say. For me, I have no idea how close or far I am from Darchen, much less Tarboche.

9:22 pm.

Nima and Rikjin are back. Nima is at my tent with my bowl of hot noodle soup! I have saved the pieces of cheese from my lunch to crumble into the hot broth. Ah, I am in culinary heaven! Nurturance and nourishment are one!

I have to say that I am grateful for each day of Khora, and I pray for the strength and wisdom to reach Tarboche.

You know, I have to say I continue to fiddle with my sleeping bag and learn about it. By Day 7 or 8 it had begun to do things by itself. I guess it got tired of waiting for me to catch on. So velcro strips were hooking themselves together while I slept, all resulting in improved warmth and comfort for me. Well tonight, as I again unpacked and set up my tent, I decided to try the bag with the zipper in a different position, on the side instead of having the zipper on top, and I must say it's looking like a promising night. If you take the time to figure out the way these outdoor types think and design things, they really have some very good ideas. Barbara, my friend who has backpacked extensively, will be so proud of me.

August 26, 2006. Day 24
8:19 am.

I am so tired. It continues to be hard to fall asleep, but then the last few days I sleep sweetly, and the alarm wakes me and it's hard to wake. I know I'm tired. My body hurts more and more, although I must say my Achilles enjoyed the rest last night!

As I start prayers, I feel more easily, with less history/tears, my heart, my human heart, as Mt. Meru, strewn with flowers and sprinkled with perfumed water. My heart is beautiful, and I can bear that. This is emptiness to take with me today. The Heart Sutra tells me that all is emptiness, and it is. I don't always know what to do with my joy in all creation. When I am attached to a particular form of creation, I won't know what to do. When joy is continuously spontaneously arising, it is all joy, and there's nothing to hold onto. Everything is a perfect manifestation. Absolutely everything.

The Troma prayer arises for the first time. I look at the pictures of Troma Nagmo that I brought with me. For the first time, I see how beautiful she is. She is so beautiful.

7:51 pm.

One hour walk back. There was a rainbow filling the same valley where it had thundered and rained yesterday, but no rain today. I took it as a greeting from the dakinis. My clock died somewhere in the afternoon. I make a point of not checking it, just continuing as best I can. But when I reached the goal of what I was going to attempt today, it said noon time. I'm sure it was six or after. I hope it hangs in. I've reset it again.

I had a wonderful lunch with Nima, a long talk about education. When we get back to Nepal, he wants to take me to lunch so I can meet his friend Pema who has better English, so I can know what he needs educationally. He is very concerned about his brother, but I emphasized that Nima has to take care of himself first, educationally and professionally, and then we can look at his brother.

Later, two monks passed, and seemed very enthusiastic. Maybe they had met me at the beginning.

It was a hard day, I am so very, very slow. I just kept asking for help in prayer, and letting go of getting to Darchen. I hope I reach Darchen tomorrow. I don't really know how far I got today, but walking back, I was impressed. I start with a very steep hill tomorrow. I don't know what's on the other side. I was very careful all day with my Achilles and my feet and knees. Achilles has been quiet, except for a few twinges. Feet are sore but not overwhelming. Knees are somewhat sore but not in pain.

I had given all the dutsi to Rikjin and Nima. I asked Nima if there was any dutsi left, and would he save two pieces for Dorjee who is not coming around the mountain with me, but is waiting back in Darchen. Nima said that dutsi is the kind of thing that they share as much as possible, rather than keep it to themselves, and he had dutsi for Dorjee. I was touched by this natural wish to share the good, the treasures.

August 27, 2006. Day 25
7:48 am.

Another very difficult night, wanting to just thrash my sleeping bag and tent apart. Around two, and again at five, I reminded myself I had slept perfectly well in this same spot the night before. I finally calmed down and got some good sleep at five a.m. I wonder if it's because I am drawing near Darchen. I don't know how near, it must be near, but soon I will be there, and then Tarboche, and then I won't spend my days prostrating in the wilderness of Mt. Kailash. Who will I be?

Another dream that Connor my dog is dead, that he has finished his work with me and moved on.

8:44 am.

I just see how I don't go for refuge! It's there all the time. But I go to time and space; I go to history, present history, past history, when refuge is right here! There is happiness in refuge. In linear time, past and present, I know what happened in the past, and I can notice what's unfolding in the present. And there's refuge, where nothing is happening and everything is happening, and I am available to everything but not attached to anything. Available to everything as love.

8:45 pm.

I've been reading, trying to work up the energy to write. I did eight and a half hours today, and I could see Darchen when I stopped. I wished I could go further, but it would have been cruel and exploitative of me. I did a very full measure today. It is what it is. Darchen has seemed unreachable. Every day for the past two days, I've thought I'd at least be close, at least see it, but no. I decided when I set out this morning that it would take me exactly the right number of days to reach Darchen, and I let it go. When I reached the rise that I had set as my goal, there it was. I should reach it tomorrow, but who knows. I am tremendously tired, not in my heart but in my body. We are doing well, holding up well, but tired.

The weather has been so beautiful today. There was one rain/hail storm, enough to get me wet but not stop me. There has been wind all day, which is a blessing, cooling me. When I finally reached the tea shop where the turn-offs for Lake Manasarovar and Darchen are, the wind came up in earnest. I wondered if it is because we seem to finally be out of the mountains, with enormous plains stretching in front of me. The wind became quite cool, and the temperature is dropping now. I don't think I'll be hot sleeping tonight!

Dorjee came to help Rikjin and Nima move today. We sat on a hillside, the four of us, and talked quite awhile. I brought up finishing the Khora, and how long it would take, and could we adjust my other schedule. We had a long discussion, and it looks doable. Dorjee said he had spent the last three days at Chuku Gompa, praying and lighting butter lamps for this Khora. It made me cry. It explained how I've gotten through the last three days. They have been so hard, yet I am not diminishing my effort. I somehow keep going with joy and kindness. I have relied on Marcus' love, which is an open channel, it's just there twenty-four/seven. And class, and the kindness of all the Tibetans, too. And there was my guide, offering prayers for me.

Dorjee is working so hard with my schedule to allow me to finish Khora. I told Dorjee that a lot of my ability to do this Khora is because of his skill and help. He brushed that aside, just saying it was his job. He is so kind. I felt a sadness there today that I have not felt before. Maybe he is just tired.

Dorjee was saying that there is a lot of talk about my coming to Darchen. Since he is just waiting in Darchen, I guess he hears things there. A woman believed I would walk there, and when she asked Dorjee today where I was on the Khora, she was amazed and now believes I will finish it prostrating. He said a lot of people are waiting in Darchen with katas. He says that a Westerner has not done this before, and people are very excited. I felt, as I've been resting this evening, that doing this Khora is opening some door. I don't know what it is, but I can feel it opening some door.

When I stopped today at 7:00 pm, I sat and ate my hard-boiled egg lunch, drank some juice, and just looked out over the plains with all the nomad tents set up. I said to myself I didn't just want an open heart, I wanted to feel. This well of feeling that I perceive in this land just came up. I don't want to just be open. I want to be present in love, and feeling the moment.

A guy stopped me as I was walking home, as they all do. One of the men kept pointing at my apron and asking about the Dalai Lama. Since he had no English and I no Tibetan, they finally just went away. I kept saying no Dalai Lama. It's the first time someone has brought him up.

Nima razzed me today about not knowing where Mt. Kailash is. Every time I point to where I think it is, I'm one hundred eighty degrees off. No sense of direction! I thought that it was pretty good that he would poke fun at me. The warmth and ease is deepening.

There is so much love supporting this Khora. It is so clear it is not my Khora, I am just a vehicle. I felt today when Dorjee was speaking that there is an international, an East-West connection forming here somehow. I don't understand anything of what's happening. I just feel it happening.

August 28, 2006. Day 26

Rain began during the night. There is a light soaking rain now. Marcus' voice is in my heart: Purification. I remember when I was moving to a new home in America. I was waiting for the moving trucks, which were already an hour and a half late, and it had started raining. The walkway from the house to the driveway was turning into a slurry of mud. Marcus happened to call to wish me a good move, and I mentioned the rain turning everything to mud. He exclaimed immediately how wonderful the rain was on my moving day, a purification. He has eyes that see.

8:44 pm.

In the fuzziness of my physical exhaustion, I remember to go for refuge. Kailash is like a living prayer wheel, streams of people always going around it.

Yesterday, my prostrations brought me along a huge stretch of the Khora path along a mountainside. When I reached flat ground again, I was looking out on a vista that held the sacred Lake Rakshas Tal, the Lake of Power. I could not stop looking at Rakshas Tal as it came into view. There is something about the color of that lake. And I also knew that it meant I was getting close to Darchen.

11:03 pm.

It's after eleven, I should sleep. Tomorrow I go out of Darchen, toward the final destination, Tarboche. Two days to make Tarboche. I hope I can. I have faith but not arrogance.

Today was hard. I had thought it would be easier to make Darchen, but it got harder and harder the closer I got. Dear Rikjin showed up probably around four in the afternoon with more juice, and explained where the turn off in Darchen toward Tarboche was. As I continued prostrating, I could finally see what he was explaining, but when he was describing it, it felt like it was all pure chance. Until I saw it, I was just prostrating blind, hoping I came across the landmarks he mentioned. I followed his instructions: Go past the tea shop and follow the path up between the houses to the bridge. There was an extremely strong wind that came up during the afternoon. I had to pull my apron under my knees at each prostration because of the force of the wind at my back. I'm surprised anyone had a hat on. Mine was tied securely, and tightened regularly. So I fought my way through the wind, past the tea shop with people staring at me, and proceeded up the street Rikjin described.

If I knew more about movies, I could tell you which director would have directed this surreal scene. It was a very busy street, with an impossible congestion of incongruous elements: businesses being built, residential homes, a tea shop, what looked like a Chinese officers club, a building where there seemed to be enlisted soldiers, too. There were construction trucks, small engines, equipment and materials being off-loaded, and all kinds of people. I continued my steady slow pace, prostrating up this steep, crowded street. An official-looking Chinese man in a uniform kept watching me, an officer, I think. I acknowledged him with a slight bow once, and kept going. He kept watching me. I did not make eye contact because I did not want questions. I kept going. He looked like he had considerable rank, and I was not comfortable with his gaze. Other people, Tibetans, looked delighted with me, gave me incredible smiles and thumbs-up encouragement. Others just looked at me with neutral expressions. Halfway up the street, one woman with wonder and joy in her eyes insisted on giving me a can of vitamin juice. She wanted to open it for me right then and there, but I needed to keep going, to find out if I was even on the right street, and to get away from the officer and his men. So I struggled to get the can of juice into my pocket. I kept going. The closer I got to the top, the stranger people were, some smiles, but mostly incredulous or neutral looks. There was a monk, many people of all ages, motorcycles, a pool table, and people just looking at me with masked faces. It was so surreal. I expected the Chinese to come and arrest me at any time. I felt my mere prostrating presence was an act of political rebellion, and they would seize me for it. I got to the top. I was trying to decide if I should go over the bridge or through a gully that ran alongside and below the bridge. I began toward the bridge and a woman stopped me, insisting the bridge could not be crossed. I think she did not realize that I knew the bridge was unfinished, that I knew I would have to jump down to the ground once I reached the end of it. I continued through her protests. My guardian angel Rikjin was standing there as I came up from a prostration, although I did not see him arrive. We discussed how much farther I should go and decided the end of the bridge. I had done eight hours, and while I would have liked to have cleared Darchen, I didn't want to make Rikjin wait, and I had done a great deal.

Rikjin and I walked back to the guest house, the same one as when we first drove into Darchen. Three women stared at me. The oldest took my hand and I took hers as I walked by. We met Kelsang who said he was staying at the same place with his group and would see us later. I had not seen him since beginning the approach to Drolma La. It was so good to see him.

I talked with Rikjin about wanting to take us all out to dinner in

Lhasa, but with his schedule change, he wouldn't be able to be there. I asked if there were any restaurants he liked in Darchen. He said there were and he would talk to Dorjee about it. Rikjin got me settled in my room, got me two thermoses of hot water so I could bathe, negotiated my deposit for a key, and left.

I looked in the mirror. I can't begin to describe what I looked like with no shower for twenty-six days. Even the bottom edge of my teeth was brown from breathing in the dust from the ground, where I spend so much time. I really had not thought how much I was breathing in the dust until I saw my teeth. I did my best to wash my hair. It needed three washings, but it got one and a sponge bath for the rest of me. I tied a kerchief around my hair so I could dump the water, get more, and give my hair a good rinse. As I went out the back steps, a young Chinese-looking man turned and motioned prostrations. I said "Yes. Two days to Tarboche." He was very excited. It was sweet of him. I sat on the steps later in the sun and the wind, and combed out my hair. Dorjee came by and I discussed dinner, and I said Kelsang was invited, too.

Later we talked in my room, and he said that Indians were coming back from Khora, talking about me, feeling the spirituality of what I was doing. I think he said several people had asked to meet me, but he said I was tired today, come tomorrow!

This morning, Jigme and Dorjee had found me on the Khora path so Jigme could give me tea. Because we are close to Darchen, there is a road some distance away, paralleling the Khora path, and they were driving back to finish moving camp now that we were again in a town with a guesthouse and therefore a road. I saw them stop, and waved. I was surprised when they both got out of the vehicle and came hurrying across the rough land between the road and the Khora path. I went to meet them, and Jigme pulled out *two* cans of tea. While I was talking to Dorjee, Jigme polished the top of one and opened it for me! He just couldn't do enough. Such a kind heart. Kelsang was saying he worked with Jigme for years, and he is such a good man and such a great driver, which is true. Dorjee later told me that after they had stopped to give me the two cans of tea, Jigme just sat in the car with tears streaming down his face, saying I was a reincarnation of Tara, he didn't know Green or White, just Tara.

On the Khora path before I reached Darchen, I met Ariel, who gave me blessing cords and dutsi from the Dalai Lama. She was there representing him to support those doing prostrations. I asked her name, and she told me her Western name and her Tibetan name. I asked her if she wanted to know my name, and she started to laugh. She said, "Everyone knows who you are!" She said I was the talk of the mountain, and she would see me soon in Darchen. I was surprised, but I guess I shouldn't be. It is a small area. I guess word travels. I guess I'm a little hard to miss. I got blessing cords for everyone in my group. When I gave these to my crew, and gave them the dutsi, they were just thrilled.

I took my crew to dinner to thank them. I was nervous to celebrate. I had not reached Tarboche, and I do not take for granted that I will. I am close, but so much can happen to prevent my finishing. But I want Rikjin to be part of the celebration dinner, and so we gathered tonight. I guess in restaurants here there are small, separate, closed rooms for parties. When I walked into our dining room, Nima, Rikjin, and Jigme were already there. I walked around the circular table to an empty seat, next to Rikjin. He seemed like he wanted me to sit there, and he just beamed as I approached. The first words out of his mouth were that I was doing better than he had thought I would! He said that people turn back, people die, and I am doing well. Kelsang talked about the parikrama, as the Indians call it. He talked about not just walking or riding around Kailash, but my doing prostrations around the entire mountain. We talked a bit about Nima's wrist. It had been sore, and I had given him my arnica and an ace bandage in an effort to help. You would have thought I had provided the height of medical science. I guess they have nothing here.

Rikjin seemed like he really would miss me. He told me he would always remember the moment he met me, and I was surprised it made such an impression on him. I was touched at his sincerity. During the conversation over dinner, I joked about how slow I am compared to the Tibetans, and he firmly, simply said that I was not slow. For the first time, I believed him. He said that people do not hold up, they can't breathe, they can't handle the altitude. I felt what a miracle it is that I've been supported physically and emotionally and spiritually this trip. When it came time for pictures, Rikjin squashed in close, and I felt his heartfelt support and friendship. Such a sweet and true young man, who holds his privacy close but who is very sincere and has watched over me carefully and generously.

At times I looked out the window of our dining room and saw the brilliant Tibetan night sky. It was easy, since our dining room was really quite hilarious. The electric lights failed quickly, and could not be revived. They brought in candles, which was nice but very dim lighting. Then the blind on the window fell off and could not be re-attached! The door knob did not work, and at times locked us in! The comedy of errors went on and on, but I was with people I loved, they were talking energetically in Tibetan, I was listening with a smile in my heart. Who cares if the room was falling apart around us!

We all shared dinner! The food was good. I asked Dorjee to order. He apparently did well! Everyone just dug in, and Kelsang, who sat next to me, simply served me, Rikjin added in this and that, Jigme reached over and added more. It was so hilarious. I would look down at my bowl, and suddenly more things would be in it. They just took my culinary inexperience in hand and fed me, much more than I wanted but they were insistent. I liked how relaxed everyone was. Everyone just helped themselves, over and over. It was polite but relaxed, kind of a free-for-all across a table strewn with several dishes, Cokes, water. Everyone was just enjoying pieces of everything.

A wonderful moment came when Kelsang said that there had been a call, and that Rinpoche from Nepal had learned I was outside of Tarboche. He had sent a message, and Kelsang could not suppress a smile. Rinpoche had said to tell me "Tashi Delek," good luck! It made me laugh, too! The understatement was funny. It would be like telling someone leaving for the last leg of climbing Everest to "Have a nice day." I knew he was praying for me, and that made me cry.

About two or three days ago, my breathing improved again. I feel maybe I'm functioning on about seventy percent oxygen. I still pant through everything, but I have more stamina.

August 29, 2006. Day 27

Eight hours today. One-hour walk back. I never said, "I've got this made, two days to Tarboche." It was always so clear that the opportunity to attempt this was a complete gift. It was never mine, and never will be. I am a vehicle, but this was and is never mine.

It's too hard. The formlessness is too hard. The emptiness of physicality and purpose is too hard. There is only love, in me and outside of me. There is nothing to hold onto. There is no holding on. There is just the moment and how I dance with it. Then that's gone. It's all gone.

8:15 pm.

I got back an hour ago, and have just been trying to rest and not be sick. I'm so tired that I'm shivering. I woke up exhausted this morning. I had absolutely no energy in my body as well, which is different from exhaustion. I went to my starting place at the bridge in Darchen with Dorjee, and halfway there Rikjin showed up, beaming. He had come to say good-bye, leaving to return to his office to lead another group. Dorjee went off on other business, and Rikjin walked me to the bridge. We chatted about his new group, and I asked him if he remembered the two fellows we rented horses from early on. He did. I told him that one had really wanted my apron when I reached Darchen. I had told him no very clearly, but he thought I didn't understand and kept asking. Rikjin asked if I was going to keep it, and I told him it was very special. It had been made for me from love by a very special person as an act of complete generosity. I told Rikjin I could certainly let any of my friends use it if they wanted to do prostrations, but that otherwise I was keeping it. When I was all suited up and ready to begin prostrations, Rikjin hugged me and said he would be seeing me "in the mail." It was so warm and spontaneous. I began prostrations, and he left. I looked up just as he was turning the corner, and he looked back. As we saw each other, we waved, and I was glad for that connection before he disappeared from view. I am so glad to know him.

It was difficult and good prostrating through Darchen. A poor man and his child came up to me, and we chatted as best we could across the language barrier. Several minutes later, he reappeared with two children. He handed me a package of noodles, and then instructed the children, who had been holding something behind their backs, to present these gifts to me. Another package of noodles. Precious commodities I would guess for a family like this. I felt like they had given me their dinner. I'm sure they had. But he so sincerely wanted me to have these. There was such a deep concern and honoring in his face and voice.

A little street urchin had been blasting away on his whistle since I began prostrations through Darchen. Now he and a much younger child, I would guess he was eight, began following me. It was clear he wanted the noodles. He kept blasting on his whistle between attempts to engage my interest. They just followed me along. Finally a young man came along and took them in tow.

There were many different reactions to me in Darchen as I prostrated through the streets busy with construction. One young man with a dazzling smile just stood at his cement mixer as I slowly made my way down the street. He just kept grinning and watching. A pair of teenage girls asked where I was from, and about the Khora, and heading to Tarboche. Others ignored me.

I had to prostrate right through a construction line, Tibetan men and women with pick axes and shovels, preparing new guesthouses, I guess. But they stopped to watch, and smiled in approval. They didn't stop all at once. It was like they took turns. But they were beaming. These are the times I felt my pilgrimage was both a spiritual and a political statement, although I had not intended it to be. A Chinese woman kept coming out of an adjacent building and going back in. I thought she was unfriendly to what I was doing so publicly. But tonight, when I slowly walked my spent body back to the guesthouse, she and another woman were still working, and she turned and asked if I had gone around the mountain. I said, "Almost. Tarboche." She and her friend chatted, and her interest in my task and in me seemed sincere.

I began this morning with no energy, and that did not change. I met Ariel again this morning, light and fresh with her companions, and she said we'd meet as she went around the mountain. It seemed to me we wouldn't as Tarboche was my next and last stop, but I let it go.

There were very few people today. I was glad. I just kept doing one prostration at a time, energyless. I couldn't seem to get enough to drink, and my initial litre of electrolyte water was soon exhausted. It made me burp at both ends, and that seemed to help something. I finally just sat down to rest, not having made my lunch time goal by about twenty yards, and reluctantly I pulled out my last source of liquids, the vitamin tea that woman had given me on the surreal road the day before. I opened it, and immediately I knew the taste did not agree with my fragile stomach. But it was all I had, and I did not want to waste her generosity, so I persisted in sipping. Nima shortly arrived with lots of juice and a big lunch. I managed to finish the tea, and tell him I would take everything else with me. My stomach heaved, and I just wanted him to go before I threw up all over the place. He was talking about taking me to Swayambu if I had time before I left Nepal, and his face was alight with pleasure and friendship. He was talking about the inner and outer Khora, and other things, but I was just trying not to throw up. In my haste to get him on his way, I forgot to give him the two packages of noodles and the fruit people had given me, so I remained laden. The only place I had to carry them was tucked under the bib of my apron, as high up as I could so they did not get too crushed when I came down for the prostration. It added one more thing to work around. But there it was: they would be continuing the day with me, an excess of generosity traveling with me.

Much farther down the path, I met the Bon lama. I hadn't seen him in days. He was alone. We came upon each other suddenly, as I was prostrating along the hairpin turns of short, sharp, tightly spaced ravines, the remains of washouts from flash floods, I expect. Neither he nor I could see what would be around the next bend. He smiled when he saw me, and stopped. He gently took my hands, and took off the hand clogs. He looked at my hands. All I saw was dust, dirt, and suntan, but he seemed disturbed by what he saw, turning my hands over as he carefully looked at them, and finally putting his head in my hands. He then seemed to encourage me, pointing behind himself to Tarboche as if it weren't far away. I appreciated that. He then insisted I take a bottle of white stuff that I thought was milk. I showed him my ample supply of fluids and that I had no way to carry more. He insisted, opening the bottle, and having me taste it. It was like kefir, and if I hadn't been so nauseous, it would have been the best kefir I had ever tasted. He then gave me four pieces of dutsi. And then he then went on his way. He was very loving and encouraging, and I was deeply moved by his kindness, his gentle enthusiasm, and his compassion. I put the bottle of kefir in my sleeve and rolled my sleeve up to try to keep the bottle from slipping out. I took the dutsi. I could immediately feel it give me strength, and I was grateful.

I finally stopped to rest again at 4:51 pm. I was going to drink what Nima had brought. I sat down and just rested. Then I began throwing up, everything from dinner the night before, breakfast, and all the liquids. Apparently nothing had digested. It felt good to just get it all out. A monk stopped by between bouts of vomiting. I don't think he realized I had been throwing up. He insisted on giving me food. When I showed him all the food I had, he pointed to Darchen, indicating he was going there and didn't need his food. I thanked him.

I personally am amazed at how far I got today, given how ill I have been today. I will be interested when Dorjee and Jigme come to my starting point tomorrow. They will know how far ahead Tarboche is.

Walking home, I must have looked a sight. I was so ill and completely exhausted that I actually had some doubts as to whether I would make it back to the guesthouse. I just kept taking tiny little steps, very, very slowly. No energy, just one tiny little step at a time. Really, even as I was walking, it crossed my mind that I must look like I was about to drop dead. Whatever I looked like, I just inched along. A little boy and his father spoke to me. I did the best I could to understand, but nothing really came through. I also really physically could not stand for long, while struggling with the language and what they were trying to convey. So I continued on my way as courteously as I could. Then the little boy ran some distance to catch up with me. He was maybe six. He kept pointing to the middle of his forehead and saying something, but I could not understand what he was getting at. It seemed urgent to him. I wish I had understood.

I had finally gotten back to the guesthouse, walking at an incredibly slow pace. I am sure I looked like I was about to fall over at any moment, because I felt that way. I'm sure I looked quite odd. However, slowly, through open land and through Darchen construction, through people staring and through grassy lands, I finally made it. I was glad and a little surprised to see the guesthouse coming into view. When I got to my room, Dorjee came and wanted me to eat dinner. I told him that what

I needed to do was sleep, and if possible get some ginger ale or if not that, then Coke. He insisted I eat dinner, and I told him, quietly and repeatedly, that I did not need food, I needed ginger ale or Coke, and sleep, and could he get me ginger ale. He said no, but he could get Coke, and he kindly left to do so. He returned shortly with two cans. He again urged me to eat, and I told him kindly and clearly that what I needed to do was to sleep, sleep, and sleep as much as I could. He finally accepted this and left. I opened a Coke, took a tiny sip, set it on the night table and went to sleep. I slept a few hours, woke up and sipped Coke very gingerly, very carefully. It made my stomach feel so much better. I risked a bigger sip, and went back to sleep. This went on all night. There wasn't much in my body to pee, but I did as needed. In the morning I woke up with diarrhea, and thank heaven for basins in guest rooms. I kept sipping Coke, sleeping, waking, sipping, and on.

One more thing. I showed my guide the kata and sadhana from the Rinpoche who had stopped me below Drira Phuk gompa and who had insisted I was a holy one. He said the kata was very nice. I showed him the sadhana, in Chinese, and he looked at it and then he did something which taught me: he held it touching the center of the top of his head, as if he were receiving the transmission of the teaching, or the intention of it, which I'm sure he was. Since that time, I have seen many Tibetans do this. When I met Rinpoche, I was so overwhelmed with everything happening to me at the time, and so uncertain of what to believe, I had distanced from him, wondered how authentic all this entourage and presentation was. I had let my uncertainty, my fear, disparage if not demonize him. With no words, my guide taught me to receive the goodness in whatever is. He is a very blessed being.

August 30, 2006. Day 28

I woke up weak as a kitten. I didn't know that until I tried to stand up, and the complete absence of energy from yesterday flowed over me again. I went back to sleep for another hour.

9:22 pm.

I need to sleep, I need to write. Dorjee told me Jigme had put some of his clothing in the cemetery as a prayer for my Khora. I had been asking why there weren't any bones, and he said often just clothing is brought, either from the deceased as a prayer, or for the living so they will have no sickness and be whole.

This morning, Dorjee and Jigme gave me a ride to my starting place. Dorjee looked disappointed when I pointed it out. I asked if I were halfway to Tarboche: No. Jigme drove off the road into the countryside to get me as close to the Khora trail as possible, but there was still a climb to it. I walked up to where I thought my place was on the Khora trail, parallel to the road but up from the roadway for cars, across wash-outs and small gorges, finally climbing up onto the Khora trail. When I got to the trail, I realized I had to walk back even further, quite a ways, to find where I had stopped the day before.

When I awoke this morning, so drained, I thought of all the Tibetans I saw on the Khora path. They didn't pant, they didn't go slow. They were sturdy and energetic and beautiful. Sitting on the edge of my bed, I decided I would do my best to be like a Tibetan today. "Think like a Tibetan today," I told myself. I did. I just kept a steady rhythm, not stopping for breathing breaks.

On Khora today, Dorjee suggested I continue to drink Coke, so it was agreed that when Nima brought my lunch, he would bring Coke. I finished my electrolyte water fairly early, and often longed to see Nima coming down the path with several cans of Coke. No food, just sipping half a can of Coke, had helped settle my system a great deal over the night. I had the other half can for breakfast, and that helped, too.

But Nima didn't come. One herd of yaks, some very kind people who stopped to watch and who wished me well, but no Nima. I felt like I was zipping along, getting to crest after crest on the trail. There was a last crest ahead and I wanted to know if I would be able to see Tarboche from it. So I kept going, with a few rest breaks.

The crest opened onto a view of prayer flags. I wondered if this could be Tarboche, but it turned out to be the cemetery above Tarboche, although I did not know there was another cemetery on the path. When I reached the crest, all I realized was that the prayer flags marked not Tarboche but a cemetery which was a mountain. I was not yet at Tarboche, or in sight of it. So I proceeded up the mountain, through the cemetery, and then began down the mountain. No Nima. No Coke. I kept going. Maybe five plus hours into my prostrations, I rounded a corner, prostrating down the narrow, rocky mountainside – and there was Tarboche. The boulder around which I came was like hundreds of boulders I had encountered on my mountainous journey. But this boulder changed everything. It gave me no warning that it was not like all the others. It was as if I descended into a prostration in a world of endless samsara, endless sameness, and I arose in a world of bliss, of possibility. As I came around that boulder, I could see the flagpole and the stupa of Tarboche in the distance. I burst into tears. It was like the dakinis were saying, "Yes, this is possible!" At that moment, for the first time since I began Khora, I felt that completion was possible, that I would perhaps be allowed to close the circle. I kept going. Two old men came by, walking Khora. They just had to touch my hands. They were so supportive of the prostrations.

Around four, Jigme's white Toyota Land Cruiser showed up on the road paralleling the Khora path. Both Jigme and Dorjee jumped out and came to the path, bringing Cokes and crackers and lunch. All I wanted was Cokes and crackers. Dorjee said he had expected me to be at the pass, which I assume was at the top of the cemetery mountain that was now behind me. But I wasn't. He looked surprised and pleased to see me this close. I was, too. I felt in another three hours, I might make it to the flagpole where I had begun, a lifetime ago. They had brought a book to pass the time, and said they felt it was the same waiting at Darchen as waiting in the car. They walked up to a prayer place while I finished my Coke, and then I got back to prostrating.

I had to chuckle. One reason Dorjee came was that it had begun to rain. He asked if I wanted a coat in the rain. I told him I had just spent twenty days being in the rain – no problem. He laughed.

I did another three hours, with good energy, and not panting! I still had maybe an hour to get to where my Khora began, although I was dead on to where it was. I had managed to pick the right paths, which is not always clear when seeing the goal from a distance. But I had navigated well. However, Dorjee and Jigme felt we should come back tomorrow, finish, go to the gompa I wanted to see which was close by, and then go back to Darchen and leave for Lhasa. They said we'd leave for prostrations early, at nine in the morning. I hope that's true. My attitude throughout has been that however it is happening is how it should be. But I would like to finish Khora early tomorrow because I have used my days here and I don't want to push that limit, and because it really feels like it belongs in today.

While I was prostrating and they were waiting for me, Dorjee had been gathering gorgeous mushrooms on the hillside. He said they were very special, and very good for the body, and I would have them for supper. I had no appetite, and insisted that whatever Nima made with them, we all get a portion. When dinner came, it sure looked like I had them all. They were delicious.

When we returned to Darchen, three young women who I think are shopkeepers came up and asked if I was doing prostrations, Khora. I said yes, and they were very excited and supportive.

I washed my hair for the second time in two days! Strategies to wash long hair in a shallow basin are improving. I also went through both ends of five cotton swabs trying to clean my ears. I was just filthy when I got back. My face was marked with dirt, my hands were covered in dirt, and my arms looked like they had been marbled with dirt. I've tried to clean up so that I won't be too grungy for the gompa tomorrow.

August 31, 2006. Day 29
7:00 am.

I've been up since five-thirty. Who knows why? Just laying here, trying to pray as I prepare to finish this Khora with prostrations, this Khora with prayer. Awhile ago it occurred to me that as I complete this Khora, I need to open myself more to sharing myself, whether it is my hands as a bodyworker or my perception as a psychologist. That would be a radical step in self-love, trusting love living love. It's time to stop running everything through psychology, which assesses, and trust love as the organizing principle, as everything.

Two days ago, when I was so sick, I was prostrating along, and I heard this mournful sound behind me. I turned, and one of the Tibetan dogs was just laying on the trail, moaning and howling. I figured dogs are allowed to get the blues sometimes, and she was just having a bluesy kind of time. She followed me for awhile and finally came right up. I gave her a good neck and shoulder rub. She liked that. Then I continued prostrations, and at one point, she lay down right where I would be coming down in a prostration. I rubbed her ribs from the ground, then rose and continued on. I knew she wanted me to take her in, to adopt her, to travel with her and her with me. I knew I could not form that kind of bond. It was very hard to let her have her path in life and stay on my path in life, but I knew it was right to do so. Eventually, she went on her way.

8:21 pm.

We have left Darchen, and are on our way to Lhasa. We have stopped to camp for the night. Let me try to recount the events of this wonderful day.

Dorjee, Jigme, and I went back to Tarboche. I found my cairn and began prostrations. As I was prostrating toward the fireplace where I had begun nearly a month ago, I could see them in the distance, walking around the site, waiting for me.

Yesterday, I remember feeling that I crossed a point in approaching Tarboche where I felt I had entered a distinctly good place, a place in the land that exuded goodness. I told Dorjee about that today, and he said that Tarboche was one of the very good places to pray. When I was getting close to the fireplace, maybe thirty yards, the bodhicitta mantra I was using sank in even more deeply. I realized how deeply I felt the commitment to be in service to everyone until samsara is empty. Approaching the fireplace, for perhaps the last twenty minutes of Khora, I suddenly realized that the bodhicitta mantra was singing in my veins. I did the refuge mantra going down, and the bodhicitta mantra coming up. At each bodhicitta mantra, it was like the mantra words were gold filaments running through my veins. My whole body was filled with a physical bodhicitta. I have known I care for other beings. I had no idea I cared so deeply. The bodhicitta literally sang in golden filaments running all through my body. I was alive with the vibrating gold of compassion for all beings.

As I was two or three prostrations away from the place where I had begun, the fireplace in front of the flagpole, I saw Dorjee and Jigme drawing something in the dirt several feet beyond. I was unsure what to do, but it seemed right to keep going toward them, so I did. They outlined in chalk the figure they had traced. Dorjee indicated I should continue into the center circle, the "lama's prayer place," and continue from there: three prostrations East, South, West, North, and those are the completion. I did this.

When I was done, I just stood there and felt the impact of what had just been completed. I felt all the love, and that in doing this, I had dedicated myself to the well-being and liberation of all beings. I had never felt that so deeply before. I let it enter me more fully than I have. I stood there a moment more, and just felt the last bit of surrender to the Khora and all that it means. In truth, I did not want to stop prostrating. I never wanted to leave that circle. It seemed incomprehensible that there was not another prostration to do, that this pilgrimage could end.

I went to get the four katas I had brought, and gave one to Dorjee and one to Jigme. Nima had to stay in Darchen with the cooking tent, but he had made a special salt tea for good luck and sent it with them. We sipped the tea. Jigme pointed out it was rich in yak butter, and for sure, his bowl of tea was particularly yellow across the surface! Then Dorjee helped me hang some prayer flags from class while Jigme took a picture. Jigme then wanted a picture of me standing in front of the flagpole. I thought his initiative and thoughtfulness in recording this was very special. He grabbed one of the extra katas and put it around my neck.

I wanted to leave a coin that a wonderful gentleman, John, had sent to the Tibetan people from America. I asked Dorjee if we could stop at the stupa. We did, and Dorjee explained that we should walk around it three times, and then I could walk inside it while praying and leave the coin where I wanted. We all walked and prayed, and entered. I tried to get it in the rafters, but couldn't. Jigme scooped it up and managed to wedge it into a rafter. As always, my guys were watching over me, supplementing my weakness and ignorance in loving support. We got back in the Land Cruiser, and proceeded up the valley to Chuku gompa.

It was a wonderful experience to drive through the territory of my first day of prostrations. Nothing is gone from my memory, nothing is blocked, and nothing was too much. I remembered where I stopped, and where I wanted to stop, and where I got lost. I remembered it all.

Jigme had to stay with the car for safety, so Dorjee and I climbed to the gompa. I don't know if it was a thousand or fifteen hundred feet. Maybe it was less, maybe it was more. What a climb! It was nearly straight up. Dorjee bought a can of Coke for me before we started and said for me to drink it on the way. I tucked it in my pocket, knowing it would be too much to ingest. Dorjee walked slowly and I stopped to rest a few times. I wondered how I could have just finished thirty-four miles of prostrations and be so completely out of breath as I climbed to the gompa.

When we got to the monastery itself, there were many steps still to climb. We did. Dorjee bounded back down one set we had just climbed, to my slight dismay. When I began to follow, he said no, to wait there, he was going to look for the monk. I sat, breathing, waiting. I saw only a doorway into the monastery. A woman came and threw out a basin of water. Conditions seemed profoundly simple and austere. I wondered what it was like in winter. I wondered at the depth of commitment to spend one's life here, in devotion. There seemed to be nothing else to keep one here but devotion. How strong and beautiful.

Dorjee returned with a monk. He was not very old, I would guess late thirties, but I find it hard to guess the age of the Tibetan people. They all look perpetually young to me. He unlocked a room, and I followed Dorjee in, doing three prostrations before the statues.

There was Amitabha, looking like he was made out of a very pale jade. But this was the rangjung, the self-manifested. He wasn't made at all, but self-manifested. I asked if I could take a picture, and I could not. I just took him in with my eyes, the Lord of the Western Buddhafield, who accepts all. The monk told Dorjee some of the stories associated with this Amitabha, how an invading army had tried to make off with it, but it had become too heavy to carry. How the statue would talk to some people. At one point, the statue had asked a man to return it to the monastery, and it became very light to carry.

At the monastery, I lighted two enormous butterlamps with Khora donations, and I looked more at Lord Amitabha. The monk told about the conch shell, which Marpa, Milarepa's teacher, had gotten from Lake Manosarovar. It, too, was stolen, and sang its way back to the monastery.

It is indeed beautiful. Dorjee told me to give him a donation and asked him to let me listen. After sharing much story about the conch shell, Dorjee told me to listen while I prayed. The monk blew the conch shell, at length. I listened while praying.

The monk also told us about a bowl, also self-materialized, that belonged to Naropa, Marpa's teacher. It, too, was stolen, and threw out the butter and things within it to return.

I was profoundly touched by Chuku gompa and the monk who kindly spent so much time with us. Dorjee told me later that last time he had brought someone to the gompa, the monk would not blow the conch shell. I asked Dorjee if he had been able to listen, too, and he said yes.

Walking down from the gompa, Dorjee pointed above me. I turned and there were a large number of eagles circling above the cliff above the gompa. My sisters had come!

Dorjee and I talked at length as we descended. It seems that Darchen feels I am a reincarnation of Tara. The girl who brings the hot water to the rooms apparently saw me and felt that. A couple who run the Chinese restaurant where we ate looked in our dining room and felt that. They are friends of Jigme, so word got back to Dorjee. Dorjee felt that only a "holy one" could have done the Khora with prostrations because it is so difficult, and I am, after all, neither young nor acclimated. He says not even many Tibetans do it, although some do. He said the Indians have a shortened form which does not cross Drolma La.

He told me I need to write a book about this, and there is a picture in my camera which will be the right picture to show people, to open them to this experience, to their possibility. I told him I was glad he had brought this up, because I wanted to write a book, and I worried how the Tibetan people would feel about that. After all, I was a Westerner, speaking of their sacred tradition. He felt there would be no problem with that. He told me I have to write a book so people will know this happened even if they don't know me, or read it after I'm gone. He said that if we didn't have Milarepa's biography, we wouldn't know what he had done, and this is the same.

We got back to the guesthouse. Three young women were out front and rather shyly asked if I had completed Khora. I said that I had, and they became very excited.

Nima, who had waited behind with the cooking tent, grasped my hands. He held my hands so strongly! I was shy. I backed up a little inside myself, which I feel bad about. I was overwhelmed with his love and excitement for what I had done. He was not held back. Is it just Westerners who are so neurotic about receiving the joy in life? I gave Nima his kata.

I went to my room, packed, and left the extra knee protectors in my room for whomever might want them. I saw Kelsang, who was so kind and warm. He said he would call Rinpoche and let him know I had completed the Khora. He said to keep in touch, and I felt he meant it.

I sat in the Land Cruiser as all the guides were milling about and talking with each other. At one point, my guide came over and pulled me out of the Land Cruiser. A young man wanted to do the Khora with prostrations and had found the knee protectors, and was asking if he could have them. He found them so quickly! I talked briefly with the young man and I said it was fine if he wanted them.

As we drove out of Darchen, I turned to Dorjee and said that when we had driven in the very same entrance road, it had been another lifetime. He smiled and nodded. I said that Mt. Kailash was in my heart. As we drove, everyone kept singing. There was so much happiness in the car. Jigme put tapes in the tape deck, and each of them sang and whistled. Even my guide commented on the happiness and the singing. As we drove, Dorjee pointed out where I had come through two mountains and followed the Khora path. I saw it, and Nima added that that had been one of our campsites. The distance where the path ran looked just enormous to me. You know, it was.

9:35 pm.

We have begun the drive to Lhasa. I was relaxing in my tent when Nima came outside the flap. I opened it and he asked how to spell "prostrations." We discussed this, and I finally wrote it down, it being a complicated word for someone learning English. He left, and I went back to relaxing in my sleeping bag. Then suddenly he was outside again, this time with Dorjee and Jigme. I opened my tent flap again, and there they crouched, holding a cake with candles. Nima had baked a cake to celebrate my Khora! He had even written on it in red icing: *Happy Holy Mt Kailash Prostrations 2006*. Nima had made a cake! So that's why earlier, he had been asking me how to spell "prostrations"! I dressed and went to their tent, which was bigger, and served the cake to us all (after a picture). I had two pieces! It was wonderful, vanilla with white frosting and red raspberry writing. Where did he ever get the red icing to write with?

September 1, 2006
5:30 am.

For some reason, my body just seems to like to wake up at this time. I've slept lightly for awhile. In the towns, the dogs seem to gather anywhere between three and five in the morning for a howling session.

It's very interesting. Here, in the rural areas, the dogs have been barking all night, back and forth across the wide open area. The larger pack finally settled down for a little while, but then it was like trying to sleep in a tuba section. One of the guides was snoring slightly. A dog to my right curled up and was snoring in short bursts just outside my tent. And two dogs to my left were doing the same! Much later in the day I realized that some of the snoring was from yaks across the adjacent pasture. It was really very sweet to listen to these sleep sounds. I had my first little dream snippet of prostrating and then realizing I didn't have to prostrate from A to B. I could just walk.

I'm so glad I did not finish Khora and get on a plane. I can feel the integration is just beginning. I spent a lot of yesterday in the car just working with feeling this experience as a victim or as empowered. I'm not there yet. I still want it to come through my oh-how-amazing-my-poor-inadequate-self-has-experienced-this. My heart is overflowing with the amount of love and kindness, and with the amount of _possibility_ that I have and am experiencing. But those heart tears are different from the tears of poor-me. My heart is not my personality. It is clear and open space, with no past and no future, just infinity held right now. Unlike my personality, my heart has no agenda, no score to settle, nothing to prove, no goal. Just joy. Just love. Just experience without judgment. My heart has no limit.

My heart is my safety, and there is never a reason to shut it down. My heart is generous and playful and serious and perceptive and spacious. Why leave that? Only to re-live history where nothing is truly happening because it is all re-runs, it has all already happened and is just being re-played. No feeling, no receiving, no joy. Predictability at the expense of being alive.

When I was lying here in the dark listening to the yaks and dogs, I realized I have already received the teaching. Why do I ever give up the focus on my heart? My heart doesn't _do_ anything. My heart _is_. My heart is perceiving, understanding, being present with. To feel truly known and truly with someone is the best there is. We don't need anyone to do something for us. We need them to truly know who we are and not turn away. To know us and be present with us. Then our hearts unfold the next step, risk engaging the next step. To do this, we need to not turn away from ourselves, to not turn away from knowing through our human hearts.

I am so glad to have this time. Khora is not over. It is just beginning. I should write this book because I am a door. We are all doors. It's not about Tracey. It's about possibility that we show each other. I am joyful in this early hour because I can feel myself choosing life. Dea said to bring home the joy. It's in showing up to respond to life: My choice, my response. For the first time, I feel like I'm consciously choosing to dance with life, not following or tentative, but dancing out of the joy of the opportunity!

How does a fifty-six year old Westerner do Khora with prostrations? In her heart, loving first, and being willing to be held in love by all the Westerners and Tibetans and people from Earth loving her. My heart feels like a diamond. That's how much joy I am this morning!

I think of Milarepa and Marpa, his teacher, who had him build and un-build a several story house nine times, gathering the boulders, assembling them, then disassembling them and returning them to where he had found them in the landscape. If the dakinis had said for me to do eight more Khoras, that would have made a start on my personality. Can I make a start on it? *When I'm in my human heart, my personality is not important.* I want to truly understand the truth of that. Love is running like the Brahmaputra River.

It's amazing and pleasing to me how much more tolerant and flexible, and really appreciative I've become. When we got back to the Darchen guesthouse, I was even vaguely glad there was a bathroom, although it had not changed. I enjoyed the bed, although it had not changed, and the electricity woke me up when it came on for its brief stint at ten or eleven. Here, I am quite happy to toilet in the out of doors. We're in Saga guesthouse tonight. There are all kinds of glitches, but I'll snuggle in and get some sleep. I'm just appreciative. Odds and ends matter less.

We drove along the Brahmaputra River today. I was just overwhelmed with the size and beauty of it. It is one of the four main rivers emanating from Kailash. Kailash is so generous, so generous. I turned to Dorjee and said the river is Kailash's love. I had told Dorjee, as we ate the cake, Kailash is in my heart. Marcus was right. Mt. Kailash is the mirror of my spiritual human heart. I couldn't stop crying through all the realizations and sharings. I wasn't crying because Kailash is enough. I was crying because I hadn't noticed it before.

September 2, 2006
7:24 pm.

I'm having a bit of a meltdown right now. I still keep meeting people who think I'm holy. When we left one city, the innkeeper told one of my guides that he could tell from my face that I was holy. When my guide told him I had just finished Khora with prostrations, he wanted to touch my hands. He was a good man, no darkness running through him. Another person kept saying I was his teacher, and wanted to give me a precious mala given to him by a very high lama who died. What have I to teach this passionate committed man who does not see his own holiness? He is giving away his treasures. He says when I pray on his mala it will be like him praying on his mala. I don't think I'm worthy of a student like that.

More of this story that I'm in, this story that I am, keeps leaking out. As we walked to Gyantse Gompa today, one of my guides told me that for the first thirteen or fourteen days, he didn't think I would be able to do the Khora with prostrations. Yesterday, we were driving through horrendous conditions on the Friendship Highway. In general, for miles and miles, the road was under construction, which meant we sat long periods in backed-up traffic, and very often drove through foot-deep mud on one-lane areas around hairpin curves going through the passes. At one point, we came down to the valley floor, and the Highway was simply closed for a section. There was no detour route, it was just closed. Vehicles had to drive off the banking and into the river, and do their best to drive through the river until the Highway was open again. We did that, pausing for an hour and a half on a little island in the middle of the river, trying to decipher where it was shallow enough to get through the river to the bank again. One truck was stuck in the mud at the edge of the river. Further down, one Land Cruiser was up to its radiator in water, immobile. On our walk, my guide told me that yesterday, as we were driving through those horrendous conditions on the Friendship Highway, making our way blindly through the river, that so many cars got stuck but we didn't. He felt that happy outcome was related to me, because I was an incarnation of Tara keeping them safe. I told him I was constantly praying to Ganesh! These speculations on who I am and my holiness are very difficult and upsetting for me. I am just a human, so very human, such a mess, really.

September 4, 2006

I just went to bed last night. So much self hate is activated when the possibility of goodness in me arises. My self-perception at those moments is invisibility: I can feel the easy lovingness toward someone, I can easily feel my act of kindness and enjoy it, but I cannot see/feel me doing it. I can only feel/see the recipient. The hard work of finding Kailash in the mundane everyday is beginning. Wilderness is hard, but it is easier than all the distractions of the everyday, all the thoughts and concepts and ideas that I confuse with necessity or reality.

So I just went to sleep.

My salvation from this old habit at present is to remind myself that there is never anything to do. The saints didn't *do*. They *were*. They were who they were. They weren't who other people told them to be. In a sense, they just couldn't help being who they were, and they were passionately themselves, even though they didn't fit or conform. They could not betray the longing of their hearts.

Tara doesn't show up and do something. She is love. She is an emanation of kindness. Guru Rinpoche didn't do something. He is truth. So Tibet blesses me by tugging at my deepest available issue, and while I am still here in this profound country, allowing me to practice, practice just being who I am.

We stopped for watermelon today! Along the side of the road, right next to fields of the melons, little stands, many little stands. We stopped and slurped melon. So good! My guides talked with the vendor. We stood around and ate. Such a simple, good time.

We finally are in Lhasa. I finally got to an internet café, intending to send a letter to Marcus for class, letting them all know I had finished Khora. But there was an e-mail waiting from him, from August 29th. As usual, he just touched that place in me where the last thread is barely holding on, and the thread gave way and everything poured out. The spiritual crescendo continues to build. It is not decreasing since ending Khora. It is increasing. The e-mail from Marcus was waiting for me:

Tracey – Been thinking about you and feeling you the last few days.
Emptiness and silence roaring through space.
Love pervades all is self-arising.
All my heart – Marcus.

The letter I had intended to send Marcus for class had to wait. When I read his message, I dissolved into wracking sobs. All the pent up uncertainty and overwhelm of the last month broke through the dam. There is little paper in Tibet, no tissues, little toilet tissue, few napkins. Paper is rare and used sparingly. There I sat, in the tiny closet of the hotel with the two internet computers, sobbing, my nose running profusely, my eyes spilling rivers of tears, using one napkin I had saved from breakfast and one overwrought tissue, and my sleeves, trying to mop up the river of fluids emanating from my sobbing heart. All the fear and confusion I had felt since Khora began, with all these people who kept telling me I was holy, just burst out. I had had no one to ask about this, to ask to help me understand this impossible thing that kept happening to me. And here was my teacher and my friend, showing up, as usual at the right moment. I replied:

Marcus, I just got to Lhasa today, and thus to internet. I had composed a letter to you, to forward to everyone in Class, but I wanted you to get it first. I just scrolled through the first two pages of e-mails, and here you are. I haven't looked further, if you've written again. But thank you so much for being there. I'll see if I can forward the letter I wrote in a separate e-mail, but your e-mail just pulled open everything.

I finished the Khora with prostrations. I was close to the end when you wrote. The dates are in my other notebook, but I finished August 29 or 30. It took me 28 days, and my guide, who is quite special, suggested I not finish the last hour or so that night, but come back in the morning early. I did, prostrated for another forty minutes or so to the place in Tarboche where I began, and he helped me through the closing rituals of Khora. Then we spent some hours at Chuku Gompa, because I wanted to see the rangjung Amitabha there.

As you'll hear in my letter, it is so clear to me that I did not do this, I could not. It was so hard. But my heart was always joyful, it was physically demanding but I was never unhappy about being there. But without all the love, which I felt, from you and Class and my friends and family, my support team here which was amazing, and all the Tibetan people, and the Europeans and Japanese and Indians, too, and from me, I could not have done this. I did not do this. We did it. East and West met in my body, and I did the Khora with prostrations (the Tibetans call it Khora with prayer). Thank you.

But that's not the problem. The problem is a lot of people think I'm a reincarnation of Tara/Drolma or a dakini. One man insists that I'm his teacher. He is a very special, spiritual person. One monk I met had a dream the night before I crossed the Chinese border that a dakini was coming to Tibet from Nepal. A very holy monk at Chiu Gompa met me and apologized he had nothing to give me. There were signs. Just before my first prostration, there was a landslide right across from me. There were other signs; too, I can tell you the whole list when I'm back. One man gave me a Guru Rinpoche medallion for the Khora – I did not know until later that his teacher gave it to him, or I would not have taken it. Now someone wants to give me a white mala given to him by a very high lama. It doesn't feel right.

Everyone keeps calling me a holy one. Aren't we all? These are these people's holy things, and they are insisting on giving them to me. I'm just sitting here, and people respond all around me to this holiness.

Emptiness and silence roaring through space is where I live. I just don't know what to do with all the rest of this. I'm no teacher, especially not to a Tibetan.

There is so much love, in me and around me. That's all I'm trying to stay with, to not numb out or forget or get complacent. I remind myself there is nothing to do. I don't have to do anything, even if all of Darchen thinks I'm a reincarnation of Tara. But it is a little much. I can't even explain to you more clearly, but I think you get it. Even though Khora has physically stopped, it has not stopped, and I'm glad about that. But there is more and more opening inviting me, and I feel like I don't know how to open more. I'm just doing the best I can to stay here, but I feel like I should be getting something more, and I don't. I'm afraid, of my own goodness. I'm just afraid.

Thanks for being there. I'm going to go rest and pull myself back together, or not. I know this whole thing is doing itself. I'm just overwhelmed with what keeps coming at me.

Rinpoche and Michael have been wonderful. I will make every effort to see the lamas you asked me to, and bring cakes for their families from you. Rangrig loves you very much, and Michael, too. You are so wonderful, you touch people so purely.

I love you.
Tracey

Marcus replied, September 5, 2006:

Tracey,

I shared my best to tell you, you would become a legend.
A Western woman doing full prostrations around Kailash
is off the charts even for the Tibetans. Have fun being
honored for persisting on following your heart and vision.
In reality as a reference you should go on Oprah and
empower and inspire a nation of women who need a model
of authenticity. When you left class I saw and felt you as
an emanation of Yeshe Tsogyal. I guess I was right, huh?
I can't tell you what to do, though I can humbly suggest
that if a pilgrim wants to give you something because of
what you represent to them, you might want to receive and
share your blessing with them. After all you are indeed
in an incredible holy land and your American history has
no reference for them. You have done the impossible, like
breaking the four minute mile. It is an achievement of
immortality. You can now have a reference of how blessed
I feel from you loving me and being generous with me.
It is you who is becoming the teacher and me becoming
the student as the space continues to open. You are the
living inspiration. Your perseverance is the rally call for
liberation. Enjoy the overwhelm and know you are loved
til the end of time.

All my love –
Marcus

6:54 pm.

I'm just exhausted. I'm sitting in a restaurant now, realizing I haven't
eaten much. Maybe that will help. Then I will go prostrate, and maybe
sort out the incense the monk gave me for Rinpoche in Nepal.

I can't even write. There are no words. Just a void with a tremendous
force of gravity pulling me through something. It's like Khora. I don't
know where it's pulling me, but I am willing to go.

September 6, 2006

I finally managed to send a letter to class through Marcus:

My dear Marcus,

I am writing to tell you there is so much love in the world that the impossible has been made possible. I felt very clearly that I could not do the Khora with prostrations as an individual. I felt it every day. But I felt so much love from you and Class and my friends and family. I have felt how my guides and cook and driver have watched over me not only physically but spiritually in the most acute way. The Tibetan people on Khora and in general that I met every day have given me so much love. And I have been loving me. I felt at times during Khora all the love from East and West meeting in my body.

With all this love, I finished the Khora with prostrations in 28 days. Dorjee, my guide about whom there is much to say, encouraged me not to finish on the evening of the 28th day. So we returned to Tarboche, where I began, on the morning of the 29th day. I prostrated for about 40 minutes, to the place where I had begun, and he guided me through the closing rituals of Khora. Then we spent some hours in Chuku Gompa (monastery) because he knew I very much wanted to see the rangjung Amitabha there. Then we returned to Darchen and started the journey to Lhasa.

It is so clear that this is not mine. I could not have done it. But held in my love and all the love of East and West, I closed the circle of Khora with my body kissing the earth and devotion in my heart. The spiritual center of the universe really is in my human heart, and Kailash is my mirror. Thank you, Marcus, and everyone. There is so much to say, but I'll stop here.

Please forward this to Beth, and I know she will make sure everyone gets this, even Patrick of the no-email.

I am in Lhasa now, leaving day after tomorrow. E-mail has not been easy to access, but I am so happy to be able to share this with you all, before I get home.

It's going to be really hard to leave Tibet.

Please give my love to Dea.

I send all my love –
Tracey

Later, in a message to Beth for herself and class, I wrote:

Tibet is for me beyond words. Everyday is a prayer. I am integrating and staying open. I am so grateful I did not leave Tibet right after Khora. The time outside of everyday routine is so good for me. The choices are so clear, past or present moment. That's it. Old habits or present moment. Present moment holds me in love as I hold me in love with no image. No judgment. A different way to be in life.

Put differently, I'm lightening up. Now that's something!

I love you all. You have no idea how I have relied on your love.

Thank you.
Tracey

We had journeyed through a few cities and many rural stops along the way in our drive from Western Tibet, which is where Mt. Kailash is, to Lhasa, in Central Tibet. Our goal after Lhasa was Samye, the first monastery in Tibet founded by Guru Rinpoche, King Trison Detson, and Shantirakshita, an Indian scholar. Samye is at the base of Chimpu, a famous mountainside with caves where Guru Rinpoche and Yeshe Tsogyal spent time in meditation. The plan was for me to do the prostrations that I had not been able to do in dangerous places on Khora, like part of the descent from Drolma La. My guide felt I would be able to do this in one of Guru Rinpoche's caves at Chimpu, which sounded wonderful to me.

September 8, 2006
7:00 pm.
We have pitched our tents in Chimpu. It's easy to sit out on the rocks in the sun and pray. This is a sacred place. I feel this place pushing at my chest to let it in. When will I accept this much love?

8:40 pm.

My crew is praying together, I am just sitting in my tent, listening to the mantras in unison! It is like listening to a bird beginning to sing again after a very long silence, like something that has been still is pouring from their hearts! I think of going out to join them but I am afraid to interrupt, to change this in anyway. I just listen, enthralled with the joy and power coming through.

8:04 am.

A slow waking up. The tea shop people came down and were quite boisterous. I thought it must be morning. So I checked my clock – midnight! I thought, "Oh my, I'll be up all night now." Then I heard them again – it was 6:30 am! What sweet sleep.

The peacefulness of this place is profound. I hope I achieve compassion before I leave. I have let fears and worries come before compassion. Trust the peacefulness of this place.

9:13 pm.

Just a few notes. I prostrated in Guru Rinpoche's cave at Chimpu for five hours. As it was, I did not fit in the actual cave, so I prostrated in front of it. There are three caves there, now enclosed in rooms.

I learned that it is stepping into the timelessness, the void that matters. Linear time always knows, always has an expectation. The moment, the void, does not know, and so is available, available to love, whatever form that takes.

In the first hour and a half, I did the Guru Rinpoche mantra. I was surprised to feel his kindness. I expect his fierceness, but I never felt his kindness before. It was like Marcus, attending with care to every atom of my experience. Throughout the five hours, I attempted to offer my human heart as Mt. Kailash, as Mt. Meru. That's all. Just offering that capacity as a gift to the deity.

There was just tremendous kindness that I received all afternoon, from Guru Rinpoche, from Yeshe Tsogyal, from Vajrasattva. It's not that it was easy to prostrate for five hours. It wasn't. But I was devoted for five hours, and grateful.

On a practical note, my guide had said that the two monks in the room would let me know "when the sun had moved," and I should stop so that I would have time to walk back down the mountain to camp while there was still light. Despite the fact that Dorjee spoke with them at length and assured me they would let me know when it was time to leave, I intuitively thought that the monks would not understand all this.

Around five o'clock, I asked them as best I could – they had *no* English – if I could continue or if it was time to leave. We got nowhere, but there was no objection to my staying, so I did another hour, and then headed out, sore knees and hands, happy, humble heart. At the end, there were finally no other people there visiting and praying, so I took the opportunity to enter the small cave and take up all the space in it, which I did. What a gift to be able to finish the last few prostrations there.

I did the last seven prostrations in the cave itself. It was completely different space. I was shocked; the difference was so palpable and so immediate. The prostrations were much harder because the cave was so small and the floor was so rough. But I am grateful for the experience to have touched and been touched by Guru Rinpoche's actual space. I don't know what would have happened to me if I did five hours in there. I think I would have disintegrated. I know I am not ready for that. I am grateful for the taste that I could handle.

Dorjee and the monks had pointed out the way down. I got through what they thought was the hard part, that is, I found the stupa on the way down. But then I got lost three times. I was rescued by a monk, two nuns, and the third time one nun. I think it took two or three hours to climb up. It took me one hour to climb down. When I got to camp, Dorjee said he was just talking with Jigme about coming to look for me. I was worried he might. There was just one trail down from the gompa, but I think there are many trails getting from the meditation cave to the gompa, with not much horizontal visibility. We could easily pass each other and never know. Yet Dorjee is such an excellent guide, if it came to it, I'm sure he would have found me. I arrived just in time to make the whole issue moot, I am glad to say.

September 10, 2006
2:50 pm.

A day of rest, the first day of rest since I've been here. It *poured*, torrentially, last night. I asked for a beautiful day so we could all rest easily, especially my support team, and it has been a perfect day, now one half over, laying around in my sleeping bag until nine-thirty. I'd been awake really almost every hour through the night, just one of those nights, but resting easy, so what if I'm not sleeping. I'm still me.

There was a very noisy arrival of some group around seven in the morning. I just lay and listened. I just didn't want Dorjee, Jigme, and Nima disturbed, although I thought I had already heard Nima up. As I listened, I thought I heard Jigme's voice, and then Dorjee's laugh, and later I learned that a group from Dorjee's company had come through, with someone from Nima's company, and they all knew each other and were just having a good old time visiting. This pleased me very much.

Dorjee came to say good morning, which is how I learned all this. He had a room up at the top of the cliff, but said he did not sleep well, "too many mouse," and his eyes were swollen, too. Nima I know got rained on, because their tent leaks. Jigme slept in the car. Maybe none of us slept well, but we are in paradise here, and the joy is not dependent on sleep.

I walked up to the gompa to get more incense to bring home for people who have loved me. It was just hilarious. I decided just to get twenty bags of incense and twenty protection cords, since I seem to be buying too little and then wishing I'd gotten more. Dorjee taught me the word for twenty, so I thought I had it made. I gave them a fifty yuan note and two fives, as it should have totaled sixty yuan. But they kept giving me back the fives, or setting them down or waving them towards me. So I gave them more fives, thinking maybe it was seventy yuan. That didn't work. It started out with just me and one nun, but little by little, more joined us, trying to straighten it all out. It was just so funny, like a vaudeville act with more confusion added with each new helper. Finally, there were about five nuns and me, and not one word of English. At last, I took out my pad and pencil and wrote, 2 x 20 = 40, as each bag of incense was two yuan. That met with agreement. But before I could get to 1 x 20 = 20 for the protection cords, another nun was called over, and she took my pad and wrote "5 = 0.5." Oh! I began to wonder how many offerings of one cent, two cents, five cents Chinese I had been giving, thinking it was yuan, not pennies. Anyway, that enabled us to straighten all that out.

I stopped at the statues of Vajrayogini and the Reincarnation of Tara, and left offerings. I left an offering at the rangjung footprint of Guru Rinpoche, and I placed my hands on the rangjung image of the seventeenth Karmapa, asking him to bless my hands, and left offerings. Then I went to the large statues in the back of the room, Yeshe Tsogyal, Guru Rinpoche, and Avalokitshvara. I was so moved to be in their presence again. I rubbed my mala on the statues, prayed, and left offerings. A nun came and found me in the middle of this and offered me a large portion of very intense dutsi, which I appreciated. Then I left to walk back. One nun asked me something. I said "Hakomasong," I don't understand, but a bit later, my brain thought maybe the word Kailash was in there. But I was already headed down the mountainside.

I retrieved some things from the car, as Jigme was re-building the gas filter or something complicated. He wanted to be sure we had no problems driving to the border. That is the level of Jigme's usual protectiveness of me, doing any little or big thing he could to assure my safety and comfort.

I washed my socks on a rock this morning. It really works. It gets them very clean. They are drying on my tent.

What a beautiful way to leave Tibet. Three days in Chimpu. Time with Guru Rinpoche and Yeshe Tsogyal. I can't live without love, without feeling and receiving your/my love. I turn wooden, dead, when I turn away from availability to love coming to love me. I become a caricature, not supple, not joyful.

7:22 pm.

There is a sadness slowly curling around me. My last few days in Tibet are here.

7:45 pm.

Leaving Chimpu. During Khora, I felt the bridge between East and West. I lived in the emptiness, which was a profoundly – not healing, but healed experience.

As I leave Tibet, I take Tibet with me. I take with me the profound spiritual tradition that I have tasted, that I have just touched and been touched by. It remains with my American culture. It is not either the blessings of Tibet or the blessings of America. It is not either/or, or I have lost it. It is the truth through my human heart. A deeper level of honesty will now note my priorities. I have stopped my life for three months – seven weeks of which has been in Tibet – to have this experience, to have this learning, to give myself over to some wisdom higher and deeper than my conscious mental thinking. It has blessed me by receiving me. Now I hold both the practical tasks of my life, and the sublime rhythm and resonance that are Tibet.

I have always felt pulled, and usually torn, in two directions. Do I focus on my relationship or my self; I have two professions that I work at, two offices that I manage, and so on, always with me living in the tension in between two. Not this time. America and Tibet will not pull. The teaching is union, union by listening and feeling my human heart first, committed to honesty with myself first. Committed to emptiness and silence and speech and sharing, and more love in me and in you. There is no conflict.

There is such quiet, expansive joy that has filled me in Tibet. I don't know what to do about the Chinese occupation. I don't know what to *do* about anything. But the ocean of wisdom in Tibet keeps welling up under my feet and sweeping me away from the falsity of linear time. I have been immeasurably blessed, and I am receiving that blessing. Teach me to be the blessing. Teach me to be the clear light.

*   *   *

I sit in the restaurant on the top floor of my guesthouse, overlooking a whitewater river down the narrow valley we descended to get to Zhangmu, the border town. I can see a waterfall plunging into the white water. I count nine valleys that I can see, looking up the river into the Tibetan evening. What a visual splendor for my last evening in Tibet. I can't bear tomorrow. I remember to keep Kailash, and Chimpu, and all the love of this country with me. My grief is rooted in joy, the joy of having come to find something that has been missing all my life. My task is to continue to keep my word, and my feeling human heart will dance along with me, will hold me in refuge as the feelings arise and melt. Emptiness first. Emptiness is so filled with love and generosity and joy. These arms of Tibet will never let me go, will never let me down, and will never hold me back. They walk with me perfectly.

One Heart. There is a universe opening.

Epilogue

It's been six months since I returned from Tibet. I kept telling myself I was back. It's been six weeks, two months, three months, Right, now I'm back. But I wasn't. At six months, I was beginning to feel that I might as well just consider myself back because it had finally become clear to me that I would never be back again. This moment of life at Kailash had become my home which lived in my heart. Nowhere else. Not my house or my country of citizenship. My love had become my home, and I loved Tibet, and I loved love, and I loved the constant possibility of more love, in my freshness and my tiredness, my clarity and my lostness, my irritability and my patience, my fearful grasping and my open-hearted generosity. I loved that all these held love for me to learn to relax into. I had always loved this or I would never have gone to Kailash. But Kailash crashed through my defenses and placed into my open hands this wider, broader love, this love that is not contained in me but which contains me and all existence.

Through this struggle to re-center myself in a life that I left, I have shifted around through space after space. I have grieved. I have adjusted. I have fallen apart. I have adjusted. I have protested. I have submitted. Dare I say that now, finally, I am back? We shall see. But these days I feel the blessing arising. As I continue to return from Tibet, more than ever in my life, I am knowing who I am. Tibet and the preparation for Tibet invited me to stand in who I am. No one could tell me what to do, or really, in the end, how to do it. It had to be all me, all my choice, all my risk.

It has taken me a long time to get to this place. I left for Tibet at the end of my July class. I remember sitting in the next class on my return, in September, thinking that in the previous class, at the end of the last day a mere three months previously, I was leaving class, going to Newark Airport, and the next morning getting on a plane to Nepal. Then, it was matter-of-fact. I was excited, I was pleased, but most of all, it was just ordinary, it was what I wanted to do. But after I returned, sitting in class and re-visiting that moment, I was horrified! What had I been doing! I didn't know how to do that, where I was going, what I was intending to do. Yet then I was simply going. The enormity of what I had decided to do hit me, really, when I returned. Then I had been consumed with the joy and passion of going, there was no room for anything other than doing it. I was afraid, sometimes terrified, but most of all, I was grateful and passionate to have this opportunity to love. Now, I guess the security of everyday life gave me an opportunity to scare myself. Or maybe the journey really was that big. I went to Tibet to change who I am. I did not know how I needed to change, or I would have just done it here. So I went into the unknown unknowing. I did not realize that the change would be manifesting, taking root, for months.

After my return, I continued to work on this book, which meant typing my handwritten journals. It meant experientially returning to Tibet, to Kailash and Khora, which might have been bearable if I had still been in Tibet or on retreat, that is, if I had been separate from the everyday world. But I wasn't. I was at home, at work, in the noisy, messy tumult of life. I could not hold myself gracefully between the purity of Khora and the stream of demands that is ordinary life. When I would sit down to work on the journals, a howling would emerge from me, thrashing and grieving in the unbearableness of being back in ordinary life, writing of the treasures I had touched and lived at Kailash. Really, it's that I was feeling the terror of the treasures that had taken me in at Kailash. Finally I wrote:

> I can't. I can't. I can't be visible in the world. People will think I'm good, and I'm ordinary. People will listen to what I say, and I make mistakes, I understand so little. I can't. I can't. I'm not a teacher. I have no knowledge to share. I can't be listened to as if I have something to say. I only have things to say to me. I can't allow people to misunderstand me. I can't. I can't. I can't.

It took me a day to calm down. As I sat down to work on the journals again, a vague awareness arose that I did not want to transcribe my journal. I persisted anyway, and the awareness that I did not feel well floated up. I realized that it was not that I was ill, but that I did not want to feel what I was transcribing. I wrote,

I don't want to feel the end of Khora again. I don't want to
leave Mt. Kailash again. I don't want to leave Tibet again.
It hurts, I hurt, and I don't want to feel that again. I sit at
my keyboard, sobbing and howling. I don't want to leave
Tibet. I don't want to leave Kailash. I don't want to leave
Khora. I think: Khora is inside me, so what is my problem?
I don't know. It is outside me, too. Things so much greater
than me are outside me. I don't want to find the great
spaces within me. I can't bear to confront my goodness.
There is a birthing struggling to occur.

Despite my efforts to come home and to adjust and do the things
that everyday life requires, something had shattered. It is more correct
to say that in the everyday realm, everything had shattered. I finally
admitted,

I'm lost. Call it anything you want. When you break
through the illusion of everything you do, and you can't
bear the meaningless triviality of most of your day, what
then? I am alive in Tibet, I am alive in Khora, everywhere
else I am a marionette, wooden limbs automatically
moving with no sense of life, of my life. Where is the next
step? I am broken, broken in love.

Very, very slowly, through each relentless day, I found myself returning,
and changed. It is like pieces of me that had been missing, levels that
reach so far below my consciousness are rising again to support my feet.
I am returning, more mature, more open, less knowing, more conscious,
more loving, more humble, and more confident. Confidence is arising
last. Me, confident. At last, the first glimmers spill over the horizon that
is me. It has taken so long to come home, and as I arrive, as I re-coalesce,
the dilemma continues to rise up: I can't stay here. I can't settle. I keep
catching glimpses, flashes, of the Khora path around Mt. Kailash, the
terrain, the mani stones, the rivers, the rocks. I remember, I remember – I
remember the trail. I remember the prostrations. It is impossible, and I
did it. My accomplishment is real. The impossible is real, and it is real in
my body. The pull away from my life continues, drawing me away from
routine, from thinking and analyzing, from the illusion of knowing. I am
more here, and the un-connecting with here continues. I wrote,

I don't know where I am. The silence is so thick. My

ears are full of thick silence. My judgment is intact. I am functioning, caring – but I am not here. Should I just let go and wander out of my life? Wander to Francis or Milarepa; wander to some place where there is only me and my heart, no distractions, no diversions – just me and all my lies, until I choose truth? I hate this world. It's a cruel, deceptive, dangerous world, and I hate having to have my wits about me while my heart is open. I am growing up, I am being more solid, I am coming into existence. My sinfulness is so present. Sinner. Perpetrator. It is only my choice in every moment that makes me different from a perpetrator. But sin is the doorway to deeper love. Seeing my sinfulness opens my humility, my equanimity. When my sinfulness is not hidden, there is no pride. However painful, it is a relief to be exposed.

One of my blessings in life is that silence is a gift and a teacher for me. Silence continued to guide me toward that next step:

I have never been in a silence this thick. I am swathed in it. I could be a blind woman, moving through the world by feel. That is how little I register the world with my eyes. I see selectively. I see what I need to see, and not in a practical manner. I see what lives, what teaches me life. Psychotherapy is too cumbersome. Love is sleek, simple, infinitely adapted to every situation. It is only and all about love. No, it is only and all about me loving. This crisis is about me loving. I hold back. I am afraid to surrender to love. I am afraid to move forward in love, instead of in role, in picture, in illusionary control. I am afraid to know love is running the show.

I struggle to set an intention. I act, I do a million things, but there is no intention. Some actions work anyway, but I am beginning to understand life from intention, as distinct from life as action. An action can occur with or without intention, and there is all the difference in the universe between those two acts.

Love stands in front of me. The door is open. I am afraid to come in. I am coming in, but not with my will or my intellect. I don't understand. This is happening not merely before I understand, but without my understanding. My old desperate frenzy that 'I'll do anything but I want to understand it first' is not in charge here. I am changing, and I don't know what the change is or how it is happening. It is just arising in me. I will never understand. I don't need to understand. Clearly, I have already agreed to this change or it would not be arising in me. It is just that I have agreed without my usual experience of will or intellect. I have agreed from intention.

*   *   *

It has been nearly a year since I prostrated around Mt. Kailash. I look at the aerial photograph of Kang Rinpoche that I brought back from Nepal, now framed and hanging over my bed. I prostrate to Mt. Kailash forever, every moment, in my heart. It is really startling to me that I did Khora almost a year ago. My mind says that it can never end, this magnificent experience and accomplishment needs to be everyday, always present, re-visited and savored, without end, without letting go. But today, I feel that I cannot freeze that event in time, holding onto that experience before anything else.

Marcus did a bodywork session for me several months after I returned home. He works very intensely. At one point he asked me where I was. I knew I was in my heart, but what came out of my mouth was "Mt. Kailash." He cried out, "No, you are here in this moment! It is not about Mt. Kailash, it's you!" What next flashed through my mind shocked me like nothing in my life has ever shocked me: 'If Mt. Kailash is over, if it is taken away from me, then I will kill myself.' Not, I feel like killing myself, but a deadly clarity that it was time to commit one way or the other. The spitefulness hit me full in the face. I was confronted with a core dynamic I have danced around, vaguely expressed in symptoms my whole life, now standing nakedly, completely, perfectly available to be chosen. Finally, because it was so clear, I saw that I did indeed, right now, have to either choose it completely, or let it go completely. There were no more places to keep suicide as some vague option. I either fully accepted life, or I fully rejected it. I either went with my tantrum that if I can't have it my way, I won't play at all, or I relaxed into loving me right now as I am. That moment showed me that it was not Mt. Kailash that was sacred, it was me, and I have never wanted to love me that simply, just for me, not for my accomplishment, but just for me. I was horrified at the intent: I absolutely and literally meant I would kill myself if I could not wear Mt. Kailash as my raiment. If all I had was the nakedness of Tracey, no fine raiment behind which to hide, then my fundamental rejection of Tracey was exposed. If I would only love myself in the shelter of Mt. Kailash, then I didn't truly love myself. That was now exposed.

After practice today, I gaze at my aerial photograph of this magnificent spiritual and physical center of the universe. I will love it always, and be grateful to it always, for devouring me and changing me forever. But I cannot cling to it. As my teacher says, I cannot rest on my laurels. There are no laurels. There is just this moment, and then this next moment, and this next moment. There is no rest. There is no time. There is just this moment.

In this moment, the only moment, am I rejoicing? Am I in joy? Tulku Thubten Rinpoche asked, "What is behind the Name of God, the Face of God, the religious symbol that we use and rely on?" He answered, "*Infinite Love.*" That is the source of the joy. Marcus reminded me, "*All there is is love…and the love is endless.*"

Mt. Kailash was an enormous, diamond-studded door through which I stepped. And now the opening won't stop, moment after moment, whenever I want it, door after door opening, drawing me deeper into the heart of love, ravished, devoured, and comforted in the infinite heart of love. I must let Mt. Kailash go so that I can be here in this moment. When I let Khora be past, it can then live in me every moment. When I hold onto it, I distort and stain both it and myself.

*   *   *

In October 2007, I returned from my second trip to Tibet, this time for a month, this time to Eastern Tibet. I am realizing now that I needed to return to Tibet to bring closure to my first trip. Although I did not know it until I was there for awhile, and even more so now that I'm home, I went back to Tibet to close the circle that arose on Khora. The circle is inside me and outside me. I have had difficulty fully grasping what this circle is. I was told to close the circle at Kailash, to finish Khora. I felt a circle closing in Tibet as I rounded Mt. Kailash and persisted in finishing Khora. I felt it in my spirit and in my body, but my mind has been unable to fully grasp this meaning that drove me to finish Korah no matter what.

This circle is many things. It is my truth with myself. As I live this moment, am I willing to become as aware as I am able of how I am choosing to live this moment? Will I close the circle of who I say I am and how I am actually living in this moment? This is a huge and ongoing task. Words and concepts are easy. Aspirations and hopes are easy. Being motivated and passionate is easy. But responding in this moment: that is the proof. It is not that I am never irritable or reactive or cruel. Of course I am and will be. But having chosen that response, will I be conscious that I chose cruelty in that moment and remain with my heart open for what is next until that moment is fully unwound, until each consequence has played through? Or will I kick into my psychological defenses, my rationalizations, my self-hate, and my other ways of avoiding or re-writing what I have just chosen to be? Closing the circle of me is facing the me that I am in this moment as my choice. There is no reaction that I can't help. On some level, it is my preferred response to that moment. Closing the circle owns this. Closing the circle owns this with love, that is, without changing it in anyway. There is no explanation, there is no blame, and there is no punishment. There is no demotion in my right to be here and to live. My humanity and blessedness is as full as it ever was. My ownership of this moment as my choice simply does not hide away from visibility. It is, I am, and love still loves me and I still love me. There are consequences to every action, but the consequences do not reflect me as good or bad. They just reflect the outcome of that choice. What I get is the experience of that choice, and unless it is the moment of my death, a new moment to choose again, the same or differently. This is closing the circle inside of me.

Closing the circle outside of me is to remember that there are no enemies, and there are no differences. Fear drives me to make separations between you and me, between good and bad, between past and future. The fears of events in my own personal history drive me to make splits, to be a victim to an abuser, to justify my acts of cruelty in an effort to avoid just feeling my fear. If such small things that I have already survived create such rifts in my ongoing responses, how will the world ever heal? How can cultures, races, and nations choose kindness first if I cannot even choose it in a dispute with my parent or my neighbor? I am not speaking of passivity here, of giving in to avoid conflict. I am speaking of becoming conscious of when my response is really a response, and when my response is really a reaction, a defense of something I am unwilling to really look at. A true response is part of a sharing, a dialogue. It remains present and open, to both share and learn. It can be angry without threatening and without cutting off, because in its anger it remains present in the discussion. It can fear and remain present rather than hiding my fear in a premature and forced resolution that is really a flight. This is what is meant by having an open heart. I stay in my open heart rather than shutting my heart and justifying this with my rationalizations, ideologies, and words.

In the terrible struggle to find who I am after Khora and what to do with my life, I realized that three years ago, before Tibet, I knew much more than I do now, much like I knew much more when I was seventeen than I do as an adult. Three years ago, I felt more assured in my direction, more on top of where I was headed, more sure-footed. I felt I was growing in understanding. As I have continued to work with my teacher and with myself in my life, I realize I know less and less. When I listen to teachings, I realize that I get it wrong most of the time when I just rely on my own thoughts and answers. I realize my teacher holds a space and an awareness that is beyond me. True, this is why he is my teacher, but on the other hand, it is difficult to hold open space within myself for that which is by definition unknown to me. Catching glimpses of how little I know, how ignorant and profoundly limited I am, is what makes me fearful to speak aloud. I can teach what I know, but what I know is nothing, is a smudge in the shadow of a truth and a reality that is nearly completely beyond my awareness until a teacher makes a comment that awakens me to see what I have not seen! It is this most of all that makes me seek silence and invisibility. I am a fool and a dunce. I trust my love but I do not trust my knowledge. I live my love but I fear to teach this miniscule world in which I live and move. I am a leader, and I have resisted being a leader my entire life for this reason. People follow me anyway, and I tell them all to go away. But I know I am a leader, and to make matters worse, I can be charismatic when I want to. How can I risk leading when I get it wrong most of the time, when the most precious and deepest levels are where I make my mind unsubtle, gross, concrete, compartmentalized, and linear?

There are different responses that have spoken to me. I say, *When I teach to you from myself I will be in error; when I teach to you from yourself, teaching you from what you show me of you in this moment, I will not harm you.* It is only in imposing my answers on you that there is risk of harm. And then a response arose on another level. In Nepal I was talking with a new friend, troubling over people's responses to me for doing Khora with prostrations. I was unable to receive their love. Finally he just said, casually over his shoulder as we walked around a corner running an errand, "*Well, three dakinis spoke to you; maybe you need to consider that.*" I still don't know why divinity asked me to do this, or what Khora really meant. But in a gentle yet direct way, he was saying that maybe I could give up trying to subsume divinity into my personal script. If divinity wanted to invite me to a portion of the dance, I did not need to run or grasp the whole dance. I could accept the invitation without feeling like I had to understand the whole thing. I could live me and let them live them, and sometimes we talk and sometimes we don't, but I don't have to know it all.

A holy one. A reincarnation of Tara. I was so worried that that all meant something. I see now, it does. It just means something. It doesn't matter what it means. Everything means something, and life goes on. Controlling it to fit some picture of what I think it means, of what I should be, is where I get off track. I don't have to worry what it means, who I am. In fact, it is impossible to not be who I am. I am being myself inevitably, and perfectly.

It has taken me two years to realize that I wanted to receive the teachings of Kailash with the same habits with which I lived before Kailash. I wanted to know them instead of live them. I wanted to keep my separateness, keep my judgments and opinions and thoughts, and go back to life as usual. I wanted Kailash to be in the past. I preferred to have tasted this magnificent destruction and remain unchanged.

That is a choice. That's all it is. It is not inevitability or a failure. How I live each moment is a choice. It is not good or bad, not better or worse. It's just what *I want.* Nothing prevents me from melting through my judgments, my opinions. *I don't want to.* So I went to Kailash, and if I had not kept a journal, I would have forgotten much of it before I even left and forgotten most of it within two years. Such is my dedication to separateness, to my resistance to change, to the illusory security that my way is right and I should not have to undergo the blessed ordeal of change, of evolution on any terms but my own. What does it take to let my teacher's teachings live in me? What does it take to receive the blessing that Kailash pours forth with no hesitation? Kailash didn't make we wait. It didn't withhold the teachings, the experiences, the beauty, the pathos. It offered it all, immediately. "Leave behind all your thoughts and concepts for all your lifetimes," Rinpoche told me before I even left. "There is an inner journey and an outer journey. You have already begun": Rinpoche told me! "The center of the spiritual universe already exists in your human heart. Meet your mirror." My teacher told me! I didn't have to go to Kailash to go to Kailash! But I did have to go to Kailash to go to Kailash. I did have to go to Kailash and recognize that divinity has saturated all time and space with itself. Call it teachings, wisdom, blessings, or whatever you will. Divinity has saturated all time and space with itself. Kailash just shows me that in incontrovertible form. It shows me that like the side of a barn: so I can't miss it, even with my personality, even with my humanness, even with my history, I cannot miss it. I can only refuse it, but I cannot miss it. I can only develop selective blindness, but I cannot miss it.

Kailash is life lived with no defenses. That is not-knowing. That is devotion and commitment. I know that I know how to do that because that is what I did at Kailash.

To close the circle, I must live differently inside myself and outside myself. I must live differently with me and I must live differently with you. This really is not new; it is not opening a new space for us on this planet. But at least, at last, it does no harm. There is the maxim 'First, do no harm.' This is a way to do no harm.

So the circle closes in my conscious ownership of who I choose to be, each moment, of what blessing I agree to be in this life. Ownership, like freedom, is a very heavy gift. All time, all possibility, sits in ownership, in freedom. All of the past and all of the future sits in every present moment. Will I hold all that while I live this moment? This is the circle closing. At times it is unbearable, and I need to remember that it is not work to do this; it is not a struggle to wrestle with. Divinity is never dissatisfied with me as long as I am in truth, in my open loving heart. My picture of how I should be doing something is irrelevant and a distraction. There is no evaluation; there is just my open-hearted trust in love loving me constantly. I will never get it, I have already gotten it, there is nothing to get, and it is a perfect moment.

Tibet taught me what is possible. It is not about Tibet. It is about what I choose, and what I commit to, what I give my word to. It is about the enjoyment I am willing to open to. Every moment in Tibet whether I was scared or nauseous or cold or hot or in pain or comfortable: every moment I was completely filled with the joy of that moment. Tibet made me forget my distractions. She made me forget to make excuses. A burning Achilles tendon was just a piece of information compared to the experience of the Khora trail, the land to be laid on, to be prayed on, with my body and my heart.

What I have called my difficulty in coming home is actually that Tibet showed me it is not the place that makes this possible. It is not the form. Mount Kailash is only a form. I realize now that that is what my teacher told me before I left. "The center of the spiritual universe already exists in your human heart." He told me to meet my mirror. He didn't tell me I had to go there to find something, but that I would go there to find what I already had. Mount Kailash is spectacular. Although I cannot see it, I have no doubt that it is streaming out constant blessings on us all. But my heart and your heart is streaming out constant blessings on us all, too. Have you ever noticed how we humans are around babies? The toughest tough guy shines forth light and joy when meeting a baby. His or her true heart suddenly emanates, shines out and blesses us all. Babies are Mount Kailash, too. It's not Mount Kailash, it's not the form. It's not the baby, either. Those things exist to remind us of our hearts, that our hearts are always there, are always working, do not need developing or training or more of anything. Our hearts constantly love. We suppress that, hide that, and keep it secret, shining it only with a special friend or in a special moment. Yet it's there 24/7.

I have had difficulty coming home only because I have not wanted to love my moments here as I loved my moments in Tibet. I loved all the moments in Tibet. Here, I'm picky, I'm fussy. I complain. I am back to good and bad moments. When my heart is open, it's all one place. It's all one moment. I don't have to love them all the same, even though they are. I just have to love them the way I want to and own it: I am tasting, chewing, digesting, receiving this moment just the way I want to, so there is no complaint.

Not being in Tibet hurts more than anything has ever hurt in my life. It hurts all the time. When I resist this hurt, there are good and bad moments. When I receive this hurt, I hurt in the arms of love.

Now, finishing this book, I am home. Home is my heart, and the responsibility of me for my life, my life in each moment of my choice. That is home. Thank God there is so much help available, so much love constantly willing to help me, support me, and teach me, until I can trust more deeply, and then more deeply again, that that love is me, and cannot be defined or limited or evaluated or owned. It can only be loved in return, and then loved again. There is truly no limit. The only limit is the one I choose. This Khora with prostrations is a door. It is not an achievement, not a thing, not a point in time. It is a door, a liminal space. Help me stay in the door!

Heart Sounds
Lessons and Changes

The wrenching ordeal of re-visiting my journey to Tibet through writing this book has left me in a peace I did not anticipate. I had no idea this was waiting for me. As I say this, I am aware it is waiting for me all the time, and always has been. I had felt like I've been wearing my nervous system on the outside of my body, usually muffled, but the reaction tripped before I was even aware I was reactive. And then the teachings would come through. Now there are teachings I must give myself. It is I who must find my feet, and stand in them. It is I who must direct these feet, moment by moment, in the not-knowing of life.

I am deeply surprised at how much I have changed since Tibet. I felt peaceful and open there, joyful and grateful beyond any possible words. But now, only some months later, I feel and see how much I have grown. I am so much kinder than when I was in Tibet. So much less fearful. So much clearer, less reactive, and more willing to rest in "the natural great peace," to rest in the wisdom of love instead of the efforts of my intellect. I have grown up more. And still, I am just beginning. Maybe I've graduated pre-school into kindergarten, maybe day care into pre-first. I don't know.

The steps before me continue to become smaller. I find the awareness of my sinfulness, to use a Christian metaphor, to be a great liberation, to be a door that opens into possibility, each sin showing me the possibility of my love. I understand why the saints said they were sinners. These holy people saw the smaller and smaller things in themselves. The smaller the thing, the larger it is. The impact of a grain of dirt stains the whole fabric. The fraudulence is unbearable when you begin to see the tiny lies. And the gratitude for the mercy and love of divinity, always there, always laughing, is profound. Only humans worry.

The teachings and lessons from my journey around Mt. Kailash came in many forms. I will share some of them here with you as best I can. I would point out that there is nothing to do with my learnings from Tibet. There is just not blocking them, not fighting or suppressing them. Just for me to let them be, let me be. Give up the effort of resisting, and just show up in this moment.

*   *   *

We lie. With language, with our faces and expressions, we lie. Particularly with nuance, and with social graces, with the sleight of hand of nuanced language, we lie. The truth is we are all naked before each other, and we all have the same mishigos, the same shit, the same blessedness, the same beauty. But we use language to create the illusion that we are different, that we are better or worse, that we have different struggles or are at a different place with our struggles. We have the same struggles, and we are all at the same place with our struggles. We are all at the beginning, and we will all always be at the beginning, and this is a relief. It is a relief. There is no illusion to uphold.

Throwing up for eight hours out the window of the Land Cruiser with my crew of four that I had just met a few days before taught me this. We would stop to pee, to stretch, and I would stand outside my front seat door, and look at the slime on the door where I had been throwing up. I had no language to make a joke. I did not know the subtleties of Tibetan culture to make a nonverbal joke or gesture to dismiss or minimize this. For lack of any more sophisticated thing to say, I said to Dorjee, pointing at the door, "I'm sorry," although I knew it was not a matter to be sorry about, it was not a matter of fault, but it was the best I could approximate to just acknowledge the mess I was creating. He was so gracious, dismissing the whole matter with a wave of his hand and a kind expression. And I was fine. I was not embarrassed or ashamed. I was in the naturalness of my body in a new land, a new altitude, and my body was adjusting. I knew that was all it was. I knew if someone threw up all over my car door, or my car for that matter, I would just love them and want them to feel better as soon as possible. But the whole situation taught me how deftly I wanted to lie with words and tone and turn of phrase. That is not a good thing. Better to be naked and real, than skilled and hidden.

Another gift from Tibet is what I call "one speed." Because I never adjusted to the altitude, which means that I never had much breath, there was no possibility of hurrying. I am happy to say that hurrying never occurred to me, and for those of you who know me, that is saying something. I am always moving, speaking, thinking, and doing too quickly, too efficiently, in this crazy pace of modern life, and in the crazy learnings of how my family of origin worked. But in Tibet, that all stopped. I did not stop it. It just never occurred to me to hurry. Then when I began climbing, between the nausea and the lack of oxygen, there was just a steady presence in which I lived. I could not do anything about anything. I could just show up in each moment, as best I could.

Eating changed. Because I was nauseous most of the time, eating became conscious. Each mouthful paused before it entered my mouth, and my mouth and my stomach would have a little conversation about whether it was a good idea to put that into my mouth. If they agreed that I could probably keep it down, I took it into my mouth, slowly. I chewed it slowly, tasting each step along the way before I swallowed it to see if my stomach continued to agree that this was possible. Having successfully eaten one or two bitefuls, this process did not change. Every bite was new. Because my stomach tolerated six bitefuls did not mean it would tolerate the seventh. So eating moved out of that taken-for-granted category into a moment-by-moment-each-moment-new category.

Then there was the gift of ignorance. Not-knowing what something is, what will probably happen next, how to manage something, has always been a primal fear for me. I have relied on my intellect as my lifeline of safety. If I just knew what I was dealing with, I could make a plan, develop a strategy, and surmise the odds. But doing Khora with prostrations around Mt. Kailash brought me into a realm where I had no mastery. It was physically demanding, it was outdoors, even! And spatial orientation is a weakness for me. I rarely can visually orient well enough to ascertain where I am in space, whether it is a department store or the wilderness of Western Tibet. Thus, I did not approach the Khora with the assumption that I understood what it would require or even what it was. It never occurred to me that I could do Khora with prostrations; it was just that I desired it. All I had was the devotion in my heart, the prayer that I could do it, and the great fear that my pride, my image, would rebel if I "failed." How can one fail at Khora? It is impossible. If I had done one day of prostrations, how blessed would that have been! But I knew my image would fuss if I was unable to complete Khora with prostrations, and I would have to commit very deeply to choose from my heart instead of from my image if that happened.

So I went through each day in not-knowing. I woke up, not knowing when to leave camp to walk to my beginning place. I did not know what to wear, or how many layers, since carrying things was not an option. I either wore it or I didn't take it. I didn't know if the rain and hail storm was serious enough to stay at camp for the day or not, or if it would pass. I didn't know anything, except that I was in Tibet to love Mt. Kailash, and everything else would have to be worked out by some other level because it was not being worked out by my conscious mental realm or my ego.

One of the hardest things I learned is that we are all doing our part. Doing Khora with prostrations was my part. People from China, Europe, India, everywhere in the world, came up to me, some crying, some touching me, most bringing some kind of gift, many expressing a deeply felt gratitude. I remember being puzzled by it. I remember thinking, 'If this is so very special to you, why don't you just do it?' I didn't understand why they didn't just do it. I understand now that it was what I was called to do. They were called to do what they were doing, and I was çalled to do this. When I realize this, my heart opens, and I feel that we are all one community on this planet. We are all doing something, not better or worse, but each our part. Like dots in an impressionist painting, we are all essential. This was my dot.

The learnings about home would fill a book in themselves. As I strive to integrate, to keep, to be changed by my Khora with prostrations, I return again and again to the love. I could not do the Khora with prostrations on my own. It is only all the love and compassion meeting in and around me, from East and West, that made *any* of that journey possible. From the start, or let's be strict, from the second day, my ego was not strong enough to generate prostrations. From the second day, there was only fatigue and ignorance, and from that everyday space, I prostrated. To keep the Khora, I have to keep the door that is my human, vulnerable, present, physical heart open to all the love flowing in me and around me. The love inside me and outside me is the same love. If I close that door and make you different from me, then I have forgotten the Khora with prostrations. I have let the world separate into East and West again, and I have told you that I can function without your love, and I can't. I can repeat historical patterns in a solipsistic world of my own past projections. But I can't live in the present moment without living in your/my love.

Myloveyourlove gave me the courage to let down barriers while still having boundaries. What does this mean? It means feeling and relying on the safety of myloveyourlove. It means opening my perception to see when you are in your heart and when you are in reaction, and loving from the appropriate level. How deep do I have to go to love you when you are in reaction, and still not be victimized by you or control you? Love is not naïve and is not blind. Love is very very accurate, and completely generous in that accuracy.

When will I get it that I am absolutely just like everyone else, so there is no one to be impatient with, no one to dislike, because they are all me? When will I finally remember that, and be kinder? Life is just one continuous stream of second chances to learn this. Thank you. Living compassion and impartiality – there is nothing else. With compassion there is no thinking required, no decision as to who is worthy. In some ways, that feels as though ignorance is my safety. It has always tormented me, and now it is the peace and safety of not-knowing which opens my heart to everything.

I have learned that the only love there is to give is the love that I allow myself to receive. From our kindness and generosity with ourselves, we are free to be kind and generous with others, to let go of the strings attached to our gifts, to open our eyes and see outside ourselves for what it is, not for what we fear or desire. I cannot say this clearly enough: we cannot love from deficiency, from a want in ourselves, or from will. Love is only what flows over the top of the brimming cup; it is never from the cup. Tibet taught me surrender, and faith, and kindness without a reason.

I realized there is enough love to make the impossible possible. I have been praying all my life like I am unworthy. I am a daughter. It is time to pray like a daughter. My teacher taught me that there is no limit. Tibet gave me an opportunity to live that in some small measure. I pray everyday for Tibet and her people, for China and her people, and for our tiny planet and her people. It was at first difficult to realize that I could not marginalize China, but love is love, love is not divvied out, love is not for some and not for others. Love is pervasive, infinite, and abundant.

For years, studying with my teacher, I kept asking what I should do. What I meant was, 'Tell me what I need to do, because then I'll do it, I'll get where I need to be, *and then I'll be done.* I'll be *there.*' One of the most difficult things for me to accept has been that there is no *there.* There is only *now.* How I live *now* is all there is. And if I get this *now* "right," it doesn't matter because a new now is arising, and I have to choose again how I will be that new now. It's never over. It can't be accomplished so that then I can sit back with the accomplishment, the prize, the knowledge, the key. It is a truism that all there is is the present moment. However, when you grasp that this is literally true, it changes everything. Then you stand no longer on a floor but on a pinpoint, and balancing for all your life with every ounce of who you are on that pinpoint, you can't see anything around you. And you can't see the net because choosing to stand there is the net.

I have learned that love is more intelligent than I am. It does not need me to understand, itself or anything else. It works without my understanding and support. For me, I no longer labor under the illusion that I know what goodness is, or how to be a loving person. I do not know how to be sure that what I deem to be love is not tangled up with my psychological pictures, needs, and defenses. As my teacher says, Love is running the show. What I am understanding that to mean is that love is beyond any cosmology, any belief system, any description. It is beyond control. There is not even the illusory control of understanding what it is. It drives, leads, shapes, teaches, breaks, and molds me. I do nothing for it. I do not please or live up to it. It has already loved me so far beyond my entirety that it is inconceivable to my intellect how completely I am loved. Only my human heart can open to this. In the face of love, my intellect can only glaze over and grow dull with overwhelm.

More than that, love cannot be anticipated. Without realizing it, I have spent much time sitting back and naming what I saw as love, as goodness, thinking I could see a pattern or a path. Now I am realizing that the outworking of love cannot be anticipated. I am finally realizing that I do not know what love will look like. I do not know what a loving action looks like, or a loving outcome. The path of love is self-arising and overwhelming. All that is left to me is joy in the face of the mystery, resting like a babe in its arms through the storms and peace of life.

This changes everything. Whenever I think I understand something, I find out there is more, there are larger arms holding what I thought was the new vista. Love is so far beyond my ability to define it that I am left only with burning passion in the void. I am left with the only choice for me being to love everything, starting with everything about myself, everything, absolutely everything. This is daunting, but there is no other path.

Finally reaching down out of the void, my toes brush the ground. Slowly, I sink my weight into my feet, held in the infinite resourcefulness and nourishment of the void, but standing in my humanness. I am realizing I had to prostrate around Mt. Kailash because my journey is to come into my body. For me, prayer without my body is incomplete. I must live my dance with divinity not through my energy field, but through every cell in this dense physical form that I am. There has been an effort to get through this life without embracing the physicality of it. But I am realizing that I must admit all of me to my life's effort and my life's experiences.

How can I love this planet Earth, this environment, the animals and plants and elements that bless and sustain us, when I do not love my own physicality, when I prefer to find God in my energy field instead of in everything about me, my body, my psychology, my heart, and of course my soul? Prostrating around Kailash on my belly, touching thirty-four miles with my outstretched body again and again, invited me to mend the separation I have instituted and maintained between my love and my humanness. I am terrified of fully living in this body, but that does not matter. I was terrified of Kailash and I went there, trusting my heart, trusting love. Love is big enough to hold me, all of me.

What is this "infinite resourcefulness and nourishment of the void"? What do these fancy words mean? The void gives me freedom, complete freedom. Free will is as overwhelming and mindbending a notion as unconditional love. But we are free, if we want to know this. The void tells me I am free to love me, not because I do not make mistakes, but because I have a right to be here. I have a right to be here, to live this life, any way I want to. There are consequences to every choice, but the choices are all available to me. There is no right way to do this. It is really open to me. Love, the void, does not judge me, does not tell me what direction to go. It supports me in complete freedom, to live the way I want to, with all the consequences of that choice. There is ever-bountiful non-judgment, love, and joy in the void for me, for the moment that I am. The complete lack of judgment or blame is the infinite resourcefulness and nourishment of the void.

A friend read an early draft of this manuscript, and said something that seemed obvious but had never occurred to me. He said that the book needed to be bigger, to have more in it, for example, who I was before Kailash. He said the reader had no context for this person who received a calling, although the sharing of the calling and what happened afterward was clear. As I digested this, I came to the conclusion that it had not occurred to me to describe who I was and where I had come from in my life because it is not relevant. My history is ordinary. It did not result in Kailash. The invitation and my choice resulted in Kailash. Nothing in my life prepared me for it, and everything in my life prepared me for it. This all brought me to think about the notion of being special. I did not do Khora with prostrations because I am special. It was just my calling. Others were touched by it, as I am touched by what others do. There is nothing in my history which would have predicted this. Of course our histories shape us, but they do not determine us. Only our choices determine us.

I am learning that nothing ends, nothing goes away. My teacher gave me a teaching before I left for Kailash. He asked me to generate some good qualities that I am, and one that I offered was, *I am whole and unbroken.* He added, *I am whole and unbroken, and my history blesses me everyday.* Yes. All that I do not love about me, all that I call wrong and imperfect and unfortunate in my life history: that is what blesses me everyday; that is what comes to be loved, to see if I will love it, or if I will refuse it. I am learning that I will never "get it," I will never be done. There are days I will be shattered, and days I will be peaceful, and these days will reflect the same history. My task is to hold these days the same. One speed.

*   *   *

Whether it has been unconsciously or consciously, I am realizing that for a long time, I have feared being visible in the world because when I am visible, I am only something, I am not everything. That is, I am coming to know my arrogance, my fear that I am better than you or worse than you. As long as I live inside myself, I am the only one who really knows me, and I can hold the vague illusion of what I am capable of. When I become visible to others, both they and I will know what part of that illusion is real. They and I will see the things I am gifted at, and the things that I don't or can't do even though I might talk about them. And then I will just be Tracey instead of being special, universal. My inflated image will come down to earth, and once again I will come back to the door that asks: *Will you love you? Are you enough, or are you holding out for more before you give you your love?* Being visible exposes my humanness, that we are both all the same and all unique. Being visible destroys the pecking order, and brings us from knowledge into dialogue. Being visible takes away my defenses and leaves me strong because it leaves me just with who I am; nothing special, nothing judged.

I am astounded at the stupor that I call daily living. I am 99.9999999% habit, unconscious, automatic habit, and I don't even know it until love awakens me. It took something the magnitude of Kailash to wake me up! And still I want to drift off again, to blur over, and to become vague.

There is no vagueness. There is joy! My history blesses me every moment. Joy is the opportunity to live. It is not just certain categories or preferences of living. It is the opportunity to live any moment, to eat this life, to sing this life, to dance this life, to suffer this life, to fragrance this life. Joy does not arise from mastery. It arises from availability.

It has become clearer and clearer to me that what I call "just being" is actually active avoidance. As I let go of trying and striving, often I feel I am not really doing anything, and I am tempted to start the cycle of striving to improve myself again. But I begin to feel that that stagnant or static state of just being is not a correct description or naming. Although it feels like I am just coasting, just going with what is there instead of expending effort, in fact in these times of just being I am actually actively avoiding. Actively avoiding what? Actively avoiding the pregnant, vibrant moment. There is so much possibility in each moment, to experience and encounter. And I am learning that *I don't want it.* I don't want change. I don't want to be open to experience. I don't want to feel. I don't want my world to change, and because change is constant, if I open myself to experience, I and my world will indeed change. The security of knowing something, of believing I know what will come next, will crack. I remember talking with a police chief once, and telling him that I never felt I could go into law enforcement because the more I looked at situations, the harder it became to be clear on what was good and bad, right and wrong. To my surprise, he just looked at me and nodded. When I open my heart, when I let love lead, when I am lead by compassion, when I have no opinion of you but only openness and kindness, when I share me without judgment/ telling you, then the whole world changes. Then I am no longer good and right, or wrong and bad. I am just living my moment. As on Khora, I am just doing what I am doing, and others are just doing what they are doing, and we honor and accept each other. Living without the hierarchy, without the opinions, is a very different way for me to live. The world does not need my opinions. It needs my kind presence and my willingness to not know.

I am still lost. I am still done with my life, which is still irreparably shattered, thank heaven. It is just that I am finally beginning to find the joy. I found the joy at Kailash. If I had not kept a journal, I would not have remembered being so sick so much, so tired, so cold, because I experienced it all in joy. The sickness and exhaustion was not a negative of the experience, it was the experience, and it is the experience and not the judging of the experience which is joy. Judging the experience creates coveting and resisting, and removes me from the experience. Experience itself is joy.

As I write this, I have a sick migraine. I feel awful, I am nauseous, I am deeply tired and quite weak, and the teaching of joy is showing itself to me. I go to rest, not in sickness, but in love, in the profound peace of this experience of the migraine. I do not rise above it. I am in it as best I can be, loving me as this experience rather than separating me from this experience. The experience is the joy.

Joy does not come to us from the surface down. It comes from deep within, and rises up, laughing, suffusing everything. In true joy, we become like one of those angel food desserts that is soaked with claret. Joy in this moment makes us heavy with delight, soaked in joy, delicious, moist, and saturated. It makes us in love with this moment, whether in the joy of grief, the joy of pain, or the joy of joy. There is no just being, no neutral time. There is actively loving this moment, or actively resisting this moment.

Before I left Nepal, I was able to see the Temple at Swayambu. Nepal is difficult for me. Tibet is poor, but I was in the wilderness where the nomads and the farmers were on the land. Kathmandu, Nepal, is a city which seems overwhelmingly filled with people. There are animals everywhere, dogs and cattle. I noticed that while I would ordinarily feel so badly for the skinny, homeless animals, in Kathmandu the animals and the people seemed to be in the same boat. Both were skinny, homeless, jobless. To me, they seemed to suffer equally.

So it was at Swayambu. I climbed the many steps to the top of the Temple, walking past beggars, hungry children and adults, those with disabilities and deformities, and walking past hungry dogs with ribs sticking out. I got to the top, and walked all around the various aspects there. In the course of that wandering, I came across a little black dog. He was shiny and joyful, and very sick. It was not just the starvation. He had neurological symptoms. Unable to keep his balance, he would bound forward happily but fall over, listing so severely to one side that he could not remain upright. Then he would stand again, bound forward, and fall. He always got up, and bounded forward again. The little black dog at Swayambu, dying in slow motion in front of me. It was clear that he came to teach me to die with joy and equanimity in the midst of the suffering. He just kept looking at me as he tried to walk, stumbling, faltering. His eyes were so big and clear, and he kept looking directly at me. He wasn't begging. He wasn't looking for food, or even to be petted. He was teaching me. I wished him a soon-death. It just pulls at my heart. So much suffering. What do I do with that? Kindness everywhere. Suffering everywhere. Agenda everywhere. Everything everywhere. Heart everywhere.

*   *   *

In Tibet I wondered, What will it be like to be home? I thought it would not be very dramatic. Life is life; it is lived as it arises in all its many forms. Yet within this ordinary fabric that I would return to, I knew there would be tiny decisions that would come to me, seeing if I would continue to keep my word. I realized then that my word was not just to come to Tibet and do Khora with prostrations at Mt. Kailash. My word also was to remain true to whatever Tibet and Mt. Kailash taught me or opened in me. That is where each day my honesty or dishonesty at honoring what Tibet has opened in me will arise. I am realizing, Tibet will never be over. Khora at this level will never be over.

It took me a long time to receive the teaching of sameness. I finally noticed that all of Khora had just been Khora. While I was prostrating, I didn't think about much, which itself was a great blessing and a lack of a waste of time and energy. But looking back, I noticed that no matter what the terrain was, or the day, or my health, or the weather, doing Khora was always the same. On boulders, through water, on flat smooth ground: prostrating was the same. On days where the terrain was endless or on days when I didn't notice, it was all the same. I was always just where I was, not in yesterday and not in tomorrow. Just there, that moment, for all time.

In the same way, I'm learning now that everyone is my father. Everyone is my mother. Every moment is my death. Every moment is my life. Every moment is my entire life. The only question is whether I live this moment with my heart open, or live it within my thoughts. What does my opinion matter? Why do I have so many opinions? Because I hide from love. I hide from the furnace of love, burning me up, burning up my self-importance, my reactivity, my uniqueness. I hide in my separateness, from the ease of love. I make loving you and loving me and living this moment separate endeavors. And really, they are not endeavors at all. They are experiences, and they are not separate.

Spirituality is not convenient. It is joyful, but it is not easy, not complacent, not known, and not convenient. It is there if you want it. It is there constantly. It does not give up on you, and it does not force you. It is always available. There are no rules. There is only love, and how much love you are willing to open to. That's all.

The spiritual wrestling match of my life is evident in these pages. It is nothing as secure and immutable as a belief system to rest in, but consists in the prying away of the resistances to faith. Faith stands poised in mid-air over the abyss, and as faith deepens, the abyss only gets wider and deeper. But the love grows stronger, and the love of self, of my existence in this form in this lifetime, and the faith that however blind, I am legitimately here: this faith deepens, too.

*   *   *

It has taken me a long time to realize that the issue about Kailash is not about me. I thought it would change me, destroy me, and devour me. It did, but that was not what was important. Kailash is a door that keeps opening. It was stepping into the door that was important. It was also important to realize that it was not *my* door. I stepped into the door, on the door's terms. To do so, I had to leave my terms behind. I had to leave knowing behind. I had to step into space knowing in my deepest heart that the wings of love would keep me from crashing on the rocks, and would steer me because I had entered a plane where I no longer knew.

Truly, I have no reference points, no points of understanding for what I have done or where I have entered, and where I am now and forever. I am writing this in March 2008, nearly two years after Kailash, and I am just beginning to realize there is no struggle of how to resolve this, how to know what happened or where I am or what is next. There is love, being love in my messy-blind-dense-reactive and -potentially-open-hearted human form. I choose to stay in the door. That is all I know. I don't know what is right or wrong, what is a correct direction or effort. I just know that I can love me as I am in this moment, or I can judge me, that is, not love me as I am in this moment. That is all it has come to. The Rinpoches may understand what I have done at Kailash. I expect they do. My teacher may understand. I think he does. The people of Tibet may understand. I think they do, too. But all I know is that my choice is either to stand on a pinpoint of love, loving with all my might in this human form in time and space and infinity, or to live in the past or in the future. In past and future, I am safe from reality and from possibility. After all this struggle and exhilaration, this abysmal breaking and magnificent rising, this is what I have come to. In this surrender to my deepening, protective state of ignorance, I trust that love will teach me further. I am now so far beyond knowing and understanding anything that all I can do is leave this moment and go to the past or future, or stay in this moment and rely on love, on the lovingness of divinity which is already present loving me.

Perhaps I took the spiritual path to my humanness. Perhaps I needed to look so hard into the eyes of divinity that I was forced to see that the only other necessary reality was the one I was standing in. That the relationships of family and friends and enemies are the relationships of my healing, teaching me that there is no deeper truth than this human life. Still I feel the pull of intellect and defenses, dissociating and victim, and yet the truth is glowing more clearly in front of me. There is this life to do, fully, lovingly, courageously, excitedly, enthusiastically, and that is all there is to know. The divinity shines through the wisdom of this life, not separate from it. Prayer is not separate from how I live this moment. If my human heart is open, this moment is a prayer. If my human heart is closed, reactive, judgmental, this moment is dead, no matter how I argue my ideology and beliefs. It is dead. Only as I live fully in the house of this life do I look out into the infinity of the universe, of god, of infinite love, of all creation in the name of god, the name of god as all creation.

Still there is magnificence in the initial path I followed, the path I followed for much of my life, the path of my energetic heart rather than my human heart. Then, where I shortchanged humanness, I gloried in infinity. Where my psychology could not hold my fear, God's hands held and guided me. There is after all only one destination and all paths lead toward it. Now I choose my humanness before my energetic or spiritual self as I continue toward union with divinity. Same destination, union, the only difference being that the path on which I walk continues to widen to include more and to fear less. The line between divinity and present moment is dissolving. Good and bad fade away in the choice to be fully in the experience. Difficult and easy are there, and true, but unimportant. Everything really is present in this moment, with no effort, with nothing to be done about it, just not to resist it. It needs no help, just not to resist this experience, whether I am singing or gnashing my teeth. Holding me in kindness in the arms of faith as I receive the experience of this moment: that is all there is to do.

That I have written this book for me has come as a deep surprise. Yet over the three years since the invitation to go to Mt. Kailash and the completion of this book, working on the manuscript has necessitated that I listen to my own words, clearly, meticulously. I have seen in the writing what is my path. Some people will be able to relate to it, others won't. But the images, insights, and intentions reach back to ground me more deeply and especially more truly, more authentically, in my own life's unfolding. When I die, only I will die my death. My life will not have been anyone else's doing. My death will be traversed only by me. At the beginning, middle, and end of the day, it will have been only about me, my authenticity, my fearfulness, my compromises, my choices. This book, like the Khora itself, has faced me relentlessly with myself, and I am grateful for this. Slowly, the old historical tapes wear thin, they are less inevitable.

We all have obstacles that make us believe that love is not available to us. This book is about my obstacles, and about my journey through them to love's open arms, devouring, digesting, and purifying me so that my availability to receive love is all that is left. Corinthians 1:13 comes to mind:

> ...Love is patient and kind; love is not jealous or boastful; it is not arrogant or rude. Love does not insist on its own way; it is not irritable or resentful; it does not rejoice at wrong, but rejoices in the right. Love bears all things, believes all things, hopes all things, endures all things.

Love never ends….

I always thought those verses referred to how I was supposed to be as a loving person to others. I see now that it speaks of love receiving me, of how love loves me.

*　　*　　*

I saw Dorjee La, my guide, in Lhasa when I returned to Tibet the year after Khora. He says he met people at Kailash who said they had heard that someone had done Khora with prostrations, but they didn't know if it was true. He said, "Yes, it is true, I was her guide." He said their response was to be hopeful, they had not been sure Khora with prostrations was possible, and now they knew it was. How wonderful a response, I thought, how wonderful an effect of my act of devotion.

As we sit together in Lhasa, Dorjee La tells me I am still at Kailash. He waves his arms, "Flying around the mountain." I laugh. I know it is true. How could I not be? I know now that Mt. Kailash is in truth my human heart. Everything is happening there, and I remain committed to surrendering to the beauty, the power, and most of all, to the unfathomable mystery and compassion of my human heart.

There is a story about Milarepa, where he tells his followers not to be in a hurry to go out and serve others, but to attend to healing themselves first:

> One should not be *over anxious and hasty* in setting out to serve others before having oneself realized Truth in its fullness; to be so, would be like the blind leading the blind. As long as the sky endureth, so long there will be no end of sentient beings for one to serve; and to everyone cometh the opportunity for such service. Till the opportunity come, I exhort each of you to have but the one resolve, namely, to attain Buddhahood for the good of all living things. (Govinda, 1969, p. 42)

I have realized that for me my embodied spiritual evolution *is* my path, is what heals my body/mind and opens my spirit. By embodied spiritual evolution, I mean my evolution as a physical human being with a personal history that unfolds across linear time. I cannot say that this is everyone's path to healing. But it has become clear that it is mine. If my history which is crystallized in my personality and my body is not loved with as much passion as my spirit, my soul, then I will not heal. For me, all levels must be embraced, not just my spiritual level.

As I deepen on this human path, as I strive to be a good person, to even know what that is, to continue to let go of striving even for this, again and again, it is not the spiritual insights or truths that change me. It is the effect of that spiritual truth on my personality, on my emotions and thoughts about all the things that have happened to me in this lifetime. I have found that I cannot keep my personality as it is, and also keep the blessing of the spiritual truth. That is, I cannot savor this spiritual insight only on my spiritual level. True, from that level I can *talk about* the spiritual truth, but unless I *live it* in my interactions with myself and with you, it becomes a little compartment where I go to feel bliss. When I come back out of that compartment and the bliss wears off, I will be the same, unchanged. Make no mistake: living that spiritual truth is painful. It is a death, dying over and over again until I release a pattern of me, of my personality, to which I have been so attached. The rigidity of my body/mind must melt and open to more lovingness, to more consciousness received in love. If my body/mind is untouched by the spiritual insight, then I am unchanged by it. While my belief may have expanded or become more articulate, the way I live has not changed.

Even though receiving the next level of truth with my body and mind as well as my spirit feels like a dying, and it is on one level, maybe it is better said that in fact the deadness begins to be cut away. My beliefs about my history, my childhood, that is, my attachments, are like parasites, sucking my life energy, making me more and more rigid. Cutting away the necrosis lets life have what belongs to it: its own energies.

I have been immeasurably blessed by Kailash. Kailash brought together my body and spirit, my density and ecstasy. It brought me home to the spiritual universe that I am, residing in this human body and personality. Now it is the joyfulpainful work to live out in the fibers of all the levels of my being the truth that compassion is infinite, and that infinite compassion is right here with me, every moment, just waiting for me to trust it. I spread my wings into life. Winds of Kailash, carry me!

Glossary

Chimpu	A mountainside outside Samye with meditation caves where Guru Rinpoche and Yeshe Tsogyal meditated.
Class	A group process experience which meets two or more days where Marcus Daniels teaches on living in the present moment, sharing one's experience rather than stories or concepts, and fully embracing all of ourselves in love through the density of the human heart.
Darchen	The base town at the foot of Mt. Kailash with supplies and guesthouses.
Dakini	A spiritual being; a self-manifesting being of love; a spiritual impulse made manifest.
Drolma La Pass	The highest point on the Khora trail at 18,500 feet; a sacred transition point of death into re-birth.
Dutsi	A sacred substance imbued with various deities that is ingested and held to melt under the tongue.
Francis	St. Francis of Assisi, the greatest saint of the Roman Catholic Church, who was born in 1181 in Italy. Francis lived a life of absolute trust in the divine.
Gompa	Monastery. *Chiu Gompa* is at Lake Manasarovar. *Chuku Gompa* is at the western foot of Mt. Kailash, *Drira Phuk Gompa* is at the top of the western ascent of the Khora

trail, and *Zutrul Phuk Gompa* where Milarepa stayed is on the eastern descent of the Khora trail as one approaches Darchen.

Guru Rinpoche	Also known as Padmasambhava. In the eighth century, Guru Rinpoche brought Buddhism to Tibet from India. It is said that Guru Rinpoche's foot has touched nearly all the land of Tibet. He tamed the demons and powers of the land in Tibet to open space for and establish the teachings of the Buddha in Tibet.
Integration	To grasp a teaching or insight such that it becomes an integral part of how one lives, not just something one knows or thinks.
Kailash	Mt. Kailash is one of three sacred mountains in Tibet. In the Tibetan Buddhist system of Body, Speech, and Mind, Mt. Kailash is Body. It stands in the wilderness of Western Tibet. It is sacred to Bonpos, the original religion of Tibet, and to Buddhists, Hindus, and Jains. For Hindus it is the home of Shiva. Four major rivers arise from it, nourishing the vast lands around it.
Kang Rinpoche	Tibetan name for Kailash, meaning 'Jewel of Snow'.
Kata	A silk scarf offered by Tibetans to mark auspicious occasions.
Khora	Term for circumambulating something. Pilgrims walk the Khora around Mt. Kailash. A small number circumambulate or do Khora around Kailash by walking prostrations, known as Khora with Prostrations, also called Khora with Puja or Khora with Prayers. The Khora path around Mt. Kailash is thirty-four miles in length.
Lhasa	A city in central Tibet, the former capital.
Mala	Tibetan prayer beads. A mala has one hundred eight beads.

Manasarovar	A sacred lake near Mt. Kailash. It is the Lake of Wisdom. It is near Rakshas Tal, the Lake of Power.
Mantra	A phrase that is repeated as a prayer and that conveys a spiritual transmission.
Meltdown	A spontaneous release often accompanied by tears when one lets go of illusionary control.
Marcus Daniels	My teacher who has trained in many arts, including bodywork, group process, states of consciousness, and Tibetan practices. Marcus works in individual bodywork sessions or experiential group trainings (class). Marcus' website is <u>marcusdanielsarts.com</u>.
Milarepa	The greatest saint of Tibet who lived in the 12th century. Milarepa attained enlightenment in a single lifetime.
Padmasambhava	See Guru Rinpoche.
Practice	A period of Tibetan prayer which consists of mantras (verbal prayers) which may be accompanied by visualizations, use of bell and drum, prostrations, or other means.
Prostration	A practice in which one joins the hands over one's head as a mantra is said, the hands pause at the forehead, throat, and heart as one comes down on one's knees, and then stretches out flat on the ground with hands extended fully outward. One then raises oneself back to one's knees, rising as one completes the mantra, pausing the hands at the forehead, throat, and heart.
Rangjung	Refers to an image in rock which is self-manifested, that is, not man-made.
Rinpoche	A high Tibetan religious teacher.

Samsara   The present state of life on earth marked by endless suffering.

Samye   The first monastery in Tibet, built by Padmasambhava, Trison Detsen, the King of Tibet, and Shantarakshita, an Indian scholar.

Sky Burial   Tibetan practice of leaving bodies and body parts out on the land to be "buried" naturally by the elements and wildlife.

St. Francis   See *Francis* above.

Tarboche   An area at Mt. Kailash with a huge flagpole covered in prayer flags. Site of major Tibetan festivals. Tarboche is a few kilometers outside Darchen.

Tashi Delek   A Tibetan greeting, also wishing good fortune.

Walking Prostration A prostration (see Prostration) in which one takes a few steps to where one's hands reached when fully extended on the ground, and then begins the next prostration from that point.

Yeshe Tsogyal   A dakini born a princess of Kharchen, she became the main consort of Padmasambhava, and became a fully enlightened Buddha in her own right. She lived for over 200 years in Tibet, studying and working with Guru Rinpoche, and after Guru Rinpoche walked through to the other side, traveling the country to care for, teach, and heal the Tibetan people.

Bibliography

Govinda, Lama Anagarika (1969). *Foundations of Tibetan Mysticism*. York Beach, Maine: Samuel Weiser, Inc.

Govinda, Lama Anagarika (1966). *The Way of the White Clouds: A Buddhist Pilgrim in Tibet*. Berkeley, California: Shambala Publications, Inc.

Gyurme Dorje (1996). *Tibet*, 3rd Edition. UK: Footprint, Bath, UK.

Snelling, John (1990). *The Sacred Mountain: The Complete Guide to Tibet's Mount Kailas*. London and the Hague: East-West Publications.

Tsewang Lama (2002). *Kailash Mandala: A Pilgrim's Trekking Guide*. Simikot, Humla: Humla Conservation and Development Association.

Dying and Living in the Arms of Love
One Woman's Journey around Mount Kailash
Tracey Alysson, Ph.D.

Synopsis

This book arose from a calling to go to Tibet and do prostrations around Mount Kailash, a towering spiritual and physical presence in the wilderness of Western Tibet. This book is about my experience of this mountain and this self that went to surrender at Kailash. I am told I am the first Westerner to have prostrated around Kailash. It took me twenty-eight days to circumambulate the mountain, and the main portion of the book is the journal I kept as I did this Khora with prostrations. It is said that doing prostrations around Kailash dissolves the karma from an entire year of one's life. This book is the record of that dissolution and re-formation of my life as I rounded the mountain, and the struggle to come back to a life and a place I no longer wanted to be in. It is a portrait of the state of this mountain, the state of the land before China opens up this wilderness with an airport, a report on conversations and encounters with the pilgrims who live and visit there, and a reflection of how the profoundly rooted spirituality of the Tibetan people continues to manifest itself and to inspire and guide others from many countries.

Biography
Tracey Alysson, Ph.D.

Tracey Alysson, Ph.D. has worked as a clinical psychologist since 1980. She incorporates mind-body techniques in her clinical practice with individuals of all ages, families, groups, and combat veterans. In 2002, she also became licensed as a bodyworker. Tracey is interested in where psychology and spirituality meet in humans, and in resolving rather than managing trauma and other symptoms by exploring and reclaiming innocence and competence in the human being. Innocence and competence bring freedom. What does one do with that freedom? Tracey's fundamental experience is that we are here to meet, love, and receive who we are; and so, while serving others, the primary person she works with is herself and the vast levels of unconsciousness within herself waiting to be met.